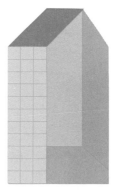

# Living Disability

## Building Accessible Futures
## for Everybody

edited by
**Emily Macrae**

with developmental editing by
**Jenny Hiseler**

Coach House Books, Toronto

first edition

Published with the generous assistance of the Canada Council for the Arts and the Ontario Arts Council. Coach House Books also acknowledges the support of the Government of Canada through the Canada Book Fund and the Government of Ontario through the Ontario Book Publishing Tax Credit.

LIBRARY AND ARCHIVES CANADA CATALOGUING IN PUBLICATION

Title: Living disability : building accessible futures for everybody / edited by Emily Macrae.
Names: Macrae, Emily, editor.
Identifiers: Canadiana (print) 20240436113 | Canadiana (ebook) 20240437764 | ISBN 9781552454886 (softcover) | ISBN 9781770568211 (EPUB) | ISBN 9781770568228 (PDF)
Subjects: LCSH: Barrier-free design. | LCSH: People with disabilities—Services for. | LCSH: City planning. | LCGFT: Essays. | LCGFT: Interviews.
Classification: LCC NA2545.P5 L58 2024 | DDC 720.87—dc23

# Table of Contents

# Welcome

This book is about being disabled in public and about the privilege of having a private place to call home. It's about the flood of feelings when a stranger asks personal questions on the sidewalk. It's about the power of disabled people coming together at a park or at a protest, on social media or on a video call. It's about how we take up space and why we're experts in how those spaces work – from the trails of B.C. to the ice-encrusted intersections of Halifax, from gyms in Saskatchewan to bus stops in Toronto. We're the experts in our own lives and our own communities. We know where the gap between the train and the platform is insurmountable, we know where the music is too loud, we know where the signage is missing or simply doesn't make sense.

Cities and towns across Canada are grappling with housing affor-dability, access to green space, how to fund public transit, and what to do about remote work. Disabled people are disproportionately impacted by all of these, but too often our perspectives are overlooked by architects, administrators, service providers, and politicians. Our knowledge offers ways to reimagine employment, transportation, emergency preparedness, and the arts.

We are the experts but we're not a monolith. A foundational piece of being disabled is knowing that other people don't move through the world like you do, don't notice what you do. We're musicians and artists, academics and activists, thrifters and gardeners, film critics and movie buffs. Every person in this book has an area of expertise beyond our lived experiences of disability. We are 'disabled and,' not 'disabled but.' We've found solutions and bridged problems that others have never had to consider.

Each of these chapters would be at home in more than one section of this book. There's real talk about the plastic bag ban in a chapter about wheelchair repair, musings about arts grants amid comments on income support, and analyses of colonialism alongside reflections about cycling. There are essays about how immigration shapes perceptions of public transit and why experiences of dating and desirability inform making art and designing galleries. There are as many voices and angles as there are ways to advocate. Some of our authors take shelter in academic tones and frameworks, others expose deeply held dreams. We use person-first language (a person with a disability) and identity-first language (a disabled person). Person-first phrasing focuses on the person rather than the disability. Conversely, identity-first language centres disability as an inherent component of a person's identity that shapes an individual's politics and interactions with the world.

Contributors embrace the nuances of both options and propose other words to assert identity. As with any marker of identity, using person-first or identity-first language is a deeply personal choice. There are strong arguments for and against each framing. Using both through-out this book reflects the diversity of perspectives within and between disabled communities. This range of voices is a response to the different ways we've been judged for being different and the crushing pressure we've felt to blend in, settle down, and keep quiet. Our ongoing encounters with ableist standards shape the way we share our ideas.

Because we're not a monolith, this book is not exhaustive. It's part of a fabric and legacy of other thoughts, advocacy, and expertise. Disability can be permanent, temporary, changing, episodic, and situational. Just as disability can be one aspect of life or a framework for understanding it, this book is one part of a larger conversation. That larger conversation includes language and concepts that many contributors build on and expand from. This book discusses different models of disability: the medical model, the social model, the charity model, and the very real threat of eugenics. The medical model frames disability as an individual failing, which is in need of correction or cure by experts. The social model views disability a product of environments or expectations that limit the participation of individuals who are in some way different. If buildings or services were designed in a way that truly accounted for everyone's needs then no source of difference would be considered a disability. The charity model positions disabled people as passive recipients of assistance rather than agents of change and decision makers in our own lives.

These frameworks for understanding disability inform how some contributors talk about barriers that are built into public spaces and private homes. Various models of disability also influence the ways other contributors write personally about bodies, feelings, and the careful expenditure of each day's resources. Some of us are pushing for accessibility one public meeting at a time, and others are dreaming of justice. We talk about advocacy and activism, sleeping in and showing up. Sometimes we use identity-first language, other times we prefer person-first. We think about what the words we choose mean for the communities we belong to. We link internalized ableism to aging and show why lived experience matters in tackling the climate crisis. We have overlapping explanations of disability justice, as we imagine, analyze, and discuss how these concepts might apply to the people and places we care about.

This book was written on crip time, sometimes from bed, sometimes (figuratively) from a dark pit, often off the sides of our desks, in a notes app, or using speech-to-text. All of us move through space on crip time. It's not just buildings and streets we move through differently. It's not just the changing seasons and shifting sunlight we feel in our bodies. Spoons are a metaphor for tiny increments of capacity. What can you do when, at what time of day? Our experiences with disability accumulate over time. Past stereotypes cast a shadow on future assumptions. There's a weight to repetition. There's an exhaustion at having to always come up with a polite response. Where do we find the insight so that every person doesn't have to be endlessly, exhaustingly advocating for themself, all the time? How do we share space and spend time with people we don't share needs with? How do we expand outward, from each individual body and every person's vantage point, to build systems that are designed from the outset with room to manoeuvre and time to decompress?

Part of what comes next is perspective: zooming out, thinking about everybody's basic needs – for relationships, for food, for lodging – and how those needs might be impacted by disability or disabilities. Solutions are prescriptive. There's no single policy, piece of technology, or design standard that will get us to our accessible futures. Part of what comes next is imagining, then taking action, toward a somewhere or somewhen that ensures we all have ways to form relationships, keep in touch, protest, celebrate. Isolation is killing people. Accessibility and mobility are ways of coming together. We're already incredibly creative in forming relationships. We're already building ways to live in community.

You, the readers, are also us. You bring your own expertise in bringing people together, your own experience of living with disability, building with disabilities. Doing better doesn't have to take a lot of money. To give just one example, the costs for accessible housing are comparable to those for conventional building methods, as long as accessible features are incorporated from the earliest stages. But doing better does take time.

So take time with this book, come back to the chapters that make you uncomfortable. Read more about the words and ideas that are new to you. Think about who else you could listen to and what decisions you could pass on to someone whose expertise you may not have initially noticed. You can jump to the plain language summaries at the end of each chapter if you're low on energy, if English isn't your first language, if you're not a big reader, or if you're deep in brain fog. Next time you're looking for a quick accessibility checklist – slow down! Flip through the essays and interviews in this book or pause to think about who else you could talk to.

## Plain Language Summary

- This section introduces the book. Two key ideas are coming together in public and having access to privacy.
- Contributors share personal experiences in different chapters. For example, people write about bustling cities and peaceful forests.
- As well as discussing disability, contributors bring many other kinds of expertise. People share skills in making music, conducting research, analyzing movies, and planting gardens.
- There are many different voices in the book. Some people are more comfortable using academic language. Others speak informally or write imaginatively.
- This section is also an invitation to readers. Anyone engaging with this book is welcome to slow down, get uncomfortable, and learn more about words or ideas that may be unfamiliar.

# Starting Out

# 'Justice Is About the Collective'

## Rabia Khedr

### Introduction and Identities

**Emily Macrae:** You bring extensive experience in disability justice at the local, provincial, and national levels. How did you get started in community organizing?

**Rabia Khedr:** Well, I'm a person with lived experience. I was born with a disability, a genetic condition that over time has reduced my ability to see, and hence I identify myself as blind. I also grew up in a household with younger siblings who also were born with different disabilities. I just went through figuring it out for myself as an immigrant child having to learn how to self-advocate. I graduated university saying I would not make a profession out of disability, and lo and behold, life happens. I found myself in the midst of a whole career path on disability.

**EM:** You're the national director of Disability Without Poverty, CEO of DEEN (Disability Empowerment Equality Network) Support Services, previous commissioner of the Ontario Human Rights Commission, founder of the Canadian Association of Muslims with Disabilities, and more! You've already given some details about your background – how else would you introduce yourself?

**RK:** I am a racialized woman, so I am a Muslim, Punjabi, Pakistani-Canadian woman. Married, wife, mother, daughter of aging parents.

I am an activist and advocate, and I came up with more sophisticated, white-privileged terms that I am stealing, borrowing, using. I used to say, 'I'm a shit disturber.' Now I say, 'I'm a social entrepreneur and systems disrupter.'

**EM:** Tell me more about what you mean when you talk about appropriating those terms of white privilege?

**RK:** Well, you know, 'shit disturber' doesn't sound that attractive and polished and professional. But 'systems disrupter' does.

**EM:** Right, so that pressure of respectability.

**RK:** [laughing] Yes, or just power! Right? It's a term of more power. 'Shit disturber' just means you're a troublemaker. 'I'm a systems change agent,' 'I'm a systems disrupter.' It's more white-privileged, social justice.

## Disability Rights, Justice, and Systems

**EM:** And what are the systems you're focusing on right now?

**RK:** Systems that exclude lived experiences of people with disability. Systems that compartmentalize disability and ghettoize it. We all have our disability politics around who's worse off. Who's more disabled? Whose needs are more significant? And I think that is reinforced by the system of supports that society has crafted, politically. Those systems split up the categories or labels of disability into different compartments. And when I say 'ghettoize,' I mean marginalize as a result. Because then we're not being dealt with as a collective, we're not being given that power of belonging to a group. We're being pitted against each other. It's that historical, colonial beast of divide-and-conquer.

For example, *autism* is a very hot term. Everyone wants the autism label. Funding is tied to that label. But if you have global developmental delay, you're marginalized, even though your behaviours might be very similar, and your needs might be very similar for supports or interventions. But if you're not labelled appropriately, if you're not categorized, if you're not catalogued, you're not resourced. I'm trying to ensure that there's a lens of equity and justice applied across the board for the full inclusion of people with disabilities, especially racialized people with disabilities and people with disabilities combatting Islamophobia.

**EM:** In terms of equity and justice, I know many of your areas of expertise are at the intersection of accessibility and cultural competency. How do those concepts relate?

**RK:** Systems treat people with disabilities as disabled people. I'm not against either term; I've matured and learned that there are a variety of perspectives. So I'm a person with a disability and I'm a disabled person. It's okay either way. Person-first language is important, however; I'm not *just* a disabled person and that's why person-centred language is important. Because I am a person who has a skin colour, who has an identity as a woman, an identity because of my choice to express my faith visibly. I am racialized, I combat sexism and ableism and all those *isms* across the board, and yet systems often respond only in a prescriptive, medicalized approach to the notion of disablements. Only. Without looking at inclusion and accessibility more broadly.

So, as a racialized Muslim woman with a disability, I require access in many different ways. Inclusion looks different for me than it does for a white man with a disability. Because a white man with a disability still has privilege. A white woman with a disability still has privilege. Because a white man is only battling disability. A white woman is battling disability and barriers due to her gender. A racialized person, like a racialized man with a disability, faces two counts of discrimination – he has to work away at two layers of discrimination. As a racialized woman with a disability, I have three layers. As a racialized woman with a disability who also chooses to express her faith visibly – and with the rise of Islamophobia – I actually face four layers of discrimination. So that really compounds the barriers I face and the things I need in order to be fully included.

As somebody Muslim with a disability, I require access to my places of worship. Depending on the disability, access can look different for people. And again, within my place of worship, I face barriers as a woman. And my disability. So I'm constantly combatting discrimination, barriers, and needing to fight for accommodations on multiple fronts. In the mainstream, in my cultural spaces, in my spaces of faith, in women's spaces. It's complex.

**EM:** In terms of those layers of discrimination, how do you explain to others or work through the distinction between disability rights and disability justice?

**RK:** Disability rights, within the Canadian context, through legislation, policies programs, and services, are really focused on the disability component only. The existing framework doesn't necessarily facilitate a conversation on equity. Whereas disability justice to me is really about recognizing the fact that disabled people are more than their disability, and if we are to create a genuinely just society, we have to be included across the board.

To me, justice is universal. Justice is something that everybody has a right to. Like we have a right to fair and just treatment. So when I talk about human rights, I say we have rights but we also have a responsibility to ensure those rights are given to all. Disability justice to me incorporates both – the right and the responsibility.

**EM:** And it sounds like justice also makes more space for many of those other identities.

**RK:** Yes.

## Individuality and Collectivity

**EM:** What I hear you saying is that there are limits to focusing on the rights of individuals. Can you talk about the role of families and communities in your work?

**RK:** I can. So, just going back to the idea of rights: rights are individual, they're not collective. They're very much about the individual, and disability justice is about the collective. Even for me, I'll go a step further and I'll say I prefer the term 'people with disabilities,' as opposed to 'persons with disabilities.' I see 'persons with disabilities' as reflecting the old divide-and-conquer principle. I understand person-first language, but who else do we call persons, what other group do we pluralize like that?

It's not 'racialized persons,' it's 'racialized people.' It's 'Black people,' right? It's all collective. Whereas as soon as it comes to people with disabilities, it's all individual. I think it's deliberate – this whole divisive system that compartmentalizes and categorizes people with disabilities by their disability and isolates them, then prescribes supports and services that cater only to that one type of person as opposed to the collective.

**EM:** It sounds like shifting from 'persons' to 'people' is a way of acknowledging the communities we're part of.

**RK:** It's putting power toward the community. We know that the disability community is unique because there are so many differences. There isn't one 'disability culture.' We talk about the notion of disability culture, but disability culture isn't just one thing. It varies from the type of disability to type of disability even, in terms of how people experience culture and express culture. How somebody with a physical disability – physical in terms of mobility disability – experiences culture is very different than how somebody blind expresses culture or experiences culture.

What I experience is by touch and texture. So something might feel really beautiful to me and my kids will say, 'Mum, that's atrocious! That's ugly. You're not going to wear that.' But it feels so good! But then I have to conform to what's visibly beautiful outwardly, because I really don't want to wear something that everyone else sees as ugly, even though it feels beautiful to me. But I also won't wear something that looks beautiful to everyone else but feels like crap to me.

**EM:** Yeah, going back to that concept of respectability you were talking about earlier.

**RK:** Yes, there isn't a single 'disability culture,' but as people with disabilities, we have all these cultural experiences that are unique to us, depending on our intersectional identities. We need culturally responsive and respectful programs, supports, and services.

**EM:** What do responsive and respectful programs look or feel like?

**RK:** One of the areas I've always been aware of – and this comes back to the families we support at DEEN (Disability Empowerment Equality Network) and my lived experience of having brothers with intellectual disabilities and my parents as caregivers – is home-care services. Home-care services are person-centred. It's great to be person-centred, but when that person is part of a family and a household, the system for instance tells the support worker they can only do the laundry for that one person. In a household, you don't do the laundry by person. You don't separate the whites and the colours by person. If you're there to take care of that person and alleviate the work of the caregiver, doing the laundry of only that one person, sorting their whites and colours and doing two loads, it doesn't alleviate the chore. The rest of that household still has to do additional whites and colours! What's wrong with throwing in a full load of whites? Then you've minimized one chore. But that's not what the rules say you can do.

## DEEN and Other Local and National Organizing

**EM:** Is DEEN Support Services a reaction to that kind of overly individual approach, which is common in a lot of health care and mainstream services?

**RK:** What informed DEEN Support Services is the exclusion of the types of activities that are a part of the daily lives of individuals with diverse cultural and spiritual experiences. Within a familial environment, a routine involves food, involves language, it may involve faith. That may not be reflected when an individual is in an environment that is providing care to them.

For example, my brother lives in a group home and he comes home for our holy celebrations. I always give him something to take back to share with his housemates as a treat. But is there a whole celebration done for him in that house as the only Muslim resident there? I don't think so. I'm not asking them to do that, but I shouldn't have to. From a systems approach, if we're to genuinely embrace diversity and inclusion and culturally responsive service, I shouldn't have to ask.

It's about belonging and connection. My big vision behind DEEN is to have residential and respite services for people with disabilities where they choose who they live with. Not waiting for the empty bed in a congregate setting or a group home that chooses a person based on their diagnosis and support needs and type of disability and behaviours. But, in fact, it's about relationships. Because that's how able-bodied people choose who they live with, right? We choose to live by ourselves or in a community or with a roommate or in a household because we're a part of a family, or we have a relationship, or we have friends, or we take a roommate, or we get married, or we choose to live together.

**EM:** Yeah, there's a denial of relationships among people with disabilities, especially people labelled with intellectual and/or developmental disabilities.

**RK:** Yup.

**EM:** So DEEN offers day programming and peer support networks. But it also has its own space now, the Muneeba Centre in Mississauga. Could you tell me about that?

**RK:** We have a house where we operate our day program because that gives us autonomy. It's something we realized is critical when we were going through the pandemic. We started to operate programming much earlier in the pandemic than larger funded agencies. Some have just resumed some programming in 2023.

When it came to people in group homes, they were re-institutionalized as a result of Covid. So all that community-living philosophy went out the window as soon as health care directives came into place. Residents' movements were controlled, who they interacted with was controlled. They didn't have the right to touch and embrace family. They weren't given the right to risk! That's a term I use from my late friend Sandra Carpenter, who lived in an institution as a young person and then became a champion and a pioneer in independent living.

**EM:** Ah, even more isolation under the auspices of slowing the spread.

**RK:** Exactly, and so despite the concept of living in the community, mainstream residential options became institutions. Just for health and safety, you cannot take away choice. Because everybody else still had choice during the pandemic. People living on their own, without disabilities, could defy wearing a mask. But residents of group homes were forced to wear a mask. Residents who exerted behaviours not conforming to infection control were chemically and physically restrained. No one else in the broader community was monitored and punished for not following Covid guidelines. The de-institutionalization movement has started to re-institutionalize people at a micro level due to the pandemic.

**EM:** And you're building an alternative model with DEEN.

**RK:** I'm building a model where families and individuals have choice. We operate a day program that has life-skills activities. We teach food that's familiar, and not 'continental' or 'mainstream.' Or whatever mainstream food participants like is there too, whatever is a part of their lived experience is a part of the life skills they're learning. For some that involves halal food; that involves a variety of cultures from north, south, east, and west.

There are hygiene and cleanliness principles incorporated too. A toileting routine for somebody is done so the personal care is provided as it would be by their family. For example, in Islam, we wash our bottoms when we use the toilet. We don't just wipe. So the DEEN bathroom is equipped with a bidet.

Some families want their family members to adhere to whatever daily worship principles they have, and we support those needs, so we support people's spiritual development. The celebrations of the group reflect participants' traditions. We will recognize and talk about Christmas because it's the season around us. We will recognize and talk about other traditions if there are volunteers and participants and staff amongst us who celebrate those. So we celebrate Eid; we've done decorations for Diwali when we've had interns who celebrate Diwali, for example.

**EM:** It sounds like those different cultural and community identities have been on your mind and part of your lived experience forever. What has it been like to build relationships with other groups?

**RK:** Oh, for sure. Well, they're all friends and allies. We all met through Ethno-Racial People with Disabilities Coalition of Ontario (ERDCO) back in the 1990s and we went off to do our own specific things afterward. Now I'm trying to bring everybody back, build capacity beyond the Greater Toronto Area, at a national level. This is what we are creating through Race and Disability Canada.

**EM:** In terms of other work on the national level, are there learnings that you're bringing from Disability Without Poverty?

**RK:** People have been working on the issue of poverty among disabled people for a very long time, but those conversations were fragmented. They were in different spaces. When policy-makers finally heard the call and the prime minister committed to a Canada Disability Benefit as an income supplement to lift people with disabilities out of poverty, that's when we felt it was important to build a collective voice. So Disability Without Poverty came into being by staying laser-focused on getting the Canada Disability Benefit into legislation and regulation.

I've deepened my understanding around strategies and tactics that have to be adopted to influence social policy. Through Disability Without Poverty, I found myself again connecting with national organizations and realizing that although some conversations have happened, not much has changed from twenty years ago, when I was nationally engaged. At least in terms of that intersectional piece. Everybody uses the term 'intersectionality' but not much has changed.

## Peace and Pause

**EM:** There's so much that you do – where do you go when you're looking for peace or pause?

**RK:** Mm-hmm. [laughs] My new thing around peace and pause is I got into watching Urdu dramas and I've brushed up on my Urdu language skills on YouTube. On the iPhone! I've discovered the iPhone. So much more is accessible to me now than ever before. The dramas are pretty good with voice-over. And then, you know, going to the mosque on a Friday, listening to a good sermon. It's hit-or-miss, depending. But there's some solace in that.

**EM:** Have you noticed or been involved in changes toward improving access to spaces of worship?

**RK:** We have been constantly advocating for that. With DEEN, we actually have an accessibility audit that we're promoting. We've also built a collaboration with a few other organizations, like the Organization of Canadian Tamils with Disabilities and their direct service arm. The Annai Thantha Illam Foundation, Accessibility for All, ERDCO – all these organizations that exist but haven't necessarily built the kind of infrastructure that DEEN has. We've kind of built a collaborative, known as Race and Disability Canada, and we've gone after a federal grant to really build capacity in the disability sector to talk about the intersection of race and disability.

**EM:** Thanks again for this conversation. Any final thoughts?

**RK:** The very powerful thing I've learned working on Disability Without Poverty is that regardless of my race, my identity as a Muslim, I have talked to small-town grandmothers who have probably never met anybody like me, who are saying: 'Thank you so much for what you are doing. Let me know what I can do to help. Because I have an autistic grandchild.' Or 'I have a disabled nephew.' To me, that connecting really restores my faith in this society and what our true Canadian values are. It gives me strength to do what we're doing; it reinforces my conviction that we're doing the right thing.

## Plain Language Summary

- In this interview, Rabia talks about how community organizing can disrupt systems. Her focus is on the ways that systems exclude people with disabilities.
- From personal experience, Rabia knows that different types of discrimination stack on top of one another. This means that a white man with a disability faces fewer barriers than a racialized woman with a disability.
- Rabia wants disabled people to choose where they live based on relationships, not diagnoses. DEEN (Disability Empowerment Equality Network) Support Services already offers a day program. Participants enjoy food and traditions that they recognize from family life.
- Rabia also talks about organizing provincially and nationally. Disability Without Poverty is pushing the federal government to lift disabled people out of poverty.

# Minding the City

## Corey Bialek

In September 2022, I was clinically diagnosed with double depression. Double depression refers to the coexistence of two forms of depression: persistent depressive disorder (PDD), also known as dysthymia, and major depressive disorder (MDD). It is a sum-is-greater-than-its-parts phenomenon that amplifies each disorder's respective symptoms.

PDD feels like an unnamed darkness flickering in the corners of my mind. Not catastrophic, but not immaterial. Some call it a veil of sadness, a poetic turn of phrase used to describe a steady undercurrent of sadness, lethargy, and disinterest in daily activities. It is a psychological baseline of unbreaking melancholy characterized by an inescapable sense of merely existing – surviving rather than thriving.

At unpredictable intervals, this baseline is punctuated by major depressive episodes. These *are* catastrophic. The kind of flare-ups that render 'normal' obsolete: despair deepens, sadness swells, and energy evaporates. If PDD is a flicker, MDD is a supernova.

The combination of PDD's veil of sadness with the acute episodes of MDD creates a challenging cycle of ups and downs, often leaving me feeling trapped and overwhelmed. The consequences of this cycle on my daily life are manifold. My relationships begin to decay as my ability to engage emotionally and maintain connections becomes strained. Social withdrawal becomes a tempting refuge, leading to a sense of isolation and loneliness. The capitalist markers of a 'good citizen' are also apt to wane, as my productivity and performance at work decline. I've often described this phenomenon as *limited bandwidth*, whereby my energy and focus slowly drain away. Altogether, the constant struggle against overwhelming sadness and exhaustion erodes my self-confidence and undermines personal goals and aspirations.

All these mental cogs – turning on and off, speeding up and slowing down – introduce acute challenges to navigating the city and its public spaces. Daily journeys, whether to the grocery store or the office, by foot or by transit, are laden with shifting emotional triggers. Public space has the capacity to compound existing mental health struggles, creating new pathways of suffering. Given that the experience of *suffering-through* is often overlooked in the design of public space, struggling folks across the mental health spectrum are forced to develop their own personal and bespoke coping mechanisms.

It is here that an interesting tension emerges: while public spaces have the capacity to exacerbate the symptoms of double depression, so too can they ameliorate them. It is in this tension that a rich possibility exists to rethink how cities can tend to mental health via therapeutic spaces that promise refuge and respite to those looking for them.

In the remainder of this chapter, I use my experience of double depression to explore the interplay between mental health and public space – how I have used public space to mitigate my symptoms, and surface lessons that have broader applicability to the enterprise of city planning and design.

## Street Theatre: A Tragedy

I hold in tension an intellectual belief in the value of Jane Jacobs' 'street theatre' with a deeply personal and emotional aversion to it. For Jacobs, streets are not merely conduits for vehicular traffic but vital spaces that foster community engagement, social connections, and a sense of belonging. She believed that vibrant streets with diverse uses and activities, such as walking, social interactions, sidewalk vendors, cafés, and public gatherings, contribute to the liveliness and vitality of a city. Moreover, she conceived of sidewalks as places of social improvisation and spontaneity. For Jacobs, this unpredictability is intrinsic to community cohesion, given that it catalyzes chance conversations, impromptu interactions, and a sense of security.

All the things that threaten my already limited bandwidth.

To be clear, I am not *always* frozen with fear when imagining sidewalks teeming with strangers. In fact, on good days, I can find enjoyment in street markets and festivals. However, when I am saddled with the heft of double depression's lethargy, sadness, anxiety, and exhaustion, my mind reorganizes the public realm into a patchwork of spaces fraught with peril.

Under these conditions, the theatre of the sidewalk fades into tragedy. Scenes of vibrancy are jarring to me. And my coping strategies are markedly anti-social: I move with haste to limit interaction with others, I keep my head down and avoid eye contact, and I walk on the side of the street less travelled.

It's not just the barrage of social activity that poses a psychological risk: the public realm itself becomes antagonistic. When filtered through my lens of depression, I see destruction in the streetscape. A world crafted in service of human conceit. Concrete and asphalt, wires and metalwork. Infrastructure. It is vital for a city to function, but its decidedly artificial nature feels like an assault on life. We cut down trees to protect overhead wires. We bury creeks to build roads. We exterminate socially constructed 'pests' – insects, rats, and other unfortunate beings – under the guise of health and safety. I cannot find promise in a slab of concrete the way I can in the buds on a tree branch. For a mind already trained on hopelessness, the juxtaposition between inorganic and organic can be ruinous.

It is, of course, easier to describe this in hindsight. When experiencing it, the combination of social anxiety, depression, and existential dread leave my emotional wires frayed and unspun. It is the fear of this feeling that makes withdrawal tempting – remaining at home, in my place of refuge.

## On the Nature of Humanity

The public realm is not antagonistic by default. In fact, when designed with nature-based intent, it has the capacity to attenuate the effects of depression. For me, this has been most evident in spaces that embrace biophilic design, a philosophy that borrows from Edward O. Wilson's biophilia hypothesis (defined as the urge to affiliate with other forms of life). In simple terms, biophilic design seeks to reconnect people with natural environments. It is, in part, a response to a rich body of literature that posits that humanity's eroding relation to nature has contributed to negative physical and mental health outcomes. As we have ideologically furthered ourselves from 'nature' – by othering it, feminizing it, dominating it – we have untethered ourselves from the very systems within which we evolved (it is not a leap to suggest that this chasm continues to propel human-driven climate change and biodiversity loss). Of course, we haven't risen above nature – we've risen within it. To be disconnected from it is at best unhuman and at worst cataclysmic.

It is this innate sense of loss, a lack of communion with nature, that worsens my own struggles with depression.

In contrast, biophilic design tends to the physical and ideological gap between us and nature. First, biophilic design holds at its core a belief that humans and nature are intrinsically, evolutionarily, and spiritually linked. Second, it argues that it is imperative to reconstitute these links, given our rapidly urbanizing world. Finally, it posits that access to nature – whether visual, auditory, olfactory, or tactile – can seed positive mental and physical health outcomes.

This feels intuitive to me. Given the choice, I would opt for street trees over street signs, parks over parking lots, and wetlands over retention ponds. Yet, as a species with over eight billion members, we cannot retreat to the ecosystems we evolved in (in part because we have indelibly altered them to serve our own needs). Nonetheless, we *can* replicate natural patterns in our urban spaces by looking to biophilic design, and in doing so foster opportunities for refuge, respite, and rehabilitation.

## What's in a Park?

In 2013, following the dissolution of my first relationship, I moved back into my parents' basement. The breakup was preceded by a month-long major depressive disorder, one of the darker stretches of time that I've experienced.

My parents live in a highway-adjacent suburb in southern Winnipeg – the sort of placeless geography that could have driven me to depression had I not already gotten there on my own. Following a multi-month withdrawal from the outside world, I summoned the willpower to cycle to the nearby Kings Park. Tucked within an oxbow loop of the Red River, the park sprawls across ninety-two acres with a perimeter all-purpose path. The path offers connection points to the park's various amenities, including a protected prairie landscape, sports fields, a lake with waterfall, and a labyrinth.

Too unsure and anxious, I needed a couple of weeks before I felt brave enough to dismount and *experience* the park. This was when I first learned about the meditative and restorative properties of labyrinths.

In the context of biophilic design, labyrinths are considered *spaces of refuge*. These spaces provide opportunities for relaxation, stress reduction, and rejuvenation. When integrated into the built environment, refuge spaces create the conditions for respite from the demands and pressures of everyday life.

This mirrors my experience.

## Walking the Rows

My first trip to the Carol Shields Memorial Labyrinth took place on one of those fecund prairie mornings in the Winnipeg spring. For those not familiar, something special happens in Winnipeg as the white-and-grey winter landscape transforms into a mélange of greens amplified by the din of life awakening en masse. The air becomes more inviting as crisp winter winds change to sporadic soft breezes. Puddles underfoot signal that the great melt has started. Squirrels squirrel, butterflies fly, and grasshoppers hop.

As my mind gorged on the seasonal delights, my anxiety dissipated enough to allow curiosity in. It was as if nature was beckoning me to join it.

As I approached the entrance to the Carol Shields Memorial Labyrinth, I encountered a stone plaque inscribed with detailed instructions. First, consider a contemplative thought or question. This came easily: *What would it mean to not be depressed?* Then, attempt to walk the pebbly rows of the labyrinth with a clear mind. Once you have arrived at the centre, remain still and identify the emotions you are feeling: *sadness, hopelessness, loneliness.* Then, while walking back to the entrance, ruminate on the original question.

I took a visual inventory of the labyrinth. The air was perfumed by the native species of flowering plants tucked between the gravel rows. Bumblebees flitted from stem to petal. The commemorative bricks constituting the outer edge of the path featured etched names and messages, memorializing death, achievement, and love. Up close, what might otherwise look like static imagery was a living landscape imbued with meaning. I started to understand Dorothy's wonderment as she stepped into Technicolor – the world was not drab by default. With a deep breath and wavering conviction, I took my first step.

My first go was not a roaring success – I wasn't *less* depressed. But the experience did trigger a sense of possibility. By way of contemplation, I noted nascent feelings of mindfulness, relaxation, and self-awareness. They were amorphous, like eye floaters: there, but gone with a blink.

Over the next four weeks, I returned to the labyrinth daily. With each visit, the process of introspection opened new spaces in my mind. Within these mental expanses, I could explore my emotions and thoughts, and through this achieve some level of clarity and perspective on my personal struggles. I found poetry in my mental awakening that coincided with the spring bloom, as each bud raced to open first. Ironically, I grew closer to my depression, learning to regard it as something I live with, not something that defines me. In this realization, I discovered the possibility of hope.

To be clear, the labyrinth was not curative, but it *was* therapeutic. The act of contemplation, set within a naturalized landscape, helped steel me for a difficult journey toward self-healing. Proof positive that nature can be more than a backdrop.

Importantly, labyrinths are only one of many manifestations of refuge space. To be sure, it is not my contention that all parks and streets be retrofitted to include unidirectional pathways (although, selfishly, I would not mind it). However, I am suggesting that we could, and should, incorporate opportunities for escape for those who need them – as simple as a street arcade or as complex as a grotto.

Even more broadly, in service of promoting healthy outcomes, biophilic design's core belief that stronger connections to nature are universally beneficial should reverberate throughout the design of public space.

## Contemplations and Conclusions

Over the past decade, I have floated between professional positions in urban planning, sustainability consulting, and development. What's been fascinating to witness, particularly as a person who struggles with mental health, is how casually *wellness* is tossed around within this multidisciplinary landscape.

Indeed, wellness has resurfaced as a topic du jour, a kneejerk response to a global pandemic that foisted the issue back into the collective consciousness. Yet the people making decisions, those responsible for crafting healthy communities, are not well-suited for the job. Sure, like everyone, I am happy to know that the air circulating in my office has been filtered more than the stories I see on Instagram. But it misses the point completely when real conversations about mental health are absent from the discourse. Yet, at the same time, we can't expect planners or architects or city officials to facilitate meaningful conversations about the topic while bereft of the requisite knowledge to do so.

But we do love to talk about it.

And here, in this superficial discourse, nature has emerged as wellness's corollary.

The narrative that nature can improve mental health has been deployed by professions across the city-building spectrum, usually to curry favour for both public and private development projects. It has become so pervasive and encompassing that its original meaning has been largely hollowed out. It is right up there with sustainability and accessibility, concepts that are presented to the public in a way that's untethered from real-world implementation. Indeed, even if they've made it into the design concepts, wellness and nature tend to be value-engineered to within an inch of their lives. It is why we continue to build concrete plazas (sorry, 'privately owned publicly accessible spaces'), streets with trees cast in concrete, and new communities named after the ecological feature they replaced – Bubbling Brook Estates, for example. Sure, I am jaded, but for good reason. These things are almost exclusively delivered in their cheapest and cheeriest iterations.

We should not lay blame for this at the feet of urban planners, developers, architects, or any of the on-the-ground folks toiling through the mucky realities of city-building. I believe there is a genuine, collective interest in exploring ways to meaningfully integrate natural systems into our communities. But this seems to me a fool's errand, at least within our current economic system. Just as capitalism has co-opted sustainability by reclassifying development as *sustainable growth* (an oxymoron if ever there was one), so too has it co-opted wellness. How many times have you encountered the term *self-care* since the pandemic? Surely it is not the *system* making us sick, but our own irresponsible patterns of behaviour. Tsk, tsk!

And all of this is to say nothing about a political apparatus that pathologizes lower socio-economic status while limiting uses of public space: encampment clear-outs, public realm disinvestment, defensive architecture, inadequate and non-existent bathroom facilities. Is it intellectually honest to rely on this system – the same system that creates the conditions for mental precarity – to meaningfully address mental health in the design of our cities? Perhaps, but only if your class-based identity card gets you through the turnstile.

This is admittedly an oversimplification of an enormously complex issue. I get it. But I am steadfast in my belief that moving forward requires eyes wide open, even if all I see is a world clad in concrete. We must understand the system we are working within, knowing where it is malleable and where it is immutable, if we are to recast human spaces as ecologically diverse, biophilic, and egalitarian. This is a worthwhile pursuit, even if we are doomed to muddle through.

On the bright side, who is more accustomed to muddling through than those living with mental health challenges?

See you at the labyrinth.


## Plain Language Summary

- Corey writes about what living with double depression means for going outside and getting around a city.
- Going to the grocery store or taking public transit can make a bad day worse. But when public spaces are designed carefully, going outside can have a positive impact on mental health.
- Corey describes biking to a park when he lived in Winnipeg. Although he had been very depressed for months, he returned to the

park many times and eventually got off his bike to walk around a labyrinth in the park.

- Walking the labyrinth was a way to reflect on how he was feeling and to connect with nature in the city. Corey gradually found feelings of mindfulness, relaxation, and self-awareness at the labyrinth.
- As someone who studied urban planning and now works in that area, Corey is critical of the way that new projects use words like *wellness* without actually creating conditions that could help people feel better.

# I'm Proud to Call Myself Tkaronto-Guyanese

## Courage Bacchus, translated from ASL by Kimberley Johnson

*Note: This chapter is translated from a video that Courage recorded in May 2024.*

Hello, everyone. My name is Natasha Bacchus. I prefer to be called Courage, and my sign name looks like this *(sign language for brave)*. You *(readers)* may be curious who I am. Let me introduce myself.

I identify as Black, female, Deaf, and queer. I prefer to communicate using sign. I use a variety of communication systems:

- American Sign Language (ASL)
- Signed Exact English (SEE)
- Gestures
- International Sign
- Fingerspelling
- A little bit of lip reading

I was born and raised in Toronto. My mom and dad immigrated here from Guyana from the city of Georgetown. I'm proud to call myself Toronto-Guyanese, but I don't feel comfortable identifying as Canadian. People of African descent settled here because of slavery and formed the Black diaspora that exists here in Canada, America, South America, and Europe. This is Indigenous territory, and this land is considered stolen land. This makes me feel uncomfortable identifying as Canadian.

I acknowledge this land belongs to Indigenous people and I acknowledge those of African descent who were brought here because of slavery, and who subsequently fought for their freedom. (*Sigh*)

## Passions

I really love sports and exercise. I am a former Deaf Olympic runner. I love working out, running, and being active outdoors.

I am passionate about advocating for my rights and those of my various communities. These groups comprise a minority and have been marginalized. I pay special attention to Indigenous, Black, and Deaf people, plus the rainbow (*International Sign for* 2SLGBTQ+) and disabled communities. They are very invisible in our society and have been systematically excluded. They have a lot of mental health struggles, passions, and successes yet remain under-represented in our society. Inclusion for Indigenous, Black, Deaf, and rainbow communities is lacking.

I want to fight for them, so they have a safe space where they can express themselves. It means a lot to have a voice and to share it, but it's not easy to do so. The experience of oppression and exclusion has made it unsafe to be vulnerable. The system has caused me harm and failed me. But I still have my voice.

## Roles

I have several roles: arts access consultant, mixed-media actress, and Deaf theatre interpreter. And I like to participate in panel presentations and do facilitation work. I have been involved with CILT, which stands for Centre for Independent Living in Toronto. I've been with this organization for two years as a workshop facilitator and have done workshops for the 519 and the Rexdale Community Centre. I have an upcoming workshop with the YWCA where I will share my experiences with ableism, disability, and CILT.

## Community-Building

'What does community-building mean to me?' Let me think about this. To me, building community means building trust. Understanding one another's background, trusting each other, collaborating, and working together. Do we have a mutual understanding of what access needs are and how to meet them to build community?

Trust is important. Community-building requires a feeling of trust in the space. Everyone needs to work collectively to ensure all access needs are met, and to ensure that no one feels left out. So, for me, number one for community-building is trust. Number two is respect, and number three is patience. We all come from different intersections in terms of our background, experience, perspective, opinion, and feelings. We see things differently. The challenge is in building trust.

For example, the Deaf community contains divisions: the white Deaf and the Black and Indigenous Deaf. It is challenging for these two groups to come together. Why is that? Trust. The Black and Indigenous people are sensitive to who is in their space. The white Deaf folks are focused more on work, whereas the Black and Indigenous Deaf folks prefer a safe space where they can discuss their personal concerns, thoughts, viewpoints, aspirations, and needs.

Do these two communities trust each other? No. They must build trust by being responsible and by their willingness to take accountability, their willingness to learn, their willingness to understand and nurture a safe environment. An exchange of knowledge requires a safe space and time. People can't jump into a relationship without earning trust first.

## Safe Space

In terms of my personal experience, have I felt safe in the hearing and Deaf communities? Not always, no. I need to take my time to build trust by learning who is in the space and by getting to know their agenda and desires. I also consider:

- Do we understand each other?
- What is their lived experienced?
- Where do each of us stand?

I need to know these things before sharing my knowledge.

It is challenging because the community is very, very small and doubly so for the Indigenous, Black, Deaf, and disabled communities, which are even smaller. It is hard for individuals to have that trust, but we must come together and build trust in order to move forward.

### Favourite Place

My favourite place is Paris. I like it because I can be outside enjoying the outdoors, dining, and people-watching. I just love Paris. I also like to visit Guyana, where my family is from and where I still have relatives. I enjoy spending time with them when I go there. I also love Toronto because of the abundance of international food on offer here. I enjoy going to different restaurants and trying global cuisines. I like Toronto big-time, it's champ (*sign language for* awesome). I like the world vibe of the city, the culture, and the food from international communities.

### Access in Toronto

Availability of access for Deaf people in Toronto is definitely challenging. Some public spaces offer basic access. For example, movie theatres have closed captioning. Public theatres such as Theatre Passe Muraille, Harbourfront, and Buddies in Bad Times provide interpretation and captioning services, so that's cool. Access is not widespread, though. The best example of access here is Canada Video Relay Service for making phone calls. Apart from the examples I've mentioned, there is very little access for Deaf people in Toronto.

What do I want the readers to know? Access should be in place for Deaf people who live and work in Toronto. Whether Deaf people want to go shopping or buy theatre tickets at the box office, make sure frontline staff are willing to communicate either by writing back and forth on paper or by hiring an interpreter. If the staff know sign language, that's wonderful. Communicating with people in public space has been a challenge.

Deaf people do live, work, and play here but are spread throughout the city. I know some of them are active in sports through organizations like Silent Voice and the Bob Rumball Canadian Centre of Excellence for the Deaf (BRCD). They also work in various locations in Ontario, such as Belleville, London, and BRCD. They are also in Barrie, Toronto, and Milton.

## Access in Washington

For the question 'So far, do you have a positive experience to share of another town/city?' Yes, I do. Washington, DC, is amazing and very accessible because of Gallaudet University and its surrounding area. There are businesses with Deaf staff such as Starbucks, pizza places, a Deaf-owned brewery, and a theatre called Atlas. Gallaudet University in Washington, DC, is an amazing space for hosting Deaf events. It's just not the same in Toronto. Here, we don't have Deaf restaurant owners, Deaf café owners, or Deaf theatre owners. It would be nice to see Toronto have some of what already exists at Gallaudet in Washington, DC.

## Sports and Art

I'm an athlete, three-time Deaf Olympian, intramural track-and-field champion, and one-time Pan-American Games for the Deaf champion.

I love running, and my specialty is sprinting. I've done the 100-, 200-, and 400-metre races and participated in the 100-, 200-, and 400-metre relays for both indoor and outdoor track.

I became an actor in … 2019 *(ellipsis indicates pause in source video)*.

My first performance was in a production called *The Black Drum,* which featured an all-Deaf cast. The director was a woman and theatre-owner from Norway. She's retired now. Her name is Mira Zimmerman. She taught me all about the theatre world. I then immersed myself in the realm of show-making, learning about the rehearsal process, run-throughs, and tech runs. I flew to Paris for two weeks and travelled to a small town located just north of the city called Reims. Every two years they host a Deaf arts festival called Clin d'oeil.

I really enjoyed being in an all-Deaf environment where I got to experience different artistic expressions. I have been in different parts of the Deaf world through the Deaf Olympics and the arts. The former is all about competition and being physical while the latter is where one can express themselves through various genres of art.

## ASL and Sign

I'd like to return to ASL and share an anecdote that made me uncomfortable.

The first language I learned at the age of four was ASL. This language was invented by white Deaf teachers, so ASL isn't the best fit for me. I am grateful, though, that I can express myself through sign; that's a positive. The negative is that ASL deprived me of my true language. I should have learned my ancestral languages: African language, Black language, Black Sign Language, and African Sign Language. These are part of my origin.

My experience as a Deaf Olympian helped to solidify my Deaf identity. I also learned International Sign and realized that I didn't have to rely exclusively on ASL as the only means of sign communication.

As an actor, performer, visual artist, and artist advocate, I embarked on a journey of decolonization. Unpacking myself through art helped me tremendously. I could share my story with others. I have struggled, though, to express my true self through ASL. It is not my natural language. It is important to express my authentic self and identity through my own artistic practice. I don't have to resort to ASL or the ways in which I have been colonized to express myself.

## Performance

I would like to add a bit about my upcoming performance. It is a monologue and will happen from July 31 to August 4, 2024, for the National Deaf Arts & Culture Festival in Halifax, Nova Scotia. I will be unpacking my Blackness and the journey to becoming me. I explore my life as a Deaf Olympian, the feeling of disappearing from being colonized to my experience with ASL. My original sign name prior to Courage was the ASL letter N at the shoulder. It stood for Natasha. A white teacher gave me this sign. I find it triggering because it references having a bad attitude (ew *facial expression*).

Courage represents who I am. I'm a trailblazer. My running is a metaphor for the challenges and obstacles I have faced. I run through the woods, breaking down barriers and running through walls. Despite all my fears, I keep pushing through.

So, please come to Halifax and watch me perform along with three other Black Deaf artists from across Canada. We will be sharing our individual journeys of unpacking and exploring our Blackness.

ASL is my first language, but it is also a foreign language.

My journey of decolonization and exploring my Blackness has been beneficial for me.

**Translator's Note:** *The process of changing spoken/signed language into written form doesn't always fully capture non-verbal/manual communication (e.g., tone of voice, facial expression). To help account for this, I made conscious* *word choices while also taking into consideration the author's voice, the audience, and the medium. My notes have been added in italics and parentheses to indicate some of the non-verbal communication.*

## Plain Language Summary

• This chapter is based on a video Courage Bacchus made in ASL. It was collaboratively translated into English by Kimberley Johnson, a BIPOC interpreter.

• Courage identifies as Black, female, Deaf, and queer. She prefers to communicate using sign. Courage explains that because ASL was invented by white Deaf teachers, it isn't the best fit for her.

• Courage is an athlete, three-time Deaf Olympian, intramural track-and-field champion, and one-time Pan-American Games for the Deaf champion. She's also an actor, performer, visual artist, and artist advocate.

• Courage developed and performed a monologue for the National Deaf Arts & Culture Festival in Halifax. It unpacks her Blackness and experiences with ASL. Courage's artistic practice is an important way for her to express her authentic self.

• Courage also brings a global perspective. She has competed and performed around the world. Her favourite place is Paris, and she enjoys visiting family in Guyana. Courage wishes Toronto could learn from Washington and Gallaudet University to improve access for Deaf communities.

# Planning for Access.
# Planning for Change.

## Sarah Manteuffel

The profession of community planning, in its simplest form, is about people. My title is Community Planner. Community is therefore the essence of what a planner works toward. The spaces planners design, the infrastructure we build, and the policies that guide us are all there to ensure that the people who make up our communities can thrive with ample access to the amenities we need. However, there is a problem in the way designers and planners talk about and prioritize access. Exposure to disability and inclusivity in planning is not ingrained in the educational process, nor is universal design enforced in the Canadian professional context. Planners work for the public but need to do more to respect, acknowledge, and amplify the voices of disabled people in our communities. The planning profession must take a step back and question how to truly practise equity by increasing disability literacy and learning from lived experience.

My frustration with my profession comes from a lifetime of fighting for inclusion. I have achondroplasia, the most common form of dwarfism and a disability that is often forgotten in typical conversations on disability. My lived experience has taught me first-hand that I must fight for access because historically my voice has not been heard. Living in Winnipeg, where many people did not know much about my disability, I was one voice of a minority community of people with dwarfism. I began fighting through advocacy work and public speaking in my final year of high school. Starting in elementary school settings, I would join mentors in the dwarfism community by standing in front of a classroom of young students to tell my story. I would talk about my disability, how I found ways to adapt, and emphasize how I was just like everyone else. I would face these classrooms unsure whether the faces looking back at me were learning and feeling empathy, or leaving only 'inspired' and grateful they were not born with my disability. The work I was doing simply did not feel like enough to make change.

After high school, I began an undergraduate degree in interior design. In my design education, I began to feel hindered – creating individual spaces would not create systemic change. I became frustrated with the design world's focus on aesthetics over human-centred and inclusive design, so I took a step away to focus again on advocacy. I reflected on my experiences as a disabled person and how they could inform my career path. During this time, I moved to Toronto and began to experience a broader range of built environments and professions. I met and learned from a larger collective of activists and listened to their advocacy work. I explored community planning as a profession and became interested in how it functions as a catalyst between policy, engagement, and design. Community planning provided a potential path for me to try changing the system from the inside through bigger-scale and longer-term projects and initiatives that could benefit every person in society.

I decided to get my master's degree in city planning to learn more about doing this work. I returned to Winnipeg to reconnect with my community and make change in the place I call home. During graduate school, the coursework was not as focused on disability as I had hoped. In classes, I pushed the narrative and encouraged my peers to think about accessibility in the work we were doing, from age-friendly urban design to law and ethics. I sought out disability studies courses but was frustrated by the primary focus on the negative effects of ableism, barriers, poor policies, and design. We shared important conversations about global disability issues, but I also wanted to see joy in disability through action. I wanted to discover more how people with disabilities continue to seek and make change, much like the activists who created the path of acceptance before us. I was so excited learning about how the World Coalition of Citizens with Disabilities (later Disabled Peoples International) was established by disabled people from around the globe at a meeting in my city. I tried to seek out more stories like this. Through my education, I began to learn that I was not alone in the fight for more accessible communities, and not the only one sharing a story to seek inclusion.

As I continued to grow more passionate about accessibility and my role as a disabled community planner, I continued to face my own barriers in the education system. I was consistently challenged by the physical spaces that made up my university. To get from class to class, I had to walk long distances. In the public washrooms I could not wash my hands due to high soap dispensers and distant taps. Though I was teetering on the edge of burnout due to the intensity of graduate school and the consistent barriers to accessibility I faced, I pushed myself to keep going. I wanted to ensure that other students with disabilities could study community planning and design and continue to make change in their communities – the way I wanted to make change in mine.

As a result, I focused my final research on a few related questions: What is holding our profession back from disability inclusion? How are professional planning codes of conduct guiding the profession and holding us accountable? How can we better integrate disability into these professional codes of conduct?

Among the sources I analyzed were the most recent professional planning codes of conduct (as of 2022) in Canada, the United States, the United Kingdom, and Australia. Each of these documents included language that did not enforce inclusion. Frequently used words ranged from *where applicable* to *may*. The lack of commitment to enforcement was further undermined by unclear language. If a user cannot understand a document, how can they fight for their rights? If a city planner is not clear on what is enforced, how will they be encouraged to make change? Of the four codes of conduct I analyzed, the Canadian document was the only one to not include any specific mention of disability. It's possible that the Canadian professional code of conduct used vague language to be more inclusive, but by not specifically naming the people and communities who are marginalized by planning decisions, the profession erases our voices from future conversations.

My research also included distributing a survey to planning professionals across Canada. Respondents supported adding more specific language to the professional code of conduct to make it disability-inclusive. When I asked about their experience in working on accessibility projects, or with people with disabilities, many of the survey participants acknowledged a lack of training, experience, and awareness.

Through my research, it became clear that there was a need for increased education and professional guidance to support current and future planners. Students and people at all stages of their careers need to learn more about disability and accessibility as it relates to planning processes and decisions. Disability legislation in Canada continues to shape new conversations in planning and design professions. However, standards such as the Accessible Canada Act, National Building Code, and Accessibility for Manitobans Act are often only a starting point for inclusive and accessible design. As of 2024, only two standards of the Accessibility for Manitobans Act are fully in force (Customer Service and Employment). These standards take years to be developed and implemented across all levels of government and businesses. In the meantime, designs and policies continue to not meet the accessibility needs of our community.

By learning from the challenges of past planning decisions, students can make more inclusive decisions as professionals. Transportation systems that consider mobility devices, connected community designs that decrease walking distances to amenities, and wayfinding systems with alternative formats for individuals with visual and cognitive disabilities are just some examples of the ways we can implement change. Hearing about existing challenges from disabled people and those most impacted by planning decisions is also essential. Through more inclusive education, students can be motivated to promote and enforce accessibility. Without this education and guidance, professional community planners may continue to avoid integrating accessibility in all aspects of their work. Without enforcement of disability inclusion in the planning profession, community planners might rely on only the minimum legislated standards. By entrusting inclusion to legislated minimum standards, community planners therefore avoid innovation and do not act on evolving needs and ideas shared by those with lived experience. The developing provincial and national accessibility legislation will push this forward, but community planners must get ahead of regulation and be leaders of change.

Through the diversity of work that community planners complete, there are many opportunities for increasing inclusion. Transportation and infrastructure, policy, community development, engagement, collaboration, urban design, and built environments can all benefit from an accessibility perspective. Inclusion does not have to wait for a disability-specific project to be brought to the forefront.

While I am encouraged to have influence in how the planning profession integrates accessibility and inclusion, the feeling of burnout that I pushed away in graduate school has returned. I am navigating being a disabled employee, advocating for a shift in internal systems, as well as a change in how we collaborate with clients. I am listening to other stories of lived experience with accessibility and disability, which can weigh heavy on my soul and create feelings that not enough is being done. There are days when I question if change will happen, and whether I should be part of the team to do it.

But then I remind myself why I decided to become a planner. Long-term, systemic change. Transforming whose voices are in the room and making that room barrier-free. This work is not easy and will take time! Putting this much stress on myself is the exact opposite of what I was trying to do for others, and I need to allow myself and others to be able to rest, to take it all in, to share and grow, so that I can do this for the long haul.

Taking things slow has allowed me to really listen to those with lived experience and ensure that what they have said has been reflected in the work we do. I have become humbled knowing that this is not work I can ever be an expert in. It is collaborative and evolving. I have learned that I will not always get it right, but being open to change and thankful for suggestions will continue to increase inclusion. I have also learned to accept that sometimes I do not have to be the only voice speaking up for change. That as professional planners and designers listen to and amplify disabled voices, more people will learn and be allies who fight alongside us to make change. Working together on education and acceptance reduces the burden on disabled people as the primary advocates. By encouraging more community planners to find passion in the opportunities of accessibility, there is hope that fewer professionals will fear getting things wrong and learn to make things right. I imagine a future where all public engagement is accessible without requests for accommodation. Where processes are collaborative and empowering for disabled voices. Where communities consider all user types in their policies and designs, to create amenities accessible to all.

A more inclusive future fuelled by the voices of disabled people will lead to change in our physical environments, our policies, and the administration of professional organizations and educational programs. If the planning profession shifts to prioritize the needs of our disability community, then change will happen. Imagine a community where every person can access all amenities and spaces independently and comfortably. Where people can choose to walk, roll, wheel, drive, or take transit without challenge or confrontation. Where we can rest where we need without being separated from the community and use spaces our way without feeling a need to conform. The (barrier-free) path is envisioned, designed, budgeted, engaged on, ready to be built – and it is beautiful.

## Plain Language Summary

- Sarah writes about her experiences creating more accessible communities as a community planner.
- In her final year of high school, she started speaking about her experiences living with the most common form of dwarfism.
- At university, Sarah was surprised that there were not more courses and conversations about disability. She also found that the campus was not very accessible.
- As a result, she researched the professional codes of planners in Canada, the United States, Australia, and the United Kingdom. She found that the language of these documents did not enforce inclusion and some did not include disability.
- Sarah describes ways to incorporate the priorities of disabled people in community planning. She shares that advocacy can be exhausting, especially when you have a disability, but explains why it's important.
- Sarah stresses that by having more education about disability in design programs, future professionals will be more inclusive in their work. And she shares that we may not always get things right or know everything, but by listening to disabled people we are on the right path.

# 'You Don't Have to Have All the Answers'

## Adam Cohoon

**Emily Macrae:** It's hard to know where to start: you're a photographer, you're a film and video maker, you lead Jane's Walk, you advocate with Walk Toronto, and that's to name just a few. How would you describe your work to create more accessible cities and communities?

**Adam Cohoon:** I'm always trying to find something tangible to anchor an idea to. [For instance,] my photography has been trying to critique the inaccessibilities of art galleries by showing art that's done by people with disabilities and pointing out the inaccessibility around us. It's telling a story, but also in a weird way giving people some nervous indigestion so they don't forget what you're telling them. And you know, photography and video look at how other people view the same thing.

**EM:** You grew up in Kincardine, Ontario, right? It's a town on the shores of Lake Huron, and when you were growing up it had a population of around six thousand. How did using a wheelchair in that community shape your understanding of what accessibility can or should be?

**AC:** In Kincardine, government was weirdly approachable. I, as a seven-year-old, talked to the mayor about accessibility but didn't realize it. He was just a guy in a golf shirt who ran into me in the street when I was out with my educational assistant. I talked to him, and after that, when they were finally deciding to extend curb cuts out of the downtown core, he decided to make the first route from my house. Because at the time, the only way I could easily get downtown was either doing driveway ping-pong – remember, driveways already have the curb cut – or I could get downtown starting from my school.

So I had seen the mayor and after I had talked to him my dad got a phone call and he goes, 'Adam were you talking to a man?' And I thought I was going to get the Stranger Lecture! And I said, 'No, Mrs. Wallace, my educational assistant, was with me' – she sort of knew him and she said I should just talk to the man and tell him about accessibility and about what I had noticed. And my dad goes, 'You know who you were talking to? That was the mayor of Kincardine!' And I go, 'No it wasn't, he was wearing one of those green shirts with an alligator on it! And, you know, the mayor, he wears that big chain.'

**EM:** It sounds like you learned the value of making people uncomfortable, of that nervous indigestion, at an early age.

**AC:** I did. And then as you get older, as a man, you start to get this idea that you don't bring up problems unless you have a solution. That was my attitude too. Even when I shared my first video, *Life Bloored*, I wasn't thinking about accessibility. I was just explaining why the video was so shaky and jerky: it was because the sidewalks are so uneven as I'm going up and down curbs. It's bumpy and inaccessible, and there are many stores I can't get into.

At first I was like, it's better [here] than it was in Kincardine, and if even Toronto is this way, I think all of Canada must be this way too. I didn't think it was my place to openly, loudly critique what was going on. Luke Anderson had just started some of his [StopGap Ramp] work. And I started to work a bit with the TTC, and there were starting to be accessibility buttons for doors, but I still sort of thought, why should I be the shit disturber? It was only when the solution was maybe slowly coming, like I could see automatic door openers, that I started to speak out.

*Self-portrait photograph of Adam Cohoon in front of an inaccessible gallery.*

Before, I felt like, why should I scream about a problem when I didn't have the solution? It wasn't until I learned a bit more about the Jane's Walk philosophy that I was ready to talk about accessibility. Jane Jacobs also believed that you didn't need to have the solution to label a problem. You don't have to have all the answers.

**EM:** What surprised you about access and ableism when you first came to Toronto?

**AC:** It wasn't magical; there were still parts of the strip that were not accessible – unlike the neighbourhood I live in now, where everything is fancy new buildings with super-wide sidewalks and easy-to-push door openers. There were a lot of these Victorian-style buildings that still have the old one- or two-step threshold, and that was just accepted, even at the start of the twenty-first century. There was no rhyme or reason; it still baffles me that there are inaccessible pharmacies left in Toronto! The city still hasn't totally solved everything.

I'm somebody who's always loved e-books and stuff, and it got really annoying for me that [back then] every year I had to go to a library circulation desk to validate my address. Slowly I started to go right to the accessibility department and ask, 'Can you help me with this?' For a while they were like [fake whisper], 'We'll mail you a card with a number and you'll call us with the number and that'll prove to us that you still live in the same apartment.' I'm like, 'Okay, I have a scanner. Can I scan my ODSP [Ontario Disability Support Program] documents with my address on them?' 'Well, that's sort of private,' they said. 'Well, I'm offering to share it with you!' Even that step of going to the mailbox and getting a card out of an envelope, that takes spoons. Use other technologies rather than make all of us dance and deal with ableism to prove our address. Access means it's accessible for people in all the margins.

**EM:** Does your interest in using technology to connect with communities like Kincardine come from stories like that, or from your own experiences with isolation during the pandemic?

**AC:** I don't think I came to terms with isolation during the pandemic – I came to terms with isolation a lot earlier. It's just I had no way to explain it to other people and so I thought it was a burden I just had to suck up and carry. The new part I had to deal with during the pandemic was figuring out what to fear with respect to the actual illness. But the isolation, I knew that from before. The loneliness.

I was once in that weird space where I sort of respected those people who were anti–smart phone. I sort of respected that anti-technology culture of both the music industry and the live-event industry.

It wasn't until later in the pandemic that I realized that for all these [in-person] live events, people were starting to use online technology. It's ironic for people with disabilities who said, 'Oh, I could do that job if I could do it from home,' that now so many people are working from home. And so [the pandemic] was sort of my reckoning with technology and saying, 'We'll do this and I'm going to push hard and I'm going to fight.' I think some disabled people are reticent to sign up for certain streaming events. It's like when you go down to the States where there are certain foods you can only get when you're travelling. You're scared to fall in love with something if it may be taken away. Because our biggest fear is that all these online events are going to all of a sudden be cancelled when things go back to 'normal.'

**EM:** It seems that you use your art to communicate that vision of a more open world.

**AC:** I don't like it when anybody can be turned away. Even before the pandemic, I might not have spoken up or I might not have spoken as openly, being critical of the culture of small music venues or some restaurants being inaccessible or having their bathrooms downstairs. I might have been the person who said physical accessibility is the answer because everything has to be done within these spaces, and I will just take isolation as the burden I have to bear. Whereas the pandemic has really taught me, 'Wait a minute, isolation shouldn't be the burden that I have to bear!'

Why should culture be only for people who can drive to cultural venues? What about high-speed internet? Kincardine is one of those places where the internet is reasonably reliable. Why can't we bring more culture there? To think that one of the highest-rated non-sports-related broadcasts in Canadian history was the Tragically Hip's final concert. That shows that [even back then] you could easily participate in that moment whether you were in the big city, whether you were in Kingston, Ontario, or a little tavern out in some village in Saskatchewan.

**EM:** Are there other things you'd like to see changed? Things you don't want to see pulled back after the pandemic or things you'd like to see more of?

**AC:** I hate that the limit for ODSP is that you're only allowed to make $1,000 per month [$12,000 per year] on top of your ODSP benefits before the government starts clawing it back. It basically just gets people up to the poverty line. Without changes, I know a few friends with disabilities are probably going to end up burning themselves out [on work where the pay is clawed back]. [With changes,] I might even go for big arts grants in my name without worrying about clawbacks.

I would like to see more old buildings being encouraged to actually make their front entrances accessible. Very few places in Toronto could argue that their steps have not been altered and are pure heritage. If you can prove to me that those steps are the exact same design that they were in 1853, when the building went up, I'll take an alternate entrance, but you can tell, some of them, that it's 1970s cement they used to redo the entrance.

**EM:** You've also already mentioned some of the ways technology has changed daily life during the pandemic. Anything else you'd like to say on that topic?

**AC:** I'm laughing because as a kid I loved McDonald's, but there were three things that pissed me off. They didn't take credit cards. (This was back in the eighties.) They didn't deliver. And all the food, you couldn't add tomatoes or anything extra to their burgers. And my dad made fun of me. He said, 'Adam, all these ideas are absolutely ridiculous! You don't want anybody putting a fast-food meal on plastic. You don't want McDonald's delivered on impulse. And a future where you can just ask for extra tomatoes on a cheeseburger is absolutely ridiculous!' Just the other day I sent him a picture of my recent McDonald's DoorDash order, which was a cheeseburger with extra tomatoes.

When I was younger, some of the accessibility experts would say, 'Well, we don't need to worry about that [barrier], they're working on wheelchairs that can go up steps.' But if you would have said that people would have computers the size of chocolate bars that could be carried in their pockets or mounted to their wheelchairs, the experts would have laughed. Things change. We don't have all the answers.

**EM:** I know you've done so much work with Walk Toronto. What do you bring to those conversations as someone who's wheeling and riding rather than walking?

**AC:** It surprises some people that on quieter streets I'd rather drive down the road than use a very narrow sidewalk. And so some of the streets where maybe somebody like them actually wants a sidewalk, I'm going to have to drive slow so I don't flip off. So I sort of bring different things. Walk Toronto was already an accessibility-viewing organization, but we're adding more women and people of colour and people from the suburbs, and when you have two people with authentic disabilities on the steering committee talking about their experiences, that's when the change starts to happen. It's made sense for our meetings to stay virtual. That's access.

**EM:** For a lot of people, online meetings might just be easier to get to.

**AC:** They are. The only thing you have to be really conscious of is the quality of the data stream coming into some parts of Toronto. Some people like me live in a new non-profit housing building that's got beautiful fibre optic cable. There is a disparity in what people can pay for. So yes, online options do make meetings more accessible, but they can also create a barrier and bring digital inequity.

**EM:** I have one other question for you: What's one thing you think everyone should ask themselves if they're trying to create a more accessible community?

**AC:** When somebody asks for an accessibility measure, should you just give that accommodation to one person? Like me and the library, getting a card in the mail? Or is it maybe important to ask if, well, maybe this policy is discriminatory enough and ableist enough that other people would benefit from it being changed?

Also, *isolation* used to be an intangible word, but I bet because of the pandemic everybody now knows the feeling of isolation. How can you make sure that whatever you're doing, you're doing your best not to isolate in an unhealthy way – yourself and others?

## Plain Language Summary

• In this interview, Adam talks about growing up in Kincardine, Ontario, and moving to Toronto.
• Kincardine is a small town. When Adam was growing up, it was easier to talk to decision makers directly. Adam remembers telling the mayor about how hard it was to get downtown because there were no curb cuts for wheelchair users.
• Moving to Toronto, Adam assumed that the city would be much more accessible than it is. So Adam found ways to help people notice barriers by taking photos, speaking up in public, and joining committees.
• Adam also talks about the isolation of being disabled. Adam hopes that the pandemic has encouraged everyone to think differently about isolation.
• From experience, Adam knows that technology can be used to reduce isolation. It can also be used to increase access to arts events and public meetings. But technology is not enough. Everyone needs to think about whether their approach to planning an activity could isolate someone.

# Making Home

# Planting Permanence

## Shay Erlich

### Visions of Blooms

Dreaming about the world that is just around the corner is kind of my thing. Following a deeply held tradition of disabled future-dreamers, I believe in the importance of imagining what a world that loves disabled people might look like. Dreaming about the ways that our future might unfold, where we all get to thrive, is a powerful force against the ways we are relentlessly pressured into accepting the world as it is, and the pittance of access and acceptance afforded to us. This is a fundamental part of who I am, and how creating art and being a disability activist are interwoven for me. My art is a place where I can test the worlds that I dream up, and my activism is the work of calling new worlds into being. I know that by playing, experimenting, and iterating, we will get to the liberatory future we are seeking.

For as long as I can remember, my coping mechanism in times of stress has been to imagine having a space of my own that I felt safe in. When I was younger, I dreamed of a first apartment and what it might be like to have more control over my own life. A world where I was completely in charge of where I went and what I did. Where autonomy was exciting and opened doors. With each action I took, a little more of my true self emerged and the path ahead became clearer.

Along the way I've learned a lot about what I need in order to nurture my dreams into bloom. To thrive, each dream requires its own unique blend of careful tending, cultivation, and the right environment. When I can act thoughtfully and intentionally in pursuit of change, I am constantly impressed by what is no longer insurmountable. And yet, despite the realities I've dreamed into existence, I still feel insecurely rooted in this world. One of the dreams for my own life that I spend the most time imagining is a near future where I have stability, safety, and permanency in my housing and care. Among some of my most radical dreams, the vision of the future I am searching for would be mundane and virtually taken for granted were I not both trans and disabled.

Now I spend most of my dreaming time thinking about a permanent home. A place that is truly mine to decide over and control. A place where I define what safety is and make the rules about how I want to live and who I get to be when I'm tucked away from the world. To set the terms of how I am perceived and who is permitted to perceive me away from the ableist and conformist public eye. For me, safety and control are the key distinctions between being housed and having a home. Despite living independently for more than a decade, I've never truly felt like I had a permanent living situation. I'm still dreaming my way toward the kind of home I want to spend my adult life in.

## Creating Optimal Growth Conditions

I experience regular ongoing oppression and traumatic encounters as a trans disabled human. My home must be a place where I feel safe to recover and heal from how the world imposes itself upon me. Sometimes I despair that this is the best I will be able to achieve in my lifetime. That as fervently as I can wish for a world where disabled people know only love, the world I currently live in regularly shows disabled people that we are disposable – a subclass of citizens without full participation in society. The experience of repeated oppression puts me, like many other disabled people, in situations daily where I weigh the risk of a traumatic encounter, trying to reduce the opportunity for harm where possible.

For example, my spouse and I have an unwritten rule that we avoid the ER unless we believe there is a serious threat to life if our medical needs aren't addressed imminently. While I have had wonderful and caring experiences in the hospital system, I have also had multiple experiences where I was not believed, and the encounter became deeply traumatic. The uncertainty of what to expect shifts us to manage medical concerns at home that are beyond what most people would feel comfortable with, to avoid potentially traumatic experiences.

Oppression is also a collection of day-to-day negative experiences. So often, navigating the world as a trans disabled human leads to an endless series of small negative interactions, including misgendering, anger over sharing space, and potentially dangerous attempts to be helpful. Disabled people deserve the control, space, and privacy necessary to recover from the weight of these encounters. The lack of safe space for processing trauma is directly related to the inadequate housing situations facing disabled people of all ages and the fact that, for many, these negative interactions occur with caregivers providing services in their homes. We do not have a guarantee of safety in any place in our lives.

Like plants, I require safety to thrive. I need to unmask and respond authentically to my sensory needs. Masking is when neurodivergent people assume the characteristics and mannerisms of neurotypical people to move through the world with greater ease. However, this is emotionally and physically draining. Most neurodivergent people require spaces where we don't have to put effort into masking. The alternative is burnout. During the pandemic hours of solitude and isolation, I learned how to have a new relationship with my sensory experience. I have come to cherish the ways that responding to my sensory needs improves my well-being.

Throughout my life, my need to be loud, dance, stim, and feel my own emotions intensely has been defined as problematic or threatening, but these are pieces of myself that I finally understand and have a good relationship with. I want the people I share space with to value what I need in order to process and be present in the world. It's an important part of me and I am incomplete without it. A place where those needs aren't met wouldn't be my home anymore, but rather somewhere I was forced to endure. This is something we should not stop advocating for until all disabled people have their needs for sensory regulation and expression met. Too many disabled people live in institutions, congregate settings, or crumbling subsidized housing – without appropriate care, livable incomes, and a modicum of privacy; without access to critical tools for well-being and self-regulation. They do their best to flourish in inhospitable conditions.

**Surveying the Growing Environment**

If all I required was privacy to meet my own healing needs, it would be simple; however, as someone whose disabilities include significant physical limitations, I require care. My spouse is also disabled, and they have their own significant physical limitations. Both of us have needed daily care for the last several years. The cyclical nature of my disabilities have meant that since my early twenties I've gone in and out of phases of needing daily care. My needs have rarely been met. For well over a decade, I've tried to establish stable care through any means and program possible.

In Ontario there are two broad options available for disabled people who require daily care: traditional home-care services and consumer-led care. Traditional home-care services are offered in a variety of ways, through larger organizations and institutions. These services can be offered within the community in the case of Ontario's Local Health Integration Networks, coordinating and sending personal support workers (PSWs) directly into a disabled person's home. Or they can be offered in the context of supported independent living arrangements. In this case, the place where a disabled person lives hires and coordinates PSW care, often across multiple apartments or supported units. With this option, disabled people have very little control over services, but also have a smaller administrative burden.

Conversely, consumer-led care is offered predominantly through organizations for independent living. In this case, a disabled person is responsible for administering a care budget; hiring, training, and coordinating their own care; and reporting back to the funding organizations about how the money was allocated. While this approach gives consumers more choice and flexibility, it also places significantly more responsibility on disabled people, representing a massive administrative burden compared to non-disabled adults.

Virtually all the adult living options for disabled people are governed by how much care someone is allocated. Generally, the more care you require, the more pressure there is to live in congregate care, such as a skilled nursing facility. Care allocations and care needs are often drastically different. Assessment procedures consider only the time the government says a task should take, rather than the time it would take for that task to feel nourishing and caring. Assessments require the skills of a tightrope walker – presenting as sufficiently disabled to get enough tasks within your profile to create the hours of care you need, but not appearing too disabled to live independently.

Rather than listening to the desires of disabled people, the system of care is rooted in making the process more efficient for the government, and it can take enormous amounts of advocacy to remain living independently in the community. Disabled adults end up tucked away in all kinds of places when they no longer have the capacity to advocate for their care: hospitals, nursing homes, supported independent living units in larger buildings. Each of these systems enact their own violence of limiting life options for disabled people in the name of institutional needs or efficiencies.

## Budding Season

Over the last fifteen years or so, I've had experience with traditional home-care services and consumer-led care but have hit limitations with both models. Within traditional home-care services, I was repeatedly subjected to ableism and transphobia. Even a brief experience this past summer with traditional home-care services made it clear that they do not meet the needs of my family. Within consumer-led care, the administrative burden and refusal to modernize the programs create further barriers. Regardless of the program, all care arrangements with the Ontario government mean disabled people have far less access to freedom of mobility. All contracts will deduct care days for time spent out of Ontario. However, there is no distinction between travel between provinces (where our rights to care are still within our citizenry rights); travel for work, medical, or educational purposes, where residency generally continues to be extended to citizens of a province; or travel for leisure (which disabled people still have a right to). Additionally, virtually all consumer-led care programs dictate the amount you can pay your care staff, directly impacting the quality of staff one is able to hire and retain.

The contract for Ontario's Direct Funding program sits signed on my filing cabinet, where it has sat for two years now. I can't bring myself to send it in and sign away my rights. Instead, I raised my consulting rates and drafted my own job posting for the care I need. I can't deny my need for care, but I'll claw my way into a position of enough privilege to control it. I have hushed conversations with colleagues about how others are trying to do the same. The system that was supposedly designed for our needs is failing spectacularly at allowing us the futures we deserve. Slowly consensus and desire are budding, nurtured by community into a cohesive demand for care systems that prioritize our needs and desires, well-funded systems that show the value and possibilities that this care work represents to our community. A system that recognizes that support is a prerequisite for success and inclusion, whether defined by economic goals or not.

Beyond the funding and logistics, I have had to grapple with the intersecting legacies of care and ableism that I have inherited. Within my family, I have been shamed for my care needs. I have been conditioned for years to believe that if I was unable to meet my care needs independently, I wouldn't receive the support I needed. I've witnessed other members of my family make their care needs as small as possible in hopes of being acceptable. I carry the legacy of everyone who told me that my care needs were gross, a burden: the obvious disgust that a person like me exists in the world.

I was lucky that when my family couldn't meet my needs, I brought myself to places with peers and adults who tried their best to be the community I needed. How lucky I was to have in my life some truly incredible adults who cared and invested deeply in young people, and how different my life would have been if I hadn't found my way to them. At the same time, I was wrecked when either my increasingly apparent disabilities or my confidence as a non-binary person made the organizations and people who stood in for my family turn away and become unsafe.

I need to reach beyond these legacies and experiences because they don't define what care is meant to be. I believe we can build something that isn't founded on shame and the pressure to hide disability from the public eye. And so I do my best to move through frustration and fear in the hope that I can find something functional and fulfilling for everyone involved. It's fuelled a lifelong quest to build communities where it is truly safe for people to bring all of their complex identities and nuance into how we move through the world together. A dream of connected, caring, mutual living is a radical proposition. I honestly don't know if I will ever truly achieve this goal.

## Harvesting

But no matter what, I can't find what I'm looking for in Toronto. By all rights, I am relatively well-off as a disabled person living in this city. I live in an affordable, rent-controlled building. I live on the ground floor and don't have to worry about elevator outages trapping me in or out of my home for weeks at a time. My kitchen and bathroom are adapted to levels that make using them possible with support. One of my favourite parts of my apartment is my garden: a small island of greenery. Spending time out there helps ward off the ways I get land-sick in the city, where local green space is often very difficult for me to access. Given the grim lives of so many disabled people, it feels selfish to admit that this isn't the adulthood I find myself dreaming of. It is so much more than most of us get, but the bare minimum of what we deserve.

Nonetheless, I increasingly reject city living. My apartment feels confining rather than safe and cozy. The chasm between me and downtown often feels insurmountable. So much of the time it is like playing four-dimensional chess to wrangle accessible transit options, the capacity to plan ahead, accessible routes, variable energy, and support needs to get downtown. Living in Toronto feels incredibly isolating. I sometimes feel like a two-dimensional being with a life collapsed down to what can fit on a computer screen. My vision of home is impossible to bring to life where I am, and so, in my own version of crip time, I am preparing to leave.

To move would mean an incredible amount of faith that I would be able to re-establish my chosen family's care and social needs somewhere else. It is daunting to imagine the task of finding care workers we would feel safe enough to bring into our home and live our lives with. It's also challenging because we lack examples of non-traditional collective living for disabled people. A lot of the contemporary imaginings about living in community for disabled people came out of the independent-living movement of the 1960s to 1990s. Too often, this movement was led by parents who wanted, once they had passed away, options for their disabled adult children who they believed could never lead their own care or have a full life. There has been little formal exploration of living options where disabled people have authority over their living conditions.

The parent- and bureaucrat-driven models of the late twentieth century also neglect what a disabled person who is queer, non-binary, and polyamorous might need to feel good and supported in their living situation. Queer disabled people struggle to find places of belonging, caught between inaccessible queer communities and risks of discrimination for being queer, trans, and non-monogamous within disability community and organizations. There is a need to dream up housing and care options that match the vast spectrum of who we are as disabled people.

As I embrace interdependence in so much of my life, I can only imagine finding home in a disability-led collective-living situation. I have always loved and sought the casual moments of intimacy that develop from shared time in a kitchen, or the brief bits of conversation that frame parallel play. In some versions of my home, the building is a live-work space for disabled artists – a community hub offering classes and performances for our broader community. Food security programming is also intrinsically linked to this vision, as I have witnessed so many disabled people struggle around this issue.

From a lack of accessible kitchens, to a lack of teaching disability-informed ways of cooking, to learning how to navigate sensory and body demands that make healthy relationships with food challenging, disabled people have a desperate need to innovate around the inter-section of food and disability. To that end, part of my dreaming involves imagining a working communal farm and farm shop café that supports disability entrepreneurship and employment.

Other versions are simpler: for example, a small, intentional community with individual accessible living units and a large shared common area. However, any version will require the types of resources and partnerships that are not common for disabled people to have access to.

## Growing into a Thriving Forest

I can see the first steps that I have already wandered down this road: this journey has already begun. My spouse and I carefully navigate being in our own caregiver-disabled relationship, where we are simultaneously both every single day. I often describe care as the heartbeat of our relationship, and it's a fully developed love language of its own. While the actions are unique to us and our needs, the way we approach and understand our needs is magical. We understand that our needs are valid and that it's always okay to ask for support. That even if the other person can't offer the necessary support, they are a sounding board for other ideas about how it could be done. We ally to achieve our everyday tasks as best we can and take a teamwork approach to the day. I don't take care of them, and they don't take care of me. We take care of our lives, together.

In line with that, we don't lose sight of ourselves as whole people who are connected far beyond our intimate care cocoon. I see the ways we invest in ourselves to thoughtfully build the careers we want to have as one of the central drivers of the stability we seek. I see how we also invest outward, identifying the humans who are a part of our family and broader network, and the pieces that each of them brings toward building this dream together. The deep commitment we all share to living in community and being in relationship. The mutual recognition that not having all the answers isn't a barrier to beginning the journey together. Although we don't yet have a fully realized vision, the act of dreaming has been enough to generate movement all on its own.

This year's garden might be one of my most tangible signs of dreaming to date. In previous years I have filled my containers with the standard annual fare: tomatoes, cucumbers, potatoes, and herbs.

This year, I replaced more than half of the garden with perennials I can look forward to watching come alive each spring. Rhubarb, strawberries, red currants, gooseberries, raspberries, and grapes. Each one reclaiming specific childhood memories of being let loose in the gardens of grandparents, friends, and neighbours. Each plant simultaneously a link to the past feelings that guide me forward, and a portal toward the future. A beacon of hope from my slowly manifesting dream world – reminding me that one day the plants and I will spread our roots: finally at home.

## Plain Language Summary

• Shay believes that dreaming about the future that we want to have is an important part of making it happen.
• This piece talks about how hard it is for Shay to dream of a future with a safe home and with care that feels safe because Shay is trans and disabled.
• Shay lives in Toronto right now where it is expensive to live, and it is hard to get around the city because they live far from downtown. It can also be scary to interact with strangers sometimes.
• They want to move and live somewhere else, but they are scared they won't be able to find other trans or queer people to help them.
• Shay wants a system where queer and trans disabled people always have support that feels good to them, no matter where they live or what their family looks like. They compare what they need to feel good to what plants need to survive to show that disabled people deserve to bloom like all living things.
• They are hopeful that by talking about their dream, it will happen for them and other disabled people.

# The Art of the Ordinary: The Challenge of Defining Interabled Relationships

## Athena Cooper

'Don't tell people your art exhibit was inspired by a *Dr. Phil* episode!'

I laugh. I sense that my friend is being only half-serious with her scandalized expression.

We're seated outside, sipping our cold drinks on a warm Calgary afternoon in the late summer of 2022. The café is directly across the street from my apartment building and I'm once again thankful for our well-chosen downtown neighbourhood that provides me with numerous opportunities to get out and about in my wheelchair without needing to wrestle with accessible transportation options.

My friend is an old work colleague who has been employed in the arts sector for many years, and I've been describing my journey to get grant funding for my 2024 exhibit project, *The Extraordinary, Ordinary Nature of Interabled Love*. Through my paintings, the exhibit will illustrate the love story of my able-bodied husband and me, highlighting the little moments that make up our lives together – from the mundane to the life-changing.

I trust her opinion on the intricacies of the art world, and there is definitely something absurd about this crossover between fine art and *Dr. Phil*. And yet, when it comes to the representation of disability in popular media, this is where we are.

The episode in question aired in March 2019 and was titled 'I Swiped Right on My Quadriplegic Boyfriend.' In it, Dr. Phil advises a couple that an able-bodied woman dating a disabled man 'can be his lover or you can be his caregiver, but you can't be both … It won't work, one hundred out of one hundred times this won't work.'

Setting aside for a moment the outrage from the disabled community over this comment alone, let's look at the entire framing that's going on here. Dr. Phil is known for sensationalizing his subjects. He's even primed the studio audience by asking them if they would date someone in a wheelchair. (Fifty-eight per cent say yes.) Would they date someone who requires full-time care? (Twenty-nine per cent say yes.) He also says at one point, 'You're a young, single, attractive female. Out of all the people you can choose, why choose someone in a wheelchair?'

Cue eye roll.

The year 2019 stands out for another reason: my husband and I were married that August.

I had met Stefan through an online dating app five years earlier, in 2014, when we were both living in Vancouver. He had mentioned on his profile that he liked to listen to classical music while working on his writing, so I sent him an icebreaker message introducing him to one of my favourite music groups, 2Cellos – a pair of talented cellists best known for doing covers of pop songs, such as Michael Jackson's 'Smooth Criminal.' As it turned out, Stefan had played the cello as a teenager, and our connection progressed from there.

Right from the beginning, we were an odd pairing. I was born with osteogenesis imperfecta (aka 'brittle bone disease') and have been a power wheelchair user since the age of six. I'm also three-foot-seven to Stefan's height of six-foot-one. While we never had anyone make embarrassing or negative comments, it did take Stefan a bit of time to get used to the stares – not so much at *us*, just at me.

I was pretty oblivious to the stares by that point in my life and was much more focused on our developing relationship. Back then I had no frame of reference for what a relationship like ours might look like, and that alone created a great deal of anxiety and insecurity for me. I'm genuinely glad that the *Dr. Phil* episode didn't come out until well after we'd established ourselves as a couple, as it would have only fuelled the inner narrative I had about being in a relationship with an able-bodied person. I was used to all the quirks and barriers that came with my disability, but asking an abled-bodied partner to take on my 'disability baggage' as well seemed like a tall order.

As it turned out, the disability piece wasn't nearly as insurmountable as I – and Dr. Phil – made it out to be.

I think one of the things that helped Stefan and me initially was that we had such a hard time aligning our work schedules to see each other. When we first started dating, I was still working a nine-to-five corporate day in digital marketing and he was doing shift work at all hours of the day and night with vulnerable youth in care. This made any in-person time we had together special and worth the extra effort required to make it happen.

Much of that in-person time involved movies or good food. If we were super-busy or tired, we would get together at my apartment and either make a meal or order takeout from the great Indian restaurant around the corner. We'd then share with each other our favourite movies or watch the latest episode of *Game of Thrones*.

Occasionally we'd go to his apartment, but that was more challenging for me since the ground-level suite he rented had a single step at the entry. Even this we made work by parking my power chair outside under cover and using a rolling desk chair to get me around inside.

I really liked this guy, so I wasn't about to let one silly step stop me from spending time with him.

When we did want to travel farther afield, we would take public transit – neither of us had a car back then – to see a movie or visit a new restaurant. For any place I hadn't been before, I'd long ago developed a habit of calling ahead to confirm accessibility, and Stefan quickly picked up the habit of doing the same.

It turned out we had a mutual love of sushi, although I wasn't aware of my own love of it until we met. Despite being born in Vancouver and living on the West Coast all my life to that point, I'd never really tried sushi. I had this irrational fear that I was going to awkwardly pick up a roll with my chopsticks and immediately drop it down the front of my shirt. There was something about Stefan, though, that made me comfortable enough to try it, knowing that if an embarrassing, clumsy sushi-roll incident occurred we'd both just laugh it off. It was

Trusty Steed, *acrylic on canvas* (2020)

this increasing sense of ease with each other that was one of the early signs of our deepening relationship.

As for that *Dr. Phil* episode, the outraged response from the disabled community was swift and came in the form of the #1000utof100 hashtag to highlight all the successful relationships built on love and caregiving. It flooded my Instagram feed with couples who looked a lot more like Stefan and me than anything I'd seen in all the rom-com movies I'd watched over the years.

The wedding photos I saw on Instagram were particularly interesting since I was up to my neck in planning our wedding at the time. I was impressed by the fashion sense of many of the brides, even if I ultimately decided not to bedeck my wheelchair in flowers and tulle.

All of this also introduced me to a new term – *interabled*, which was frequently used alongside the #1000utof100 hashtag.

*Interabled* is most commonly defined as 'one partner has a disability and the other does not,' and this was the definition I used in my grant applications for the 2024 art exhibit. It was only in diving into the exhibit's actual research work that I realized how messy that definition actually is.

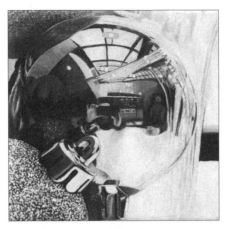

An Unconventional Couple,
*acrylic on canvas (2023)*

For instance, let's say you have a couple where the woman has a physical disability and uses a wheelchair and the man is able-bodied. This would seem to fit the definition. However, let's say the man is also on the autism spectrum and neurodivergent. He might handle the physical tasks that would be challenging or time-consuming for her, like mopping the floors or doing all their laundry, but she might handle tasks that would be challenging or frustrating for him, like keeping on top of the budgeting or the couple's busy schedule.

Would you still call them an interabled couple?

Is the assistance he offers her physically somehow more significant than the assistance she provides him?

Is this simply the most logical division of household tasks based on their respective strengths and weaknesses?

Another example: let's say you have a young lesbian couple who are both able-bodied when they get married. Then, one is in a car accident in her thirties and suffers a spinal cord injury. She becomes a wheelchair user, and the now interabled couple continue on with their lives. They both have successful careers. They buy a house and adopt a couple of kids together. At sixty, however, the remaining able-bodied partner develops complications from diabetes and chronic pain in her hips that makes it difficult for her to get around without a walker.

Do they go from being an interabled couple to *not* being an interabled couple because now they both identify as having a disability?

And, even more confusingly, what's the crossover between disability and aging?

It took some time for Stefan and me to find the right balance between skills and preferences when it came to organizing our domestic tasks. For instance, Stefan makes the majority of our breakfasts. I am not someone who has the best reflexes first thing in the morning. I think this is partly due to my disability and partly because I'm simply not a morning

Deck Chairs in the Snow,
*acrylic on canvas* (2023)

person. Regardless, having me try to pour hot coffee or cook eggs on the stove is more likely to result in burns than breakfast.

I do, however, make most of our dinners, which surprises some folks who don't realize it's possible for me to cook at all. We live in a rental apartment without an adapted kitchen, which has its challenges, but I am able to negotiate many of those, thanks to my power chair's elevating seat. I've learned to play to my cooking strengths and I tend to favour recipes that are more about assembly, like casseroles and meatloaf, as opposed to speed, such as a stir-fry. I also love my slow cooker since I can take my time putting everything together and cook large quantities so we'll have leftovers.

These days, Stefan is employed as a clinical counsellor and often works into the evening with individual clients or facilitating groups. By having a hot meal ready when he has a brief window between sessions, I can support him with his dinner needs in the same way he supports me with much-needed coffee and sustenance as I groggily roll into breakfast.

At the end of the day, this is the real beef that I have with Dr. Phil's attitude toward romantic couples and caregiving: unless couples are planning to throw away the 'in sickness and in health' line from their wedding vows, then caregiving is likely to be a very real component of that relationship as the couple ages.

As a society, we don't bat an eyelash if an elderly woman tenderly pushes her elderly husband down the sidewalk in his wheelchair or helps him by cutting his food, or with grooming, toileting, or other tasks that have become too difficult for him.

And yet, if the couple were fifty years younger, they'd be fit as fodder for Dr. Phil?

Again, cue my eye roll.

## Plain Language Summary

• Athena is an artist who lives in Calgary. She is putting together an exhibition of her paintings that show ordinary moments in her relationship with her husband.
• Athena uses her art to challenge the idea that her love story is extraordinary just because she uses a wheelchair. She and her husband each have different strengths. They help one another throughout the day.
• *Interabled* is commonly defined as 'one partner has a disability and the other does not.' Athena explains that it's hard to say for sure who in a relationship is disabled because people's needs change over time.
• Every couple needs to find the right balance of skills and preferences to live together, regardless of whether they identify as disabled.

# Ship of Theseus: The Power Wheelchair User and the City

## Angelo Muredda

'Remember, they're your legs.' That's what my doting mother would say over the years whenever my power wheelchair fell into a state of disrepair due to worn-out tires or drained batteries. The way some people remind you to moisturize or brush your teeth.

The mantra, designed to jolt me into action whenever she sensed I was procrastinating, always made me feel a bit defensive. I'm a partial lower limb amputee and I've usually gotten around inside my own home on my own legs, shuffling across the floor and transferring onto chairs using my right arm as a kind of supportive crutch. Maybe because I'm often misidentified by outsiders as having 'no legs,' which is, strictly speaking, not true, there's long been a proud distinction in my mind between my actual limbs and my wheelchair – a mobility device I use to circulate outside my apartment in downtown Toronto.

Despite my quibbles with my mother's phrasing, I've had to accept that it's hard not to think of your wheelchair as an extension of your body when it's the primary way you engage with the city in which you live. That's especially true the moment you can no longer trust it, and the prospect of being stuck inside goes from a theoretical nightmare to a real one. When they're working fine, wheelchairs are an essential tool for independence for an urbanite like me. They can take you to the grocery store or the pharmacy or the doctor's office across the street, if you're in a densely populated neighbourhood like mine. They can take you to a movie or an art gallery, opening up worlds beyond your apartment. They can propel you down the sidewalk on a stroll, indulging your fantasies of being some kind of nonchalant *flâneur*, wandering as far as you can go in any given direction, to any given shop, provided there are curb cuts and ramps along the way. They can get you onto the subway train so you can get to work. It's when they're failing and you have to replace them that they feel the most like an uncooperative appendage staging an active revolt.

Ask any power wheelchair user and they'll tell you that the process of getting a new wheelchair is fraught, more akin to setting up an experimental surgery with a highly sought-after specialist or finding the right psychotherapist than, say, getting a new laptop. It's a delicate, months-long – in some cases years-long – tightrope act featuring you, your currently overtaxed chair, and a cadre of agents from both the public and private sector, many of whom you will never meet. Throughout the process, you find yourself at the mercy of both your current mobility aids, wheezing with age and overuse, and the kindnesses and professional competencies of others, not to mention the current provincial government.

That tenuous network stretches from the occupational therapist who first assesses your need and articulates it to the government funding bodies responsible for saying yes or no to the new wheelchair. It extends even further to the vendor who translates that need into a product that you may or may not get to test out against other such products. This convoluted web includes the case worker or insurance agent, who has the final authority over how much you'll end up paying or being reimbursed for your troubles. For the uninitiated, getting a new wheelchair seems like an automatic upgrade, a subscription service that happily renews itself. But for those with lived experience of the process, it's an anxiety-ridden ritual that exposes the vulnerability of urban disabled life, the precariousness of living in a city to which you might at any moment lose access.

I entered the hardest part of that ritual in the spring of 2023, when the chair that had seen me through numerous personal milestones suddenly wouldn't turn on – at all. Though its abrupt end came as a shock, it was still a long time coming, which I had tried to anticipate by starting the application process for its replacement at the earliest possible moment. The right side of the wheelchair's frame had already been repaired just a few months into its commission, after a serious car accident that left us both the worse for wear. My inanimate companion and I both survived that trauma, but the severity of the injury cast my chair's longevity into doubt, and before long, my suspicions came true. My old chair became a personal ship of Theseus, with motors from here and a joystick from there – cobbled together out of replacement parts sourced new from the shop and old from my previous wheelchair, now good only for emergency harvesting.

Recalling my mother's mantra, I had first filed the paperwork with Ontario's Assistive Devices Program (ADP) just over five years into my time with my old faithful, long before it eventually stopped working. I went through an unexpected number of starts and stops along the way, amidst my changing status with both the Ontario Disability Support Program (first eligible and then not) and my employment (first part-time and then full-time). On top of these changes, ADP was marked as a non-essential service at various stages of Covid lockdowns, even while vendors themselves remained open. Amidst these developments, my ADP funding was approved, expired, and then extended as part of a pandemic-related grace period. The new chair eventually arrived just over four years into the process, in July of 2023 – just in time for my birthday.

The waiting period was a blur, marked by the need to maintain the good health of my old chair through the shifting waves of Covid. When you live in a city as a power wheelchair user with an unstable chair, much of the time between applying for a new one and receiving it is spent holding your breath, making conservative cost-benefit analyses about the kinds of activities you can afford without compromising the thing that keeps you moving through the world. For a wheelchair user on the edge of total machine failure, these gut-check questions become a second-person voice running through your mind, second-guessing every trip that might be inessential. Can you leave your place to go to the nearest grocery store, or will the slight bump to get onto the elevator jolt something loose in the wiring? Will you be stranded before you can even exit your building, pressed against the elevator call button until someone finds you?

Rain is one of the most common risks. Mindful of having had previous chairs damaged by flash rainfalls, each spring and fall, you stuff your coat pockets and totes with spare plastic bags. They're now an endangered species, thanks to single-use plastic bans that some disability activists have called ableist. Plastic bags serve as do-it-yourself rain covers for your joystick. A device familiar to gamers who use it to control their avatars, the joystick might be the most critical part of a power wheelchair, the thing that takes you in the direction you point it. It's also one of the most expensive to replace, often well in excess of a thousand dollars, and the first thing to go when exposed to bad weather.

In the winter, the few blocks you normally dash across on the way to the nearest accessible subway station (the one in your building isn't, and won't be for a few more years, if then) become interminable. The distance stretches on and on as the mix of slush, ice, and hard snow uncleared from crosswalks gets compacted into the electronic casings under your chair. Ice melting and evaporating into electrical components is a problem you'll have to deal with later, if the snow-filled treads of your tires can even push through the frozen intersections in the first place. You become paranoid, accounting for every minute sound your shuddering front castors make as they pass over the slightest crack on the sidewalk.

If all of this sounds like the fussing of a hypochondriac, it's because as a wheelchair user caught between windows of funding, you are effectively the doctor entrusted with managing your aging chair's care. A wheelchair may not be exactly equivalent to a pair of legs, but there's a similar slow-burning body horror to the way you feel its aging as a series of banal transformations that stack up over time.

Suddenly you're in an altogether different body than the one with which you started.

As a film critic and horror lover who parses my life through genre narratives, whenever a wheelchair starts to change, I think of the marvellously and then grotesquely altered form of Jeff Goldblum's scientist Seth Brundle in David Cronenberg's 1986 film *The Fly*. I think of the way, before the horror of his new insect body consumes him, he zealously charts his transformations on video and collects his lost appendages in a medicine cabinet he self-deprecatingly calls the Brundle Museum of National History. I also think of the 1952 exploitation film *Chained for Life*, starring conjoined twins and popular vaudeville act Daisy and Violet Hilton as young women on trial for one twin's killing of the other's husband. It isn't the most progressive or accomplished depiction of disability I've seen, but the symbiotic, codependent, fraught relationship at its centre – the mechanics of which are beautifully captured in the title – can't help but ring a bell.

A fickle wheelchair with an early expiry date is not a sibling for life, to be sure, but it's a complicated collaborator all the same. Likewise, a degrading wheelchair is not quite so dramatic as a rapidly metamorphosing body, but it's about as mysterious. There's a creeping uncanniness to the way a chair's premature senescence reveals itself through a procession of new sounds and altered gaits. Each new detail becomes a harbinger of what's about to be the new normal.

Though I'm a sucker for science fiction, I've never fully embraced the idea, appreciated by some disabled folks, that the wheelchair user is a kind of posthuman cyborg, as my knee-jerk resistance to my mother's wisdom about my chair might suggest. I'm too attached to my singular, old-fashioned fleshiness, I suppose, to fully entertain the possibility that this technological aid is more body than the one I was born with, which goes through its own share of unpredictable alterations as I age.

Still, it's undoubtedly true that the symbiotic relationship between a chair and its user is a kind of partnership, a covenant that is tested, if not broken, when the chair gives up on you before you can seamlessly transition into your new one. You can't help but feel betrayed, as though your partner in a relay has given up on you just shy of the finish line. When my old chair started to go, I thought of the moment when I was loaded into the ambulance after the car accident. I stared back at my wheelchair left in the street, which the first responders assured me would follow me to the hospital later, and felt, of all things, guilt, followed by embarrassment at my guilt. Did my old wheelchair remember that betrayal when it wouldn't turn on? Was it getting back at me?

You have a lot of time to fixate on these strange biotechnological entanglements, which inevitably turn to personification, while waiting for a new wheelchair. That process starts out of a medical necessity and ends, like so many things, in an obscure dance with capitalism. Unless you're independently wealthy and can buy it outright, in Ontario the process involves applying for a new chair through ADP. If the occupational therapist who assesses you approves the application, ADP may fund anywhere from 50 to 75 per cent of the purchase. That's provided the rest of the cost is covered after coordinating any remaining benefits you might have – or if you're willing to foot the bill for the 25 to 50 per cent that remains, typically in the range of several thousand dollars.

Nobody tells you that buying a new power wheelchair – if you are lucky enough to be funded through ADP and social services like ODSP or through your or your partner's or guardian's insurance – isn't like buying a new Apple Watch or Peloton bike. It's not like selecting a high-powered armour set in a role-playing game, for which an entire community of seasoned advice-givers on Reddit or YouTube awaits you. For one, there's no obvious repository of product reviews or walk-throughs. For most chairs, there's no Subreddit to speak of, and thus no sense of what it drives like in a punishing Canadian winter. Worse still, only a few short, chirpy vendor-approved videos with Muzak await you on YouTube; you're lucky if the person in them even looks like a wheelchair user.

If you can't make your way to the showroom, you're reliant on the sales rep to bring you a demo model, creating an unbalanced power relationship that feels more like waiting for a letter of reference from a superior than buying an expensive, life-changing device that you're going to have to live with for the better part of a decade. Through all the humiliation and puzzlement of this liminal stage that stretches on and on, there's just you and your aging maybe-cyborg pal, waiting out the winter and early spring. You diligently cover the joystick with a makeshift rain cover, a black plastic bag that is itself endangered – full of minuscule tears from all the times you've stretched and compressed it. Tiny holes let the faintest LED light from the joystick bleed through, a little bit brighter at night.

When you finally get your new chair, the excitement and relief quickly fade into something like low-key anxiety. The five-year preamble to the ritual begins again. You listen for the first repetitive rolling sound that indicates a newly loosened ball bearing and wonder how long you can get away with not fixing it before that front castor needs repairing. (*Remember*, your mother says, *they're your legs.*) You clutch your rattling armrest as you descend the rickety ramp outside your apartment, wondering if it's normal to feel like you need to hold your new chair together this tightly, this early. You wince at the flimsiness of your new joystick, already bent into an unusual position when a door briefly closed on you as you exited your classroom. It's your new set of legs, already feeling old, and it'll have to do until the next set.

## Plain Language Summary

• Angelo writes about using a power wheelchair in Toronto and the complicated process to get a new one in Ontario.
• He starts by recalling his mother's reminder to take care of the wheelchair as he might take care of his own body.

- He points out that while he feels there's a difference between his body and the wheelchair, the wheelchair is key to his mobility in downtown Toronto. It helps him get to work, experience culture, and stroll.
- He writes about how challenging it is to apply for a new wheelchair, despite its importance. The process involves many people and too many steps. It only got worse during the pandemic.
- Angelo writes about the anxiety of keeping his chair working while waiting for a new one. He has to look out for rain, snow, dangerous drivers, and mechanical issues.
- Angelo reflects on the relationship between his wheelchair and his body. He makes comparisons with science-fiction and horror movies based on his career as a film critic. While he resists seeing himself as a cyborg, he says there is a unique connection between wheelchair users and their mobility devices.
- Angelo concludes by returning to his mother's comment that his wheelchair is like his legs. He says the new wheelchair will have to be his new legs for now, until the next time the process begins.

# Desperately Seeking Dry

## Dorothy Ellen Palmer

You're about to read the most difficult and embarrassing essay I've ever written, but I don't want your sympathy. Instead, I'm inviting you to join me in collective discomfort. I'm asking you to refuse to see my experience as purely personal. When the barriers disabled seniors like me face get labelled 'personal,' it lets everyone else off the hook. It tells individuals, communities, event and city planners, businesses, and governments that they have no responsibility to fight alongside us and no culpability when they fail us. I'd much rather offer you fair warning: it's not in your self-interest to ignore the harm awaiting you and those you love. It's a life-altering harm, one unfortunately and unnecessarily shrouded in shame and silence, ridiculed as hilarious and humiliating, and dismissed as dirty. A struggle we all know exists but have agreed to ignore. Welcome to my desperate search for dry. Welcome to the tell-all tale of my life in adult diapers.

Please let me first introduce you to the millions of us who live here. Most of us are women who experience incontinence in pregnancy and again in our senior years, thanks to childbirth. Although a small army of women in yoga pants endorse exercises to strengthen the pelvic floor, no, you cannot Kegel your way out of incontinence. As the Mayo Clinic explains, '[T]he involuntary leakage of urine ... is a common symptom that affects 50% of adult women. Prevalence of this problem increases with age, as up to 75% of women over 65 report urine leakage. A woman's physical, social and psychological well-being is negatively impacted.'

Any and every one of you may become an adult diaper user. Diapers may be needed during illness or post-surgery, by those living with irritable bowel syndrome, diabetes, dementia, mobility issues, and other disabilities. *Global News* estimates 400 million worldwide users, with the market 'up 9% last year to $9 billion, having doubled in the last decade.' As Ulrika Kolsrud, the president of Essity, the Swedish global giant behind TENA diapers, explains to *Global News*, 'If incontinence were a country, it would be the third-largest country in the world.'

Big sales mean big bucks. As global marketing consultant SkyQuest reports, with a single diaper costing between fifty cents and eight dollars, 38.9 billion diapers were sold in 2021. Given our aging population, SkyQuest expects sales to hit $52.53 billion by 2028. *Fortune* magazine expects adult diapers to soon surpass the sales of baby diapers.

This widespread use of adult diapers is one reason I refuse to use the current euphemism to call them 'underwear.' It's nonsensical. If I entered any store seeking underwear, they'd correctly send me to aisles of bras and panties. In the language of disability justice, demonizing the word *diaper* only reinforces shame and stigma, just as the refusal to use *disabled* and *disability* reinforces the historical shame and stigma of these terms. Recent marketing campaigns featuring young women sporting sexy black 'underwear' are to be commended for attempting to reduce the stigma but criticized for perpetuating the ageist, ableist trope that looking old or disabled must be avoided at all costs. Euphemisms patronize and infantilize adult diaper wearers, as if we're toddlers who need made-up words for our filthy bodily functions. No thank you. Adults use adult language.

I'll be the first to admit this isn't always easy. The improvisor in me longs to fill this essay with a stream of pee jokes, to use juvenile humour to minimize the pain. But I can't ask you to join me in discomfort until I use the adult words to put myself there first.

Back in 2018, I stood at a store display of the pads I'd used for years, knowing the Good Ship Pink Pee Pad had sailed. Like period underwear, the all-the-rage newcomer to the world of bodily fluids management, pee pads are for people with *stress incontinence*, for those who dribble, a teaspoon or two, the way I'd done for years whenever I laughed or sneezed. But, thanks to two exuberant 1980s episiotomies that delivered my children, by sixty-three I also had *urge incontinence*: the uncontrollable urge to pee immediately.

I still dribbled; I also gushed full volume, pluming into the air like Old Faithful. A pad had insufficient absorbency, and I couldn't always replace one immediately. Living with whole-body arthritis and the congenital anomalies we once called birth defects in both feet, pain and decreasing mobility made it unsafe to quickly access my washroom. Forced to wait until I could summon the energy to stand up, I soaked through pads and ruined chairs. After the repeated public embarrassment of drenching two giant half moons on either side of a leaking pad, convinced a pee-scented cloud enveloped me like the stench that damned *Peanuts* character Pig-Pen, I had begun inventing reasons not to leave my apartment.

That day in the store, I knew I needed to switch to diapers if I wanted to live in the world, but pride stayed my hand. I saw diapers exactly the way the ageist, ableist world wanted me to see them: as old lady, as defeat, as shameful. Fearing that diapers made me an invalid and a joke, I told the cashier they were for my eighty-three-year-old mother. Once home, I cried for hours.

For months, I knew the planet was pointing at my already generous butt and snickering. I worried that every movement revealed indicting bulges and rustles. Extra-absorbent diapers proved a mixed blessing. When a drenched, ballooning diaper between my legs made it harder to use my walker, I imagined catastrophe. When I fell, whoever helped me up would get a handful of wet diaper and the world would never stop laughing. Please understand, in 2018, I'd been a proud member of the disability community and a disability justice advocate for years, but when it came to diapers, I was utterly slayed and silenced by my *internalized ableism*. That's when disabled people turn all the shame and guilt of ableism against ourselves, internalizing the inferiority ableism preaches and weaponizes against us in everything from everyday language to marketing slogans, from inaccessible buildings to inadequate government services. It's a constant and sometimes losing struggle to feel worthy. When it came to diapers, I felt shamefully unworthy. I stayed silent.

It's no surprise to this redhead that change began with getting angry. Outrage at injustice fuels all my politics, sits at the core of my angry adopted self. By 2019, my ventures into the city exposed a newly infuriating kind of inaccessibility. Even if the meeting, store, museum, gallery, park, or restaurant was physically accessible, even if I could drive my scooter into a washroom stall and lock it, there were never any garbage receptacles in the stalls large enough for a diaper. At the sink, there was often only a slot for paper towels, too narrow for a sodden diaper. When there was a garbage can, it often came with this lovely sign: 'No diapers.' That left me two choices: leave my bodily biohazard on the floor or bring garbage bags to secrete the sopping mess in my purse and take it home. Please imagine just how angry that would make you.

Being very nervous at one of my first literary events as a diaper user, I soaked two diapers but hadn't packed a third. It was one of those eureka moments where I realized we should all be angry that there aren't menstrual products, baby diapers, and adult diapers available in all washrooms. Then I noticed what else was missing. Not every diaper user can toilet themselves. To be truly accessible, every washroom also needs to have an adult changing table equipped with a harness to lift the diaper wearer up to the table.

Please let me be clear, this is not a discussion. No one has the right to debate anyone else's medical needs. My ability to change and dispose of my diapers controls the livability of my life. It affects everything. Being able to manage my diapers in public spaces, in both built and green environments, is a non-negotiable prerequisite to being able to enjoy any and all my city has to offer: transportation, housing, arts, culture, recreation, public space, green space, food, and fun.

After trying multiple brands, I found that those that fit my budget and my body best were made by Walmart. Don't tell me I shouldn't shop there unless you're going to make and buy my diapers for me. I already know they're evil. Like all vendors of clothing, they charge fat people more than thin people. In 2018, all Walmart diapers cost $11.99, but my extra-large pack held only sixteen diapers, whereas large packs had eighteen, medium packs had twenty, and small packs had twenty-two. At my five diapers per day, a small user spent approximately $82.89 per month, or $994.63 per year. An extra-large user spent approximately $114.06 per month, or $1,368.75 per year.

When the pandemic hit in 2020, it levied new physical and financial barriers. Given that I live with a repaired heart and a compromised left lung, my doctor made it clear that Covid would be a death sentence, so for four years, I've had to use a grocery delivery service, had to buy all my food from Walmart, and add diapers to my order. In the sourdough days of Covid, much like toilet paper, adult diapers became costly and hard to find. I spent hours scrolling the internet, had to overbuy and stockpile expensive diapers from Amazon when my Instacart shoppers sent me photos of Walmart picked clean. During lockdown, desperate diaper users on social media reported resorting to towels, garbage bags, and duct tape. Of course, that didn't work.

Over the pandemic, diaper makers raised their prices multiple times. Today, my extra-large Walmart pack of sixteen costs $14.94. Five diapers per day costs approximately $141.44 per month, a whopping $1,697.25 per year. With a yearly Instacart fee, per-use delivery fees, and a 10 per cent tip, my diapers cost over $150 per month, $1,800 per year. If I live another twenty years, it's $36,000. A user who isn't fat and doesn't need delivery pays $1,300 per year for a twenty-year total of $26,000. The disability community refers to this lifelong extra expense as a *disability tax*.

When you did your monthly retirement planning, did you budget $150 for diapers? I certainly didn't. I never expected to end up like many disabled seniors, living alone on the poverty line. Diapers decimate my food budget. Today, thanks to the rising costs of groceries and diapers, if I want to eat, I have to restrict myself to three diapers per day. I sit in wet diapers. I sleep in wet diapers. I've got open sores on my bum. It's a health-risking calculus no one should have to make, but I'm not alone in making it, and it's not the only one I'm forced to make.

I've had to cancel my delivery service. In terrified fury, in my N95 mask, I ride my scooter into Walmart when it opens at 7:00 a.m. To reduce the risk of multiple trips, I buy eight packs of diapers, storing three in each of two shopping bags on my handlebars, one in my backpack, and one clenched between my legs. I ride home on high alert, fighting panic attacks but losing the battle. Pre-pandemic, mobility scooter users practised the wisdom of never displaying our purchases. We bought only what fit in our backpacks and zipped them shut. Today, I'm an easy target on display. A sitting duck proffering enticing wares for bullies or muggers.

I worry that once they see what's in my bags, they'll think it hilarious to scatter my diapers like the insides of the Scarecrow of Oz, and I'll have to replace the $119.52 from my already-insufficient food budget. But that public humiliation and extra expense are the least of my worries. I fear an assailant will be so enraged that what they've grabbed is worthless that they'll drag me off my scooter, trash it, steal my phone, and beat me senseless. Injured and helpless, I'd be completely marooned. Even if a passerby wanted to help, they couldn't. They'd have to call the fire department to rescue me.

Before you think this unlikely, I had to call the fire department when my scooter battery died, and disabled people face higher rates of all kinds of abuse and assault than abled people. I'm constantly insulted on my scooter, especially because I always wear a mask. I've been stalked and sexually threatened by creepy men more than once. Physical violence, my frailty to it and my inability to escape it, never leaves my mind, and I'm not alone. The full trauma of struggling to access, purchase, afford, transport, change, and dispose of diapers affects millions.

I'm sure you're asking, 'If this is such a problem, why does no one talk about it?'

There are several interwoven answers to your excellent question. First, incontinence largely affects women, and women's health is never seen to be as important as men's health. Second, as the stealthy double-agent brainwashers of commodity capitalism, ableism, and ageism conspire to villainize and invisibilize diapers by spreading interconnected lies. That diapers are merely a 'personal' problem. That diapers are an unspeakably dirty, niche product used by few, so of course they should be a profit-making commodity. That diapers aren't an accessibility issue, an equity issue, an inclusion issue, a medical necessity, and a human right. That the prudish 1950s morality that keeps us too ashamed to discuss diapers isn't harmful.

That silence lets diaper companies get away with the economic extortion of vulnerable customers. It permits city, building, and event planners, even in progressive urban environments, to pretend diaper wearers don't exist. In the fourth year of a pandemic that neo-liberal capitalism has successfully hoodwinked the planet into pretending is over, it's the same ageist, ableist gaslighting that tells the young and abled that it's fine to go unmasked because only disabled seniors will die. Let's use all the adult words. The combined, collective silence on diapers and Covid embodies and fuels the vile concept of 'life unworthy of life.' It's the ideology of Nazis. It's eugenics.

But here's the good news. Words matter. Renaming the problem empowers solutions. When we call diapers a collective problem, we can call diaper wearers disabled people. We can embrace both terms without shame. Because the problem no one talks about is one that existing urban logistics, government infrastructure, and caring communities can solve. As necessary as surgeries and vaccinations, diapers are health care. Their costs should be fully covered by provincial health plans. They should be delivered by pharmacies, just like prescriptions. These changes could easily be made by those who value disabled lives and quickly implemented by governments when told by voters that delay is not an option.

Aye, there's the rub. I promised you discomfort with a full warning. Having delivered, I'm now asking you to act. Have you reached out and spoken up? Will you now? Will you help deliver a neighbour's diapers? Will you contact your elected officials? Will you investigate and ensure that every public space accessible to you is equally accessible to diaper users? If you do nothing, if you remain silent and complicit, when it happens to you, next week or thirty years from now, when you are desperately seeking dry and find yourself ashamed, isolated, medically at risk, impoverished, hungry, and alone in your sopping, stinky diapers, you'll know exactly who to blame.

## Plain Language Summary

• Dorothy writes about adult diapers. She warns readers that this is an uncomfortable topic. Most people are scared of thinking about disability or aging. This chapter combines both.

• Half of women accidentally leak urine. This number goes up with age. People also need adult diapers due to surgery, irritable bowel syndrome, and other medical conditions.

• Adult diapers are difficult to dispose of. Most public washrooms do not have appropriate waste bins. This creates a barrier for people going out and attending events.

• Adult diapers are expensive to buy. This is an affordability issue for people with fixed incomes, especially seniors. Most people do not plan for this cost as part of retirement.

• Dorothy explains why these are systematic problems that need coordinated solutions. Event planners, city planners, architects, and other professionals all need to do better. Without the ability to buy and dispose of diapers with dignity, a large number of people are isolated at home.

# Accessible Housing Is a Human Right

## David Meyers

What could life be like for many of Canada's 6.2 million people who identify as disabled if all levels of government took action to realize our right to accessible housing? How much more independence and choice would we have with the right to choose an accessible home in which to live? And what about those of us whose names have languished for several years on accessible-housing wait-lists, with no promise of a unit, never mind one that suits our access needs or is near communities where we live?

If this Canada actually existed, would cities like Toronto still be funding new public rental housing in which over 80 per cent of homes are not built with universal design features – resulting in residents being unable to safely live or age in place as their abilities decline? Would far fewer seniors, adults, and even youth across this country who have transitioned to life as wheelchair users be shipped off to long-term care homes because their actual homes are no longer fit for them to live in independently?

There is compelling evidence that most disabled people would live with far greater independence, health, and dignity were we afforded our right to stay in our homes and age in place. Yet, during Canada's current housing crisis, our governments and private and non-profit builders continue to construct apartments, condos, and houses that fail disabled people's right to homes that are accessible.

Canada recognized housing as a fundamental human right way back in 1976 when it signed on to the International Covenant on Economic, Social and Cultural Rights. We did so again in 2010 when Canada signed on to the United Nations Convention on the Rights of Persons with Disabilities. In 2019, the federal government's National Housing Strategy Act declared that all residents have the right to safe, affordable, and inclusive housing. Canada committed to take meaningful steps to realize that right, and although all provinces and territories signed on to the act, none – with the exception of Newfoundland and Labrador – have declared housing a human right. Like most disability justice advocates with a disability, I know well that unless all levels of government commit to take action, disabled people will fall further behind in realizing our right to housing.

As a Black, cis, senior man with an acquired disability, I have lived for decades in Toronto apartments and condos that were built without my body in mind. When I used a wheelchair a few years ago, I could only partially navigate kitchens and bathrooms that I saw non-disabled people use with barely a thought. In more than fifteen years of doing disability advocacy and programming, I've seen up close, and in cold, hard statistics, disabled lives profoundly harmed because our communities deny us the adequate accessible-housing options to which we have a right. This has made the right to housing a top disability justice issue for me. In my day job, I work with disability-led and non-profit organizations advocating for governments to act on priorities like disability poverty, health equity, and adequate housing for disabled people.

The lack of adequate, affordable housing is shaping both deeply personal decisions and council debates, from small, rural towns to larger metropolitan cities like Toronto and Vancouver. One example of structural barriers to progress on accessible housing is Canada's patchwork of extremely ableist and unharmonized building codes. A building code is a basic set of rules for the design and construction of buildings, including housing, and has minimum requirements for public and private housing. Canada has a National Building Code, and some provinces have developed their own. In Ontario, my home province, the building code requires that a minimum of merely 15 per cent of units in newly built multi-unit residential buildings be visitable, not habitable. This low standard allows housing developers to construct 'visitable' units with basic features that include a level entry into a home, a wider entrance doorway, and an accessible washroom, but without bedrooms or a kitchen that would be sufficiently accessible to most wheelchair users or people with other physical or sensory needs.

So here we are in 2024, and many provincial building codes do not mandate that a minimum percentage of homes be built to universal design guidelines. The benefits of homes built this way are documented and well-known by our governments. Such homes have design and adaptability features that enable people to stay and age in their homes as their accessibility needs change, without expensive renovations. Their kitchen facilities, bathrooms, and common areas may meet a variety of disability needs and may require minimal future adaptation to accommodate wheelchairs and other devices. Universally designed housing also increases independence and quality of life for occupants while reducing major health care costs that come with unnecessary hospitalizations and living in long-term care facilities. Despite these feasible modifications, our building codes remain designed to leave hundreds of thousands of disabled people with few or no adequate housing options.

It is also commonplace in cities like Toronto for people with physical disabilities to report waiting for well over ten years for an accessible unit. The crisis has grown so severe in recent years that an epidemic of homelessness has developed in many jurisdictions. Recent data estimates that 45 per cent of unhoused people have one or more disabilities. Furthermore, there have been several reported cases of disabled people who applied for medical assistance in dying, citing inaccessible and unaffordable housing as among their main reasons.

## Disability Demographics

Before diving deeper into other key drivers of disabled people's housing insecurity, I'll highlight some population demographics to provide more context. Some 6.2 million Canadians have a disability and comprise 27 per cent of Canada's population. That's more than one in five people, and a 5 per cent increase over 2017's figure. In Ontario, approximately 2.6 million residents are estimated to have a disability, and its seniors population – estimated at 2.8 million in 2022 – is projected to increase to 4.4 million in 2046.

This demographic trend should be alarming given the housing crisis hitting disabled people in cities and towns across Canada. A society's accessibility needs increase as its population ages, and there are few areas where accessibility matters more than it does for housing. Despite this truism, housing continues to be designed without disabled people in mind.

Disability and seniors advocates have been ringing alarm bells about Canada's accessible housing crisis for well over a decade as accessible and deeply affordable stock has steadily lost ground, even as demand soars. Across all levels of government, disability advocates have seen calls for action ignored. After years of warnings by activists and organizers, the accessible-housing gap is now urgent in communities across the country.

## Affordability

Disabled people in Canada disproportionately live in poverty. In 2021, 16.5 per cent were estimated to live in poverty, twice as many as the general population. Also, disabled people who receive provincial and territorial disability incomes are made to endure annual incomes 40 per cent or more below the official poverty line, and lives of legislated poverty. At the same time, 16 per cent of disabled people were reported to live in households with core housing need, compared with 10.1 per cent for the general population. Core housing need refers to whether a household's housing conditions fall below at least one of three conditions: housing affordability, suitability, or adequacy, which includes accessibility. While many disabled people's households check all those boxes, high and rising rental costs in recent years have made the lives of too many in our community far more vulnerable. The reality is, most disabled people across the country pay market rent due to an inadequate supply of non-market or subsidized housing.

A major contributor to this affordability crisis is our governments' failure to restrict the financialization and commodification of housing. Financializing and commodifying housing means that mortgages, rents, houses, and apartments are treated as investment assets. The proliferation of Real Estate Investment Trusts has been a major contributor to this problem. A REIT is a company that buys and manages properties using money from investors. This approach turns units of housing into sources of revenue – not for the people living there but for investors seeking income-earning assets. It's not just a big-city phenomenon. According to a 2023 article in the *Globe and Mail*, 'more than 40 per cent of condos in Ontario are investment properties, with investor ownership in excess of 80 per cent in smaller metropolitan areas such as London, Sarnia and Woodstock.'

Across Canada, affordable apartment buildings are being sold to REITs. Too often, REITs then demolish the housing and displace the residents, only to build apartment buildings or condos on the same sites whose rent, or mortgage payments, are far out of reach of the low-income residents who previously lived there. Current data shows that for every affordable rental unit being built, we are losing at least three due to financialization. This problem reduces access to housing for equity-deserving groups who experience higher rates of poverty, including seniors and disabled, Indigenous, Black, Queer, and newcomer communities.

Having explored the human rights case for governments in Canada to build housing that meets the needs of disabled people, what is the record of different levels of governments on building accessible housing?

## Federal Context

As I mentioned earlier, the Government of Canada has recognized that everyone in Canada has a right to adequate housing that is affordable, secure, accessible, and habitable. Despite its duty to help realize the right, Ottawa has taken no action on housing accessibility during the housing crisis. Disability-community advocates have called on the federal government to pursue joint agreements with provinces and territories that boldly strengthen and harmonize the universal design requirements in their respective building codes. Ottawa has yet to act. Community leaders have also requested genuine consultation processes that provide meaningful input from disabled people in cities and towns of all sizes across Canada.

Federal governments past and present have erased accessibility from housing policies and investment priorities for decades. As part of the 2017 National Housing Strategy, Canada committed to invest more than $82 billion over the following decade. In his many December 2023 announcements on Ottawa's new 'war effort' housing plan, federal housing minister Sean Fraser encouraged builders to rapidly scale the existing catalogues of housing designs so as to speed up the building process. His lack of mention of the modification of existing designs or the development of new ones to prioritize universal design features alarmed many disability advocates – including me. The omission gives a green light to developers to maintain the home- building status quo. It's yet another colossal government erasure of disabled Canadians on the housing file. As the most significant investment in housing by any federal government since the 1990s, this housing plan represents a huge opportunity to build the accessible housing Canada needs now and in the decades ahead, when our population of seniors is expected to almost double. Yet, just between 10 and 20 per cent of the housing planned for construction within the federal government's various housing plans is required to be accessible, a target that falls far short of what the country needs.

## Ontario Context

Then there's Ontario, whose accessibility legislation and building code read like open violations of the Ontario Human Rights Code and the United Nations Convention on the Rights of Persons with Disabilities. The current Ontario government – unlike the federal government and some municipalities like Toronto – has yet to even declare a right-to-housing approach. Notably, there is still no Ontario law requiring housing to offer barrier-free access to key living spaces, like bedrooms and kitchens. Instead, the standard of 'visitable' units allows government bureaucrats and housing developers alike to get away with the bare minimum. The Accessibility for Ontarians with Disabilities Act (AODA) has five standards, but housing is not one of them. This is a massive failure by the current PC government – and the Liberal government that preceded it – that disproportionately affects disabled Ontarians, especially given that housing is one of the biggest social determinants of health. Without stable housing (or an adequate income), people with and without disabilities are more likely to experience higher rates of illness. This wilful failure is not just egregious but ironic, given that Ontario's deadline to become a fully accessible province is 2025.

In 2019, the late Honorable David Onley, in the Third Review of the AODA, described the speed of Ontario's progress on achieving that target as 'glacial.' In 2023, Rich Donovan, the fourth AODA reviewer, gave the current government an overall failing grade in his report. Sustained policy and advocacy efforts by disability rights organizations and advocates – and even the Ontario Human Rights Commission – have consistently been met with a non-response. The government has refused to implement any fundamental reforms to accessibility legislation that is fundamentally ableist.

As the current Ontario government rolls out its housing supply plan, More Homes Built Faster, the province's existing laws and record of inaction almost guarantee that few people with disabilities will benefit from such homes. The plan does not mention any change in the government's policies on building accessible or deeply affordable housing. Instead, it defines affordable housing as 80 per cent of market rates. Given the disability poverty that too many people endure and the urgent need for accessible and affordable housing, More Homes Built Faster slams the door shut on countless disabled Ontarians who badly need both.

## Toronto Context

The City of Toronto, six months after the federal government recognized housing as a fundamental human right in 2019, took a leap and reaffirmed this right in its HousingTO 2020–2030 Action Plan. Toronto's Housing Charter states that 'all residents have a right to housing that is accessible and takes into account the specific needs of historically disadvantaged and marginalized groups.' This declaration came after years of sustained engagement from housing rights advocates. Community groups lobbied the City to ground its housing approach in human rights. Besides this sustained grassroots pressure, City Hall was pushed by the meteoric rise in home purchase and rental prices, the crushing housing crisis among low-income residents, and a growing homelessness emergency that continues.

Toronto does not currently have a housing accessibility standard. It has a 5 per cent minimum guideline that, being voluntary, is therefore not enforceable. Its current housing plan requires no more than 20 per cent of new multi-unit residential buildings be accessible, a target far below what a city of over 2.8 million residents requires. Moreover, the City's Housing Secretariat does not currently have a reliable estimate of the number of accessible units in its portfolio of over 60,000 units, nor does it have an idea of these numbers in the private and non-profit rental housing markets. Meanwhile, the average wait for an accessible unit on Toronto Community Housing's wait-list is thirteen to fourteen years. These are just some examples of existing government structural barriers that impede our realization of a right to accessible housing.

## Signs of Hope for Accessible Housing

So, having laid out some of the local, provincial, and national issues, what are ideas for solutions and who are some of the thinkers and doers working to make progress? The right to accessible housing remains an outlier in the housing rights sector. Pressure for policy and legislative change still rests mainly on the shoulders of disability community advocates. It's been encouraging to see mainstream organizations that advance housing rights, like the Canadian Centre for Housing Rights and Maytree, start to integrate accessible housing rights into their policy and strategy work, collaborating with some disability community organizations. This cross-movement solidarity needs to happen Canada-wide.

The primary interest of housing developers and builders is profit, and, to date, the vast majority have been opposed to integrating universal design features and other accessibility best practices into home building. Most home builders hold a strong bias against modifying the architectural design and construction of buildings at the scale required to build adequate accessible housing stock. Developers choose to believe that doing so will substantially increase overall construction costs and thereby decrease profits. In contrast, research from 2023, done in some Canadian jurisdictions, revealed that when accessibility considerations and features were incorporated from the design stage, the cost of building multi-unit housing that meets barrier-free standards was approximately the same as or only marginally higher than building conventionally.

One coalition working to influence systemic progress is the Accessible Housing Network, a rights-based coalition of over sixty non-profit organizations and groups with representation across Canada. AHN strategically lobbies and petitions all levels of government to exclusively fund housing that is built 100 per cent with universal design requirements, citing human rights and legal obligations. For many years, AHN has conducted educational events and campaigns on this issue. It has effectively influenced key players in human rights like the Office of the Federal Housing Advocate and the Ontario Human Rights Commission to pressure elected officials and major political parties to enact bold structural change that can realize the right to accessible housing.

Another organization advancing change is the Accelerating Accessibility Coalition (AAC), a pan-Canadian network launched in November 2022. It includes disability-led organizations such as the StopGap Foundation, the Accessible Housing Network, and the Rick Hansen Foundation. Another coalition member is the Daniels Corporation, a home builder with experience building to universal design specifications. The AAC is working to educate home builders on the necessity and sound business case for building the millions of access-ible multi-unit homes Canada needs, both in the short term and in the decades ahead. The AAC has called for building codes at all levels of government to mandate high accessibility requirements in residential buildings and for loans and grants that incentivize building and universal design to be provided to developers.

An example of innovative municipal government and disability sector partnerships, in big-city Toronto, is the Accessible Housing Working Group (AHWG). This group is mainly co-led: on the one hand, by disability and senior rights organizations – including the Accessible Housing Network, Citizens with Disabilities–Ontario, and the Centre for Independent Living in Toronto – and, on the other hand, by senior policy and urban planning staff from Toronto's Housing Secretariat. Approved by Toronto City Council in 2022, the AHWG has been working to research Toronto's accessible housing needs. This includes developing both human rights and evidence-based recommendations for Toronto City Council on the minimum percentage of universal design units to require in multi-unit buildings in Toronto's Housing Plan. The AHWG is to formally present a report to Toronto council in 2024. Most of the group's disability community members advocated for the group to recommend that Toronto City Council vote for 100 per cent of all units to be constructed using universal design principles. Were this to happen, it would be a housing game-changer at the local level, with the potential to be repeated in other cities and towns across Canada.

Writing this chapter reminded me that just fifty years ago, in Canada, it was common for people with severe physical disabilities to live out their lives in institutions offering them minimal autonomy, choice, or dignity. During the early days of the independent living movement, in the 1970s, disability rights activists in Canada fought for and won the legal right to live independently in their communities. This influenced a supportive housing revolution that resulted in more disabled people living in their own homes with the aid of personal support workers or other community supports. Today, as we see more and more people becoming precariously housed or warehoused in long-term care institutions, disability justice advocates view the current erosion of accessible and deeply affordable housing as a clear threat to our hard-fought independence. We'll continue telling our governments to fulfill their obligations to protect our right to it.

## Plain Language Summary

• David explains that accessible housing is a human right. This right has been recognized in Canada and around the world.

- Despite this, governments across Canada are not meeting the needs of disabled people for accessible housing. This need will only grow as the population increases and ages.
- For decades, federal funding for housing has not prioritized accessible housing.
- In Ontario, the building code does contribute to the construction of housing that people with disabilities can actually live in.
- Disability-led groups are starting to partner with other organizations and work with cities, such as Toronto. This community advocacy creates hope for change.

# The *Depression Cooking* Manifesto

## Sonali Menezes

*Depression Cooking* began as a humble project in 2020 in response to complaints from my hungry and depressed friends and family. It felt right to make it into a zine, a do-it-yourself mini-magazine. Zines are by definition self-published. Zines make everyday people into artists, cooks, and poets. Zines create space for us to make things and share information while rejecting the title of 'expert' and complicating the idea of needing to be an expert on something to write about it.

Here's how I formatted *Depression Cooking*: Most recipes have two main formats or options. The first is under the category of 'Less Spoons (energy)' and the second is a remix of the first recipe under the category of 'More Spoons (energy).' These two categories are based on 'spoon theory,' which was developed by Christine Miserandino to help define what it feels like to live with a chronic illness. In Miserandino's case, she used spoon theory to describe what it's like to live with lupus. The basic principle is that a spoon is used as a metaphor to describe how much energy you might have. The spoon represents a finite amount of energy that needs to be rationed each day to survive. In the zine, I'm applying this theory to depression.

Imagine that each spoon represents a task. Let's say you need to shower, eat breakfast, and go to work. If you have low energy one morning because of your depression, we might say you have started the day with five spoons. Showering and getting dressed might take one spoon of energy, preparing and eating breakfast might take another spoon of energy, and travelling to work and putting in a full day will take up more spoons. Once you're out of spoons, you must rest to recharge your spoons. The zine shares meal ideas that take 'less spoons,' or require as little energy as possible. If you're having a better day, or find yourself with more spoons, you can try the 'remix,' or second version, of the recipe.

I didn't include preparation times because that varies for everyone when making things, and there's no such thing as a standard time to scramble an egg. I also didn't include servings because one serving of food for me might be two servings of food for you; we all need to eat different amounts. What I did include was an estimation of the dishes that would be dirtied during food preparation so you can decide how many dishes you'd like to wash. That's an important part of cooking.

I decided to turn my idea for the new zine into a couple of artist residency proposals, which were swiftly rejected. Accustomed to the frequent rejection of the art world, I continued on my way, and *Depression Cooking* grew through conversations with friends and family, notes on my phone, and a few sticky notes strewn across my desk. Eventually, with the support of artseverywhere.ca, PS Guelph, and Hamilton Artists Inc., *Depression Cooking* grew to become a zine of eight letter-size pieces of paper. It launched into the world with a virtual Zoom dinner in February 2022.

The zine blew up across the internet in ways I never could have imagined. The initial 150 copies that were mailed out for free were snapped up. My Instagram direct messages and email inbox filled with inquiries for more copies, along with personal stories of disordered eating, depression, survival, and resilience. I wasn't able to respond to everyone. With help from the Disability Justice Network of Ontario, I quickly launched a second print run. Disability Justice activists I look up to, like Alice Wong, suddenly knew me by name and were posting about the zine on their social media. Strangers approached me at events and protests to say, 'You wrote *Depression Cooking*, right?'

In an effort to meet demand for the zine, I turned to Riso printing with soy-based inks as a lower-cost alternative to Staples photocopying.

I enlisted the help of friends, my partner, and sometimes even my parents in hand-collating, folding, stapling, and packaging around two thousand copies. I sold through Etsy and shipped across the world. I've had requests for the zine to be translated into Spanish, French, and German. People have asked for a second edition, more recipes, and, of course, more copies. Because I was unable to keep up with the demand, special requests, and accommodations, while managing associated costs and scraping by with my own mental health, the zine is currently not available in print. It is, however, copyleft, and exists as a digital zine for the world to use and distribute entirely for free. I am in the process of working on an expanded version, which will eventually become – *fingers crossed* – a book.

This zine offers low-energy meal solutions for depressed humans, with the younger version of myself as the primary audience. I've compiled it first and foremost from cooking tips and tricks I've picked up in the past ten years, discovered through the pure willpower and curiosity involved in survival. Because surviving late-stage capitalism and climate change takes gumption. When you're feeling low on depression resources – or spoons – *Depression Cooking* is meant as a low-cost or free tool to support and comfort. It is a love letter to my depressed kin.

### Plain Language Summary

• Sonali writes about making a zine called *Depression Cooking*. The zine responds to requests from hungry and depressed friends and family.
• A zine is a self-published, do-it-yourself magazine. Zines allow people to share information. Zines challenge who is an 'expert' and who knows 'enough' to write about something.
• *Depression Cooking* provides recipes in two formats. Sonali categorizes lower-effort recipes as 'Less Spoons.' More complicated recipes are called 'More Spoons.'

- Spoons represent the amount of energy a person needs to survive each day.
- Readers from around the world connected with the tips and tricks in *Depression Cooking*. They ordered copies, shared personal stories, and requested translations. Sonali is now expanding the zine into a book.

# THE DEPRESSION COOKING MANIFESTO

is it edible? Cool. Put it in your mouth.
it's better to eat something than nothing
we're in the business of surviving, baby
we eat in the face of depression! Fuck you and you + you!
meal categories? No thanks.
breakfast for every meal of the day, we say!
in the depression cooking meal-plan, there are no bad foods
all foods have nutrition and all foods feed our bellies + bodies
individually wrapped microwavable TV dinner? Bring it on.
and individualist consumerist choices are not going to save the planet. Large-scale
systemic change does. Industries are our largest polluters, not you- you are one depressed
human trying to survive under the crushing weight of capitalism.
You, you are doing just fine sunshine.
mac and cheese is the very first food group.
Fuck Emma W**** and any white vegan who will shame you into believing otherwise
Shame will get us nowhere
Remember to worship the Holy Trinity: the Mac + Cheese, the instant ramen and the Holy Toast
This is the foundation! Start here and the meal possibilities are
absolutely endless
When too depressed to chew, make a smoothie
When too depressed to blend, drink an Ensure
Remember, a bowl of popcorn will sometimes suffice
cheese and crackers will always do
a bowl of ice cream too
Is it edible? Cool. Put it in your mouth
It's better to eat something than nothing
We're in the business of surviving, baby

# Moving Bodies

# What the Eye Doesn't See, It Walks Into

## Claire Steep

Three people using wheelchairs, a neuro-diverse person, and one partially sighted person head into Toronto's Union Station. This is not the beginning of a joke.

It *could* be the beginning of a joke. In fact, it's the beginning of one long, vexed saga about the largely inaccessible journey to the accessible boating service in the neighbouring Town of Oakville. It was organized as part of a week-long conference, and the idea was to break up the seminars and think tanks with a bit of levity. It did, but it also gave everyone the kind of story that beggars belief in the retelling.

We begin at Union Station. It's Toronto's nexus of buses and trains. It's also the point where the subway starts turning into a horseshoe as southbound becomes northbound again. And it's almost always under construction.

It's also chronically busy. But it's a Wednesday mid-afternoon, which makes it not horrendously chaotic. Helpfully, there's a distinct lack of information about where to find tickets, which puts us off to a successful start. Or maybe it sets the tone for this expedition.

I can't see well enough to navigate, and the desks are at the wrong height for the people with wheelchairs, so the neuro-diverse participant (my co-leader in this venture) gets to negotiate the help desk.

We come away with tickets and head off to the platform. But we don't get there, because there is trouble at first in finding the elevators, and then, having found them, figuring out which ones go where. But we're all clever people. The wheelchair users are on delegation from Germany, and the rest of us from Toronto are working collaboratively with them on accessible mapping software. We should be able to catch the right train.

We don't. The conductor realizes this and sends us racing across the platform with seconds to spare. But there's a catch. The catch is that you cannot race from train to train using a wheelchair. Although there are doors on either side of the train, they have a large step, which isn't great for our wheelchair-using travellers. There are two accessible doors on the train, but they're too far away to help us much. Luckily, we're still clever people. The two of us able to navigate the inaccessible doors get the guard to hold the train. The people who cannot keep up because the accessible trains are not actually accessible make it to the far end of the platform, descend one elevator, ascend another, board what we all sincerely hope is the right train this time, and we are on our way.

It's not the best start to what's supposed to be an afternoon's entertainment, but it's only mid-afternoon and there's lots of time for the day to improve. Our accessible destination shouldn't let us down. I've even got my trusty symbol cane in tow, to help my fellow train passengers understand the different accessibility needs of us travellers.

A word about the symbol cane. Here in Canada, we sometimes call it the ID cane. It's slim, looks a bit like a flute, maybe like a conductor's baton. I've heard it mistaken for all sorts of things.

Whatever you call it, it's a thin little thing that you hold at a diagonal across the chest. It's the partially sighted pedestrian's warning to oncoming traffic that while we can see, we can't see well.

It's different from a guide cane, which is thicker, heavier, and lets you test the depth of stairs and curbs without damaging the cane.

Neither the ID cane nor the guide cane is the same as the navigational cane. That's the one everyone associates with the partially sighted, courtesy of *Daredevil* TV series and other media coverage. As per television, the navigational cane is, apparently, the only white cane anyone uses. If you've somehow missed it, it's the long cane often with a rounded ball at the tip. You swish it back and forth to find obstacles.

I have news for TV. Not all partially sighted people are equally partially sighted. Some of us have limited light perception and others are entirely blind. A good friend has full vision but in the murky, cataract-quality way Monet is supposed to have had. To balance her, I have good-quality eyesight but a restricted field of vision. Unsurprisingly, we all have different navigational needs.

In other words, canes come in all shapes and sizes, but the only one anyone is attuned to is the navigational cane, maybe because it's the most obvious, maybe because it's got its own TV agent.

But here's a funny thing. When I go out with an ID cane in Toronto, I'm still invisible. Maybe commuters think it really is a flute. Maybe no one has seen one before. They do exist as a commodity; every so often I encounter a fellow ID cane carrier and we nod at each other before moving on with our day. Sort of a silent *You too have been mistaken for either a sighted person or a completely blind one, but not by me.*

Conversely, I lived for eight years in Scotland, and if I had a symbol cane on me when I travelled, I couldn't move for helpful strangers. Train conductors, airport security, bystanders at crosswalks or on the London underground, they all knew the ID cane signalled partial sight.

At some point, as part of Britain's nationwide campaign to make accessibility for the partially sighted integral to the British transit system, awareness had snuck in. Interestingly, British travellers and pedestrians tended to swing the other direction and, not knowing how much I could see, overcompensated. Over the years, I was handed through airport security, onto trains, off trains, and guided – unsolicited – across crosswalks.

This culminated in the benevolent train conductor who threatened to cancel the outbound Paddington train I had boarded if someone didn't give me a seat. It was late, the train was stuffy, and we had all been standing in that station for hours. Everyone wanted that train to leave the station. No one moved. The benevolent conductor reverted to bribery. Anyone who gave up their seat would be discounted their next fare with the company.

I got a seat, but then couldn't read the book I'd packed because I didn't think that would go over well with the public perception of partial sight. Mind you, I'm still working out how limited vision requires you be seated on a moving train. Maybe he thought there were balance issues that went with the cane?

Here's a tip: ask how you can help before helping. We all have literally different perspectives, so it's not bad manners, it's best practice.

Otherwise, I end up in the kind of situation where the only people who understand how much I see are other partially sighted people. More than once, I (with my symbol cane) have guided people with less vision across roads and around roundabouts. There's nothing wrong with the blind leading the blind. We're witty types with a great sense of humour. Between us we can average a fully sighted person. Sometimes. We still feel safer if/when we need assistance, a sighted person steps in and offers to safely guide us.

Accessible navigation is more than white-cane literacy. The cane is as much for sighted people as for us, and that's true of other accommodations too. Take, for instance, the strange case of Britain's ubiquitous Little Green Man.

If you've never thought twice about this universal sign for crossing roads, you're in good company. Neither had I until I moved back to Toronto and discovered the Little Green Man was white.

Six of one, half a dozen of the other, you say. Not so, say I, because I have stood on Yonge Street, squinting into the sunset, unable to tell if the Little White Man is there or not. I dare any sighted person to say they too have not had this experience.

City planners, take note: If you cannot see the thing that makes you safe, then it's not keeping you safe. Not consistently.

What's interesting is that while the effect of sun on the little white – and sometimes invisible – man needed slightly more thought, the same people who created him also *overthought* the issue of the auditory crosswalk cue.

The scene is Bloor and St. George in downtown Toronto. I've just walked up from the subway. It's summer and overhead a bird is chirping. I hear it and think, as I think every Sunday, that I should find out what kind of bird that is, because birdwatching isn't one of my hobbies.

That same bird is apparently overwintering. It's still there in the fall and it's definitely still there when I finally remember to ask someone about it in December. I don't hear it every Sunday, which is probably why I keep forgetting to identify it.

To the endless amusement of everyone – from the friend I'd asked, to myself, to some city planner somewhere – it's not a bird at all. It's the auditory crosswalk cue. I didn't recognize it because half the Toronto intersections have the bland buzzing audio cue I expect when I press the button at the crosswalk.

They would, says my resident traffic signal expert. It turns out that in a moment of spectacular overthought, the east-west crosswalks got one noise (my chirping bird) and north-south got the bland buzzer.

CBC assures me that as of 2010, Halifax began phasing out the chirruping bird. Its reason? Everyone, not just I, was mistaking it for an actual bird and walking out into traffic. Exit chirruping bird pursued by accessibility advocates. Well done, Halifax. Not only does the chirrup sound too authentically birdlike, but I can't hear it over the Bloor Street traffic nine times out of ten.

Here's another tip for the planner at home: you want your auditory crosswalk cue to be – how to say this gently? – audible.

So why, more than ten years later, hasn't Toronto followed suit?

The funny thing is that I'm not sure you need distinctive audio cues for different directions. Britain has only one. It was very loud, very definitely a buzzer, and unlike the Toronto signal, it started buzzing when it was safe to cross the road.

I've been back for six years and I still hear that buzzer and think I can cross the road. I can't. Canada does it backwards; the buzzer/bird entity sounds only until the Little White Man deigns to appear. If he appears. Even if he doesn't appear.

Despite thoroughly castigating the chirruping crosswalk noise, I'm prepared to concede that getting multiple countries to agree on what sound their accessible crosswalks should make and when they should make it is probably an ask too far. Herding cats would likely be easier.

That said, I don't think you need two sounds. You certainly don't need two if one of them is doing its best impression of the Northern Canadian cardinal.

What Britain got right decades ago, when it implemented its campaign to make the country more accessible, was that it went for simplicity. Visible button. Tactile pavement. Buzzer sound to signal crossing you could not miss for trying.

That came about because the mission to turn Britain, overnight, into the friend of the partially sighted relied on the heavy involvement of the Royal National Institute of Blind People. The ensuing design, which ran from Penzance to John O'Groats, wasn't built on what sighted planners thought people needed. Planners and designers turned to the people who needed it and went from there.

The people who needed it said they could tell north-south crossings from east-west ones with the right sensory feedback. And while I don't think they asked, I don't think anyone anywhere suggested the right cue was the sound of the North Canadian cardinal.

So, no automated birds for Britain. Instead, the accessible crosswalk button faces the direction you intend to cross. For added clarity, immediately above the button is a display that features our friend, the Little Green Man, in case your vision can't do distances. And until the Little Green Man appears, his counterpart, the Little Red Hand, is visible.

Under the button, in a feature I've never seen elsewhere, there's a spinning cone. The idea was that if you were blind-deaf, chances were you couldn't hear the auditory cue or see the Little Green Man.

The best systems work to everyone's advantage, and while I'm not blind-deaf, I have lost count of the number of times I stood at a busy Oxford crosswalk as a partially sighted woman and fell back on that spinning cone. This was accessibility at its enhancing best.

To use it, you feel along the bottom for the cone. It's knobby and easy to find. Once the button's pressed, all you have to do is keep your favourite finger on the nub of the little cone and wait until it starts revolving against the pad of your finger. Then it's a green light and safe crossing.

The cone has another advantage too. If you are somewhere busy, like a roundabout, or there are multiple green lights close together, your buzzer may not sound. That's to prevent Britian's partially sighted pedestrians walking into the wrong crosswalk. Enter the spinning cone for clarity.

It's surprisingly simple but effective infrastructure. It had to be, because the impetus for launching the accessible crosswalks campaign was nationwide. This was one instance where Scotland would not be doing one thing while England did another and Cornwall debated doing something else entirely.

Canada, take note. We are, it must be said, a bigger country, and the kind of accessibility overhaul we would need to reach the British standard of accessible crosswalks would take tremendous effort and planning. It might even involve ongoing discussions with the people whose accessibility you're enhancing about what exactly we need.

A good place to start would be with the Canadian National Institute for the Blind (CNIB), established in 1918. I have every confidence they have opinions on transportation, because accessible transport is one of their major projects as of this writing. Frustratingly, the only opinion people seem to remember is that they should put Braille on everything. Our money, our bathroom doors, our elevator buttons. Not all partially sighted people read Braille, so sticking it on your buildings does not an accessible building make. We need highlighter tape on steps for those of us with limited depth perception. We need tactile pavement to help tell us where the sidewalk ends. Large print, especially post-physical-distancing awareness, wouldn't be amiss either.

And we really need to agree on that crosswalk sound. Or at least pick one that is both obvious and audible over traffic.

These things take time. That's okay. It would be great if we got the partially sighted navigation problem solved before 2118 though. Even better accessibility would be a great way to celebrate the CNIB's second century.

Maybe we could start by taking a hint from Halifax and agreeing that the North Canadian cardinal is a less than helpful tool for successful city navigation?

In the meantime, let's get back to that boating trip. It might help clear up why we need accessible wayfinding solutions if not yesterday, then at least by tomorrow.

I left off with us on a theoretically accessible train. Once we're on board the right train, the journey is uneventful. Disembarking isn't too bad either, once we reach the accessible doors. Finding the boating place goes smoothly until we reach an access point to the river. We're now in Oakville and looking out for our destination: the accessible boating service.

How, then, to explain the ramp? It's so steep that the young woman using the manual wheelchair is too nervous to navigate it alone, and we end up pushing her. We don't mind, and she's gracious about it, but it's neither a dignified solution nor an auspicious or accessible start to the purportedly accessible ferry.

These are the kinds of mundane quandaries an imperfectly accessible city lands you in.

The expedition reaches new levels of absurdity when, unable to find the ferry, I, the partially sighted person, get delegated to search for it, because my neuro-divergent colleague is helping the manual wheelchair user steer down a muddy lane. We should probably swap, but if you've never pushed a manual wheelchair through mud, it requires physical strength not everyone has, and I don't have it. Pro tip for those at home: when possible, always use a fully sighted scout, especially if you want to find the thing you're scouting for. Unless, of course, you want to wander aimlessly for half an hour, maybe walk past your destination two or three times. In that case, by all means send out the person with the symbol cane.

After all, I'm told I make a very good guide. My best partially sighted friend says so.

## Plain Language Summary

• Claire writes about trying to catch a train at Union Station with a group of other disabled people. Union Station is a large transportation hub in downtown Toronto. It was hard for the group to find information about accessibility or get help.
• Claire describes many train trips in the United Kingdom, where she did not have these problems. In the U.K., people recognized her signal cane. They knew to offer help to partially sighted people.
• When she moved back to Canada, Claire was surprised that people didn't know what her cane meant. She was also puzzled by the sound the pedestrian crosswalks made. In her experience, these sounds didn't make it easier to cross the street safely.
• Claire uses humour to show that partially sighted people can solve problems and help each other out, even if sidewalks and train stations are not well designed.

# Cripping Recreation: How Disabled Athletes Get Left Out of Urban Planning

## John Loeppky

I started playing wheelchair basketball because a group of athletes were too disabled.

Shortly after moving to Canada, at age eleven, I phoned the Saskatchewan Wheelchair Sports Association and asked if I could play wheelchair rugby. Something about banging and crashing into other disabled people, as opposed to the floor, seemed appealing. Probably easiest if we just blame preteen aggression.

The answer came quickly... No.

And not no because they didn't want me, not no because it would have been hard to be deemed eligible (in para-sport parlance, classifiable) at the time. It was a no because every member of the provincial rugby team at the time was injured. The how and the why have been lost to time, but let's just say it was because of what I would later deem 'typical quad shit.'

My runner-up prize was to play wheelchair basketball.

The history of para-sport, like many activism-tinged movements, is littered with tales of people taking up space in ways that weren't intended or, in some cases, welcomed. Wheelchair rugby was founded in a Winnipeg gym in the 1970s. Wheelchair basketball was created, in large part, to rehabilitate those coming back from war. Boccia, para ice hockey, table tennis. It doesn't matter the sport: rather than kicking down a door, disabled athletes have – time and time again – chosen to drive their power wheelchairs, scooters, and sports chairs through them.

But that's at the elite level. That level of inclusion – the type that leads to bidding wars between British television stations over commercial rights for the Paralympics – is usually reserved for athletes, teams, and coaches who can make headlines.

When I was growing up, I think we played in every high school in Saskatoon. We played in gyms where athletes needed to be carried up the stairs. We played on as many rubber floors as wood ones. If you're wondering what that is like, imagine trying to play a very fast sport while slowly sinking into the ground just enough to make you feel agonizingly slow.

Unless we had a sustained relationship with a practice venue, we often played in gyms without traction and buildings without even rudimentary accessibility features. Even on the junior national wheelchair basketball team (I got to go to a bunch of cool stuff but never anything important), I once took a trip where the only accessible transit was a yellow school bus. That was a fun nationally funded game of bumper cars – we (mostly) ignored the safety warnings and spent most of the trip slamming into each other for fun. In an airport, I was once asked if this basketball trip was my Make-A-Wish. Every trip was an opportunity to add to my comedy routine. One time I got so tired of an airline employee asking me if I was okay to go up a wheelchair ramp by myself that I gave her my phone and told her she could call my coach and tell him to cut me from the team if I couldn't propel myself up the ramp. I paid for my bravado – one push later a front castor came off and I flipped forward.

To put it bluntly, recreation isn't available to most disabled people. Data from a group of Dutch and Canadian researchers found that more and more disabled people are sedentary, especially during the ongoing Covid-19 pandemic. In the tech sector, efforts by companies like Apple – via their watch tech – have alleviated, but not eliminated, the lack of information we have when it comes to movement. Still, our public narrative around disabled activity is (unfortunately) often boom or bust. Paralympics or bust, medals and acclaim, or a spot in the corner with your name written all over it. For every Paralympian, there are a thousand disabled kids being told they can't attend gym class.

And a large part of the issue is how local decision making – including municipal budgeting, investments in architecture, equipment access, and transportation planning – treats disabled body-minds. Even something as simple as your local accessible transit provider not allowing additional equipment (say, a gym bag or sports wheelchair) on board could mean you can't attend a practice or game. If you can't get on the bus, or you can't get out of an already inaccessible home, or you can't find appropriate sports equipment, or you can't build community with other disabled people, then you have little hope of an active lifestyle.

Despite the challenges of getting in the door, gyms might actually have a more accessible baseline than most recreation spaces. Good luck if you're one of those brave souls who prefers outdoor recreation or purely recreational competition. Online products and services have popped up in response, all while activists like Mary Kate Callahan continue to fight for accessible stationary bikes in gyms. Disabled people, particularly those of us interested in sport, shouldn't be pushed online simply because it's easier to ignore us there.

On top of that, at the root level, disabled people are not taught to enjoy fitness, nor are we given space to figure out how fitness can help us feel more like ourselves. We're taught physiotherapy by default. Good physios make the crip world go round, but that approach is fairly clinical and, in many cases, devoid of joy.

In fact, I'd argue that our public narratives around movement and disability are far more interested in cure than they are in care. I've seen time and time again where people not raised around para-sport immediately connect discussions of physical activity with remarkably unhelpful suggestions, as if a consistent yoga practice will remove your brain damage. Many disabled people end up disliking para-sport, not because of what the athletes stand for, but because of what the movement represents.

And when those actually in power, including members of municipal government or local bureaucrats, are given a glimpse into the disabled experience, it's often through the lens of disability simulations. They're given a wheelchair for a day and told to bump, and crash, and learn. Problem is, research has proven that these exercises are, at best, ineffective, and at their worst they actively harm disabled people. In fact, research that looked into the social impact of the 2012 Paralympic games found that, in some segments of the population, the Paralympics hindered the public's view(s) of disabled people. Paralympians became the 'good cripples,' as if not wanting to play a sport is a character flaw. For all the reasons listed above – bus schedules, old buildings, lack of equipment – too many disabled kids, teens, and adults are simply unable to play a sport, get to the gym, or even enjoy a local park.

'So, which cripple is yours?' were some of the first words spoken to my now-wife when she came to watch me play for the first time. While that might sound like a horrifying phrase, with decades of vitriol behind it, in reality it was said by a friend. It beat the hell out of another phrase used that day: 'So, you're the one who made the bad life choice.' One undeniable truth is that para-sport folks tend to have a – ahem – very particular way with words.

When most disabled athletes congregate in a space like a gym, there is this odd synchronicity. On one hand, you'll hear all the textbook wording of a disability activist-led space. There will be the typical complaining about para-transit schedules, maybe someone's chair got busted on the most recent plane trip, and there will often be very frank discussions about how their bodies are working. A friend used to say that there are only two conversations wheelchair rugby players have – who they are playing next and when they last took a shit.

On the other hand, you'll also usually hear the words that make non-disabled policy-makers, and some disabled policy-makers, quake in their boots. *Cripple, spaz, quad, gimp,* and the like. There have been many times in my playing career when I had to warn people about the openness and bluntness of para-sport spaces. But on top of all that activist-like activity (say that three times fast), there are also key differences between your typical para-sport environment and, say, your average disability justice social media thread.

For one, many disabled athletes will end up using person-first language. They often want to be known as athletes with disabilities (at least publicly). I think this is part of the nature of athletic spaces as communal spaces. By definition, a para-sport is very rarely an insular activity, the suffix *para*- meaning beside or alongside. The administrators and coaches often aren't disabled. Para-sport may be fairly inclusive to disabled people, but historically (in Canada, at least) it has not had the same level of racial and gender/sexuality inclusion. A gym can be a very private place, where griping about ableism is part and parcel, but it can also be a very public space. All the old biases of sport do tend to creep in. Far too many disabled athletes have destroyed their bodies (and their brains) chasing perfection. Bending to the will of a non-disabled world, while it can sometimes catch the ire of disability justice activists, is usually about survival.

In many ways, para-sport is an impossible quandary. It is built on the medical model of disability but espouses a social model ethos. The entire axis of para-sport is the classification system, where athletes, depending on the sport, are sorted into different categories and assigned 'classes.' In some sports, you see classes play out as divisions, like in track and field or swimming. In team sports, like wheelchair basketball and rugby, your class is represented as a number. Generally, the more disabled you are, the lower the number. There are then a limited number of points allowed on the floor at any one time. It doesn't take a dyed-in-the-wool disability activist to identify why sorting disabled people into categories based on their crippledom can be seen as problematic.

And sometimes that classification system, supposedly rooted in fairness, leaves out entire groups of disabled people. When para-sport deems those with conditions like Ehlers-Danlos syndrome and complex regional pain syndrome ineligible, it doesn't just harm the elite sport level, it harms those who never had any intention of going that far. You're removing kids' ability to even comprehend themselves as active, let alone at an elite level. Those athletes who are still included in para-sport's criteria are rarely equipped to interrogate that contradiction. Challenging that paradigm requires intense vulnerability, a removal of safety that most para-athletes simply can't afford. They've already had to fight to be seen as both athletes and people, so challenging these spaces, not just physically but socially, so radically feels out of the question.

So, how do we change things? If local decision making is preventing recreation and para-sport development, but para-sport keeps failing to get out of its own way, how can things shift?

For starters, we need to be thinking of recreation as an ending point rather than a beginning point. If we start with the understanding that many disabled people are active in spite of barriers, then we can think not just about whether gym equipment is accessible, but if the transport to get to the gym is; we can think less about para-sport development and more about how few disabled kids get an equitable gym class experience; we can make accessible fitness the default rather than the exception.

Para-sport teams are a bit like flowers in the cracks of sidewalks. They will always exist, they will always find a way, and they will (almost always) do so in ways that make you notice. The Canadian women's para-hockey team exists despite a lack of funding. Entire para-sports have continued long after the Paralympics have deemed them unworthy of inclusion in a particular cycle. CP football – an adaptation of competitive soccer for athletes with cerebral palsy and other neurological labels – is another example. The athletes who compete on those teams? A lot more fragile than the out and proud people who end up on posters and in Own the Podium commercials. Women playing para-hockey or athletes competing in CP football have even less financial support and public recognition than disabled peers in other sports. Para-sport creates an ethos of invincibility that is an impossible standard to live up to – and one we shouldn't want to live up to. The unpacking needs to happen from the ground up. We need to understand how to nurture athletes, build recreational capacity, and create situations where movement can develop for people.

That starts, more often than not, with talking about physical spaces rather than inclusive intentions. A gym can be perfectly accessible, state-of-the-art, with the best signage imaginable, but if there's no way to get there – or no way to see ourselves as worthy of taking up that space – it will just gather dust and make for a really good line item in a municipality's annual report.

## Plain Language Summary

- John writes about his experiences playing wheelchair basketball starting at age eleven. He participated in local and national competitions but did not compete at the Paralympics.
- He explains that many gyms were not accessible. This was not the only barrier facing him and his team. Poor public transit, inter-city bus options, and customer service at airports are other issues that continue to this day.
- Many of these accessibility issues are under the control of local decision makers. Municipal councillors choose how to invest in recreation facilities. They also vote on bus schedules and sports programming for residents.
- John reflects on the reasons many disabled people have negative experiences with sports. Too many disabled kids are excluded from gym class. Some disabled people also associate movement with physiotherapy rather than self-expression or fun.

- Disabled athletes build community using humour, but they also face pressure to be tough and succeed at competitions. Better supports for sports would reduce pressure and encourage more disabled people to get active on our own terms.

# Healing in Suburbia: A Black Woman's Cancer Recovery through Cycling and the Diaspora

## Nicole Hanson

The Caribbean is known for beautiful beaches, sparkling seas, whistling palm trees, slow-paced living, uplifting conscious music, a rich palette of architecture, and African diasporic cultures and cuisines. But what does this narrative omit? Transportation. Transportation plays an integral but overlooked role in the islands. As former British, Dutch, French, and Spanish colonies, small islands such as Jamaica are now having road infrastructure built by foreign investors through the Belt and Road Initiative: 10 billion dollars are flowing from China to the Caribbean to support six countries and their infrastructure projects. The highway investments and improvements increase automobile dependency and sprawl. The initiative also guides investments away from low-income areas of the islands and into higher-tourism areas, which can prevent tourism and investment from reaching local small businesses and cycling infrastructure.

Within this globalized hierarchy of tourism infrastructure investment, cycling – and active transportation more broadly – tends to be overlooked. Neither European colonial powers nor contemporary Chinese interests in the Caribbean recognize the ways that local people choose to move around beyond the car. Securing active transportation infrastructure as part of the Belt and Road Initiative has been a missed opportunity because islanders have long-standing practices of mobility that have spread across the diaspora. My passion, research, and lived experiences of cycling practices in the Caribbean and African diaspora have guided my commitment to strive for the implementation of active transportation infrastructure in my hometown of Mississauga. This grassroots passion for inclusive, equitable, and culturally appropriate cycling solutions intersects with my professional expertise as an environmental planner and my personal journey of recovery with surviving cancer.

What is often understated as being inherently Caribbean are the cycling options across the diverse terrain of the islands. Each nation is defined by a strong tradition of ancestral landmarks and intergenerational means of wayfinding spaces and places. Walking and cycling networks connect locals and tourists to low-density island settlements, ever-blooming biodiversity, watersheds, beaches, ports, and luscious green spaces. In Bermuda, Railway National Park is a 29-kilometre coastline trail people can walk, hike, and cycle on. This trail is an example of adaptively reusing and programming a decommissioned railway corridor into a public amenity space. It promotes the full range of active transportation modes – cycling, walking, hiking – and offers shaded pathways that respond to the local climate. St. Kitts and Nevis boasts forty-one cycle routes and bike tours for active transportation cyclists, from road bikers to triathletes. Jamaica offers 172 cycle routes, most across hilly terrains. Aruba has a 4-kilometre linear park in Oranjestad, which is an oasis for biking. The path begins at the airport and follows the shore, so you can get a glimpse of the ocean as you pass by.

In Curaçao, the Jan Thiel Lagoon is a nature reserve with various trails, including a challenging mountain-bike trail. This trail was created for the 2006 UCI Mountain Bike World Cup. In Curaçao's colourful historic neighbourhood of Punda, local cafés offer city bikes to engage the community with cycling as a sustainable means of transportation. Punda's Van Gogh Specialty Coffee & City Roastery is known for its rack of bright sky-blue accessorized commuter bikes, which are available for rent. It's extremely unusual to see a small business, particularly a café, offering active transportation as part of

their services. It's a beautiful novelty that is inherently Curaçaoan. This attention to comfort and detail demonstrates the vibrant cycling culture that has grown as part of the socio-economic framework of Caribbean neighbourhoods.

The approach to cycling across the islands differs from mainstream Eurocentric models and metanarratives, which predominantly inform new urbanist city-building and transportation

*Bike rental rack in front of Specialty Coffee & City Roastery in Curaçao.*

policies and practices in North America. Places like Bermuda and Curaçao demonstrate that 29-kilometre coastal trails and tourism-oriented cycling are inherently a part of the islands' ways of life: cycling can be celebrated here, just as much as coastal trails are romanticized in Croatia and Italy. There is a sense of deep pride and homegrown enthusiasm for solutions that support cycling in the Caribbean. These islands are not always comprehensively planned and designed by top-down planning and building departments in the creation of expanded cycling networks, repurposing of curb lands, and the building out of kilometres of multi-use trails or on-street bike lanes. Yet the at-times-uncategorized rural-road networks, on-shoulder and off-shoulder pathways, dense-canopied agricultural mountain routes, and path-making practices along gully roads all form an important diasporic mobility system and culture that informs transformational solutions to active transportation, modelling the planning and policies required for implementation. This is because, while local, these cycling systems, cultures, and narratives integrate and invite the global audience of tourists to cycle with them.

These cycling narratives speak to the sphere of everyday lived experience of various road users, whether local, competitive, or transitory. The approach to cycling in the islands is in deep contrast to North America's fixation with luring white-collar workers to cycle downtown to office buildings and neighbourhoods that prioritize the hierarchies of cycling infrastructure investment. Caribbean countries exude a refreshing and clear narrative that doesn't treat active transportation as a novelty. This juxtaposition has been my point of departure as a Black woman cycling in the suburbs through cancer recovery.

In cycling throughout my suburban city of Mississauga, I often reflect on long-standing practices of mobility and transportation culture across the African diaspora. Questions I ask are: What makes our communities empowering places to cycle, even though infrastructure is limited? Are bike routes an affordable way to get around, considering the vast agricultural land uses, distribution of density, and location of community amenities? Because the islands are small, roads usually support one-way traffic for cyclists or cars. Although bike lanes that go against the direction of car traffic are now being installed in Canadian cities, the question of how direction of travel supports safety is worth continued study in the North American context. It appears that committed cyclists, urban planners, and transportation engineers don't know, and refer to the benefits of cycling in the islands because professional practices prioritize 'adequate' infrastructure over transportation culture. We can explore 'adequate' as a selective qualifier through the historical and colonial practice of redlining.

Just as urban planning practices in the United States historically redlined Black neighbourhoods, resulting in infrastructure deficits and housing disparities, contemporary urban planning and transportation practices prevent racialized people from accessing cycling infrastructure in their communities, while prioritizing such investment in whiter and wealthier communities. The determination of which 'cycling user' should have cycling infrastructure in suburban, urban, and rural areas is inherently Eurocentric. Eurocentric models restrict cycling practices from being understood as a universal language, activity, and deeply historical means of mobility for racialized people across the Caribbean-African diaspora.

While island cities might not have formal cycling infrastructure, they do have trails, wayfinding paths, naturalized landscapes, road networks, and gentle rolling hills that provide scenic routes; beaches that are key elements for connected communities; and island-wide cycling races. More important, cycling in the diaspora inherently contributes to the growth of the economy, mobility for each household, each generation's storytelling and wayfinding technique, memory economy, and lived experience. Which begs the question of why so-called 'best practices' for cycling infrastructure in cities are based on the assumption that European and North American cities are the most bike-friendly and favorable sites worth documenting. Too often, transportation standards privilege affluent communities on the grounds that these neighbourhoods are closer to the idealized urban conditions of Western cities such as Amsterdam or Strasbourg. Taken together, these dynamics are why it was important for me to cultivate, contribute, and build on new ways of knowing and equitable approaches to adopting cycling infrastructure that could be supported collectively in Mississauga.

*City-building* is a term used to describe the process of guiding development in communities. Through the land-use planning process, the potential opportunities, constraints, and impacts of proposals for new construction are assessed through planning policies, technical reviews, and meaningful community engagement. In Ontario, this process is based on the legislative policy framework of the Planning Act and other applicable laws. There are 444 municipalities in Ontario, and residents of these communities can access planning policy documents that inform active transportation – including cycling – and can review studies, master plans, and development applications to determine if additional cycling infrastructure should be considered for potential new developments. In the quest to understand and support active transportation equity in the City of Mississauga, I reviewed policy documents that set the vision, guidelines, and funding priorities for cycling infrastructure. These documents are created and informed by policy planners, engineers, transportation experts, the community engagement process, advisory committees, council priorities, and municipal budgets. Further, Mississauga's Transportation Master Plan was developed through Mississauga Moves, a study that integrated policy review, transportation and transit data analysis, and public consultation.

Active transportation policy documents are important to livability because they shape transportation priorities, address cycling issues, influence and guide development outcomes for communities, promote safer roads and multi-modal mobility, integrate community engagement, and inform infrastructure investment by municipal and provincial governments. Regional planning authorities add another layer, administering their own active transportation policy documents. Peel Region's Sustainable Transportation Strategy, for example, provides a framework for how the region will increase walking, cycling, and various forms of mobility to accommodate suburban growth, both infill and greenfield development, in a way that prioritizes public health, and environmental and socio-economic sustainability. Key themes identified by the region's strategy include implementing cycling networks, prioritizing solutions to and removing major cycling barriers, improving year-round maintenance standards for cycling facilities, and developing priority winter maintenance networks for such facilities.

The Peel Region has one of the largest Black suburban populations in the Greater Toronto Area. The Black community in Peel represents the second-largest visible minority, after the South Asian population. Peel Region's Black community steadily increased from 116,265 in 2011 to 137,295 in 2021. Demographic analysis indicates that the top countries of birth of Black newcomers to Mississauga and surrounding communities are Jamaica, Nigeria, Trinidad and Tobago, Somalia, Ghana, and Ethiopia. This raises the question of why there has been little to no representation of Black people cycling in the suburbs. Where was the ownership in the suburban cycling space? Peel Region's large Black population provides a case study and opportunity to link the inherently diasporic cycling practices of the islands with a planning practice and policy framework that empowers Caribbean-African people in suburban communities.

This was the crux for me as it relates to recognizing the interconnectedness of planning and public health, especially as a Black woman. Black women in Ontario are disproportionately affected by the social determinants of health in urban and sub-urban areas compared to non-racialized women. This is because Black women experience more chronic illness due to the systemic inequities of the health care system when it comes to diagnosing illnesses and providing timely and adequate treatment and care. This was my story. So, in empowering people of colour and the broader population to cycle and connect with the active transportation planning processes in Mississauga, wouldn't showing up as my authentic self – riding a flowered commuter bike – communicate a shared and deeply rooted diasporic experience of cycling, while promoting new pathways to the intentionality of recovery, health, and wellness for Black women? I needed to be that voice, and hold that space and carry this lived experience, as an entryway to equitable active transportation practices in suburbs.

My equitable approach to cycling contrasted with the overrepresentation of whiteness in cycling spaces, practices, and planning policies in North America. Who hasn't heard that some of the best bike-friendly cities are Amsterdam, Copenhagen, Utrecht, Berlin, Bordeaux, Strasbourg, Oslo, Paris, and Portland? However, what constitutes the best example of urban and suburban cycling infrastructure for racialized people? To understand who the space is for, it's important to ask questions about what and who informs the makeup of the cycling space and infrastructure investments. The dominance of whiteness in cycling omits cities like Atlanta from being recognized. This is notable because Atlanta has had a strong Black cycling culture since 1986, with such well-known groups as the Metro Atlanta Cycling Club, Civil Bikes, and the ATL Pedal Bikers. Uniquely, rather than leading with advocacy, these groups focus on social and physical well-being, riding to support school drives, and encouraging people to vote.

*Nicole riding at the Lakeview Promenade as the Region of Peel Bike Month representative.*

Groups like Bonafide Riders prioritize cycling knowledge in the Black community, where they also endow scholarships to community members entering college.

In London, U.K., the Black Unity Bike Ride hosts a 24-kilometre annual bike ride, and they empower the community through cycling, running, spinning, healthy nutrition, and yoga throughout the year. Here, active transportation practices visibly and culturally prioritize the health and wellness of the Black community in urban and suburban areas. This level of omnipresent diversity and deeply rooted diasporic cycling traditions across urban and suburban areas begs the question, why are white middle-aged male cyclists dominating the space and conversation in planning policy and practices?

Haven't we all seen cyclists of this description blazing through the streets and sidewalks on high-tech bikes, flashing expensive accessories, wearing spandex? While these cyclists have their own lived experiences, motivations, and stories, they always appear to be training for the Tour de France. This hypervisibility renders whiteness as being seen and understood as the dominant demographic for active transportation in urban and suburban areas. This is how whiteness disproportionately informs the cycling space and does not reflectthe Afro-Caribbean diasporic experience.

Around the world, cycling is the most common and efficient way to stay active and maintain one's health while reducing our collective carbon footprint. While countries like Jamaica still require prioritized cycling infrastructure to ensure safety and sustainability, and to enhance mobility and enable health, it's still evident that cycling is deeply rooted in the Caribbean culture and lifestyle for both locals and tourists. Recognizing how centring Eurocentric narratives of cycling displaces Caribbean practices brings to light the power dynamics of infrastructure investment and the broader erasure of Black community cycling narratives. Speaking truth to power through my lived experience of cycling in the suburbs recentres the visibility of the Black experience.

My commitment to making cycling safe, visible, and celebrated across racialized communities in Mississauga has been based on my erasure and invisibility as a Black woman in the health care system. After being diagnosed with an aggressive form of thyroid cancer, I became the inequitable statistic of a Black woman between the ages of twenty-five and thirty-five facing chronic illness with a low chance of a good prognosis. Faced with this statistic, health equity became the driver that pushed my commitment to healing, wellness, mobility, self-discovery, and community empowerment through cycling. The ability to ride my bike after surgery, as a natural and first form of mobility, allowed me to make and claim my space in the city as an everyday Black cyclist. Elevating my urban experience during my recovery was crucial to my health as a Black woman. So why not cycle therapeutically like we did back home – in style? I gave myself permission to be hypervisible, and pedalled my story festooned with flowers as I rode through the streets on my commuter bike. My goal was to encourage, inspire, and start public conversations about Black women as everyday suburban cyclists, and show how claiming space on the streets could support our overall recovery and resiliency.

My recovery journey coincided with a greater public conversation about cycling safety due to an increase in cycling fatalities in Mississauga. Layered on this was the Peel Region's Road Safety Strategic Plan 2015–35, which tied into the City of Mississauga's adoption of Vision Zero in 2018. The Vision Zero framework equitably prioritizes zero fatalities and safety for all road users by slowing speeds, educating people, and enforcing laws to support safer behaviour on the roads. Further, according to Mississauga's Vision Zero action plan:

> There is evidence to suggest that often communities most in need are also least likely to report collisions, injuries or other serious concerns. They may not have the same access to their local representatives, the same amount of time to allocate to voicing their concerns and providing their input, or the belief that they will be heard to the same degree if they present an issue. Vision Zero efforts must account for this and look for opportunities with equity at the forefront of decision making.

Given the limited data on Black cyclists, the rise in road rage, and the politics of the war on cars, I felt it important to demonstrate the need for cycling safety for Black people in the suburbs. That's what it means to truly build frameworks based on transportation equity. As a result, I supported the continued work of the Mississauga Cycling Advisory Committee, whose main responsibility is to increase the safety, quality, and quantity of multi-use recreational trails in the City of Mississauga in line with the city's Cycling Master Plan. In the end, my efforts, both independently and collectively, supported equitable outcomes for vulnerable road users. These contributions were recognized by the Peel Region and the City of Mississauga by celebrating my efforts during Bike Month and conferring on me the Phil Green Recognition Award in 2017. The award is presented annually by the Cycling Advisory Committee to people who have demonstrated exemplary effort to further cycling activities. The award provided me with a platform to broaden my reach to various marginalized communities and support active transportation goals in planning policy and practice.

All of this recognition created visibility, not just for me as a woman navigating suburban streets, but for Black people as everyday cyclists across the diaspora. By engaging with local decision-making, contributing to the planning process through policy deliverables, and drawing on my personal recovery experiences, I was able to centre the Black woman's experience of cycling in the suburbs as a form of partnership and evidence to secure cycling infrastructure investment. After all, as a woman of the diaspora cycling in the suburbs, I want to see Caribbean practices of active transportation remain a vibrant part of life in Canadian communities.

## Plain Language Summary

• Nicole writes about where and how people bike in the Caribbean. Her descriptions draw on her experiences travelling and belonging to Black communities.

• For Nicole, it's important to learn from Black biking culture to make cycling safer in her hometown.

• Nicole has worked in urban planning and volunteered in Mississauga. She explains how cities in Ontario make decisions about cycling.

• She also explains that cycling was a key part of her cancer recovery.

• For Nicole, it's important that people cycling in the suburbs and seeking health care are visible. In hospitals and at community meetings, Black people are too often invisible.

# Survival of the Fattest Disabled 2s in the North

## Valdine Alycia

Tansi kiya, my name is Valdine Alycia. I am a fat Two-Spirit Michif with roots to Treaty One and Two at Lake Winnipegosis, but I was raised and live on Treaty 5 adhesion land in Thompson, Manitoba, a town that is closer to the Arctic Ocean than it is to the Canadian border. My pronouns are they and them, and I was diagnosed with a disabling chronic illness when I was twenty years old and living in British Columbia, near the Pacific Ocean. When I was first diagnosed, I had lost partial vision in one eye and developed many impairments that affected my ability to move in the world. I was fortunate to be diagnosed while I was living in B.C. for school, because my diagnosis took a matter of weeks in B.C. while it would have taken years while living on Treaty 5.

Since then, my life has changed dramatically. I moved home to live with my parents in order to be able to access newly discovered disease-modifying injections. My B.C. doctor had told me how lucky I was that the first medications had recently become available. Back in Manitoba, I was able to access provincial pharmacare a year sooner than I could have in B.C. Public pharmacare was the only way I could cover the several thousands of dollars per month for groundbreaking injectables with hope of slowing neurodegeneration. Since starting medication, I've been able to build a career as a Michif professional and I've embraced disability justice principles instead of relying on my ability to push my body's limits. I travel with all my meds and my mobility aid, and I've learned to rarely disclose my condition, because

I deserve to be in all the spaces without being reduced to my condition or my body size. I'm learning to take up space just as I am.

Now when I have a flare, I know that my life is not ending and I work through the sudden changes in pain and mobility, although it takes me time to accept increased pain and less mobility. I've been in a flare for a few days as I write this, and the amount of pain I am in and my dramatic decrease in mobility are so upsetting that my rage is going to boil over into my writing. This flare is a result of the stress caused by my coming out as Two-Spirit to my bio dad, who yelled at me about his religion and my gender assigned at birth, and refused to believe that I am the expert on myself. I have to be hopeful that one day he'll be able to trust my telling of who I am. I am frustrated that the stress of coming out to him is affecting my health, and it reminds me of my mom, who died at sixty.

A few years ago, before my Indigenous mom passed in hospital after her hysterectomy, I naively thought that having her white-passing family tending to her would be enough to show medical professionals that she deserved conscientious attention and care. Unfortunately, I could not account for the disregard for fat people's lives demonstrated by the health care system; she died of medical neglect. A few years later, another Indigenous woman, named Joyce Echaquan, died of medical neglect in Quebec but recorded and shared the video of hospital staff before she passed.

After Mom passed, my only pain relief and mobility improvement took place in swimming pools. When I'm in a pool it feels like nothing else matters except my breath. I can trust that the water will catch me if I lose my balance and the water temperature will keep my body from overheating. The nearly instant sense of safety and connection to my body is empowering and helps me build strength for life outside the pool. In 2019, my community pool closed permanently, and I plan my work and union travel around pool access when I'm able.

The loss of the pool, nearly two years after Mom passed and shortly before Covid-19, stopped my pain and mobility management strategies completely. It accelerated my disease at an alarming rate, resulting in ongoing losses that I struggle with. When I'm able to exist without pain, I can get in touch with other parts of myself, the hidden but real parts that I barely know. Survival forces me to focus on tasks of daily living, and since the Thompson pool closed, my mobility has decreased, and so has my leg strength. The nearest pool now is 400 kilometres away, one way, and when I have the chance to access a pool, I go through a roller coaster of emotions, from gratitude and relief to joy.

In a world where fat, disabled, Indigenous people are not supposed to exist, I have been lucky to find creative, fat, Indigenous people like me who continue to live despite a society that polices our existence. Because of our shared experiences, we've formed a creative community around our writing and art. The collective I joined as a short-term distraction from grad school has become a beloved group of friends I am connected to across Turtle Island. Because of my fellow fat Indigiqueers, like Jess Murwin, and their incredible creative vision, I have hope that our shared existence will mark a path for younger ones like us. Our shared joy is invigorating at a time when simply existing is stigmatized; as fat Indigiqueers, we celebrate ourselves and we do it without shame.

My fatness and disability are publicly weaponized when I use a mobility aid – I am accosted for the amount of space my cane takes up. Strangers are comfortable calling me out in public for the space my cane takes up rather than criticizing my fat body, and I know ableism and fatphobia are empowering them to believe they are entitled to critique the way I exist. I am seen as 'less than' for being fat and using a cane. According to ableism and fatphobia, my fatness has caused my disability, and I am frustrated by the lack of consideration for me as a disabled person entitled to legal accommodation. From assembly gatherings to pool change rooms, spaces must take my need for access into account, regardless of my body size. I do not have to shrink my body to be entitled to accessibility and full participation; I am a human and deserve to be treated like one at all times.

I was recently accosted for the amount of space my mobility aid took up at the Manitoba Métis Federation's (MMF) Extraordinary General Assembly. Entering the crowded assembly gathering as a fat person with a cane was a challenge in itself, but for someone who is overstimulated by noise, fluorescent lighting, and heat – in addition to having a disease that affects my body's ability to regulate its temperature – participating in the assembly was challenging for me. I was pushing my limits to attend the gathering 700 kilometres from my home. Fortunately, another queer friend from my community invited me to sit at their table. But when I sat at this table and asked where the water was, a stranger criticized my nosiness about hydration, then proceeded to complain about the space my cane took up at the table. What started as a historic day to mark the passing of the first MMF Treaty ended with me feeling excluded, unimportant, and unwelcome as a fat, disabled Two-Spirit. My day revolved around getting away from the ableist complaints of other MMF members rather than focusing on our Treaty. I hope the MMF Treaty does not allow others to unenroll me simply because some members deem me unfit to participate, simply because I show up to assemblies and regional meetings in my fat, disabled body.

Disappointingly, the community members who criticized the space my body and mobility aid take up belong to the Red River Métis, a Nation I also belong to. An ancestor of mine was given scrip to the land of the original Red River Settlement in exchange for being displaced, so that John A. Macdonald's Canada could expand west. I have many kinship relationships in the Nation that originate in our shared ancestral ties to the Red River Settlement of the 1800s. And I have just as many kinship connections to other Indigenous people in the north. The most inclusive relationships I have are outside of the Nation I belong to, which seems set on celebrating conformity in thinking and ability despite all our different ways of embodying space. This is how the Nation enforced disabling conditions on me at the assembly.

I have learned to appreciate the way I see the world after years of building communities around each of my identities, from my fellow Indigiqueer creators to the friend who offered me a seat at the assembly to my kinship connections across Manitoba. It's hard not to see value in myself when I see so much value in the people around me and the tips and tricks they share to live well, like walking in swimming pools. By walking laps alone at my own pace in shallow pools, I have gained enough strength and pain management to tread laps in any depth of pool. I go much slower than a lap swimmer but achieve great results that allow me to move more freely outside of the pool.

Just as the MMF excluded me from full participation in the historic passing of our Treaty, my town has created a disabling environment for me and others like me who relied on the pool for disability management. Shortly after the pool was closed, a new physiotherapist commented how 'they wouldn't have known' about my disability by the way I walked. Now, when acquaintances see me in public using my cane, they ask me what happened. A series of disabling events took me out of my able-bodied-passing life, and while I grieve the strength I used to have, I appreciate the self-compassion my disabled body requires of me.

Access to wellness support and health care is so poor on Treaty 5 that the many Indigenous peoples who live here die much sooner than their southern kin. Preventable deaths as a result of untreated chronic illness are not uncommon in the subarctic, where funding is limited and government resources are few and far between, despite the natural resources here that fuel the economy of the entire province. Canada's advertised quality of life is not shared with many residents of Treaty 5, and the wealth extracted from natural resources by the Government of Manitoba is withheld from the region entirely.

Interdependence and community care are keys to living well as an Indigenous person, and I am grateful for the many Indigenous friends who have stepped into my life to ensure that fat, sick, Indigenous people are not left behind in a time when I am told – at MMF gatherings and by Canadian bureaucracies – that I do not deserve to exist. Indigenous peoples deserve to be enabled to live well in Canada's systems – including disabled and chronically sick Indigenous people like me and my late mom. We deserve accommodation to participate and access spaces and services not designed for us. We deserve accessible health care that does not require commuting hundreds of kilometres for treatment. The generations that follow us deserve the same access to clean water, food, education, and health care that Canadians enjoy.

Despite the barriers imposed by the Canadian government, Indigenous peoples' connection to the land and water revitalizes us and gives me a sense of purpose and calm. Sitting alongside many lakes this summer reminds me that I'm part of a life bigger than my fight to survive or the loved ones I've lost. There has to be some quality-of-life sharing in Canada, and I'm hopeful that in my lifetime, Indigenous nations will be free to govern themselves without micromanagement from the Canadian government. Every time I can be near the lakes, rivers, and waterfalls that were important to my late mom, I'm reminded of how the waterways care for me and remind me to breathe, just like when I'm at a swimming pool.

In the same ways the closure of my town's pool made my chronic illness dramatically more disabling, Canada's laws and systems create disability, death, and chronic illnesses in many Indigenous folks. Sickness, disability, and death are the result of ongoing harm, land theft, and the methodical elimination of Indigenous rights. Unceded territory and disrespected treaties – or no treaty at all – enforce Canada as the legal decision maker for waterways that Indigenous peoples across Turtle Island have relied on and cared for since time immemorial. As these lands and waterways are further exploited for natural resources, Indigenous peoples get more chronically ill while the Canadian government enforces laws and systems that ultimately eliminate us. As a nation, Canada continues to maintain its polite narrative of wealth extracted from stolen land, water, and resources.

The Canadian way of life necessitates in perpetuity that Indigenous peoples survive large-scale land theft and denial of self-determination across the land. To survive Canada as an Indigenous person is to survive a disabling country.

## Plain Language Summary

• Valdine writes about living in Northern Manitoba on Treaty 5 land. Valdine is a fat, Two-Spirit person with roots in the Red River Métis Settlement.

• Valdine describes managing illness and disability in a town that is closer to the Arctic Ocean than to the Canadian border. Valdine's local pool was a place where they could breathe and trust the water to help with pain and mobility.

• Valdine felt excluded in the Manitoba Métis Federation's Extraordinary General Assembly, but has found care and community among Indigenous friends.

• Valdine compares the closure of the town pool to the impact of Canadian laws on Indigenous people. In both cases, Indigenous people know what they need to live well, but Canadian governments deny access to water and land.

# Listening

## Jacqueline Valencia and
## Alexandria McDonough

'My name is Alex. I am smart. I am beautiful. I am awesome. There is only one me in the world, and Mommy and Daddy love me.'

It's Wednesday, which means a day of commutes for Alex, my adult autistic daughter. She wakes up at six o'clock in the morning to shower. She finishes her daily affirmations, enunciating every word in front of the bathroom mirror. She calls me to show me that she is done. I look in and see that she's put her clothes on in the right direction. A pink blouse and purple leggings frame my daughter, who is taller than me. On tiptoes I see that she's combed her dark curly locks, and as she smiles to show me that she has brushed her teeth, her brown eyes glow as if to say, *See? I'm awesome!*

Alex then goes to her room, turns on the neon OPEN sign next to her bed, and reads the business hours she's written below it.

'Six o'clock. The breakfast is?'

In the living room, I serve her a breakfast of oatmeal and chopped-up strawberries. I remind her to eat slowly as she shovels the food into her mouth. She looks out the window and spots her favourite neon OPEN sign across the street.

Alex's world isn't internalized, it's actually a very interactive one. Her senses take in so much. She eats fast because flavours can be overwhelming. She screams and cries when she is overcome with emotion. She listens fiercely to life around her. It's so big, wonderful, and all so loud.

'Open open open open opennnnn. Green, yellow, blue, purple …
O. P. E. N. Open!' she sings. I pack her lunch and get ready for the
long ride to her day program. It's two buses and a half-hour subway
ride away.

Alex is autistic, low verbal, and she has sensory issues that include
auditory processing. When Alexandria was younger, she would watch
VHS tapes of her favourite shows on endless loops. She would also
sing along to jingles on television and didn't mind the peripheral noise
others made. The only indication that some noises would bother her
was when she pressed her index fingers to fold in the bottom of her
ears. This would usually be in response to the sound of a plane overhead, a fire truck approaching, or the beep of a construction truck.
Her hearing has always been exceptional.

The first bus we take is relatively empty and we easily get seats. Our
bus passes a neon sign in a pizza joint window. 'PEEZZZAH! P! I! Z!
Z! A!' Alex exclaims. She says it a little too loud, and I indicate with
my hands to lower her volume, as if I were lowering the volume on a
stereo system. She frowns at me and says, 'Shhhhh.'

Sometime around twelve years old and the beginnings of Alex's
puberty, her school assistant noticed she would run out of the classroom screaming when they started a movie. At school performances,
Alex would participate, and even sing, but she frequently plugged her
ears. Her audio sensitivities started to interfere with her schoolday.
Some of her fellow autistic students wore headphones or earplugs,
and Alex started wearing them in class as well. Over time, wearing
headphones became more common at home and outside too.

For many disabled folks, much time is spent commuting to ther-
apies, school, and day programs. Many of these spaces are located
in the suburbs, since government cutbacks make it unaffordable to
rent in the city. For Alex, a commute on transit involves blaring

announcements, the continual noise of rush-hour crowds, and loud sounds that inform passengers of stops and delays. At home, while she loves having a television in her room, Alex rarely abides people having the television on in a room she's in.

People who know Alex understand and will test out if turning down the volume or simply turning off an appliance will make her more comfortable in a room. Maybe for Alex it's just a matter of controlling the audio stimuli. She's a very creative person and uses an iPad with GarageBand and YouTube to create music and videos. Her music features loops on beats and dropping heavy bass lines. Her videos combine edits of television broadcasting station bumpers, her own versions of kids' shows, and television commercials. She gets no greater joy than watching and listening to her own art. Alex is like Prince that way, who claimed to only listen to his own music.

However, using the iPad requires using headphones. After an assessment, Alex's audiologist suggested trying not to use them as much. We wanted to see if we could reduce sensitivity to the peripheral noises that trigger negative responses. Audio therapy started with morning meditations that slowly introduce sounds like traffic and nature via YouTube videos. Eventually, we started going out for morning walks and leaving the headphones at home. At first it was really difficult. But after taking off the headphones in the quiet spots on our walk, Alex realized she didn't need them for part of the walk. According to the audiologist, Alex's participation and consent were key to desensitizing her to the noises that aggravate her. By making the choice of whether or not the headphones were needed, Alexandria was in control of her exposure to different sounds. She controls her audio world, much like she does her iPad.

During today's commute, Alex has chosen to wear her headphones for only part of the subway ride. She has also chosen not to use her iPad for most of the ride. The hardest parts of the trip are St. Patrick's station, St. George station, and the tunnel from Dupont station to St.

Clair West station. These stations are hubs, so a lot of people tend to board. As for the tunnel, there's a fifty-second screech. Most people might not notice, but Alex counts down the seconds out loud.

For the rest of the subway ride, she either beatboxes or talks in a singsong voice with non sequiturs. We pass by Lawrence West station and, for the first time, she lets out a big scream. Most of the people on the train are startled and stare. My first instinct is to give Alex a hug and tell her I am there and it's just a few more stops. Alex sobs and calms down when I offer her the iPad and headphones so she can listen to her own music or the music of Dua Lipa instead of the screeching of the subway.

The world is full of audio stimuli. Hearing someone whistle nearby causes Alex to abruptly turn to the person and say, 'Be quiet!' This has been an ongoing thing from the time she was little. Her screams on the subway during a delay or on a crowded bus end up with me focusing on quieting my daughter and apologizing to those around us. 'She's autistic! Sorry!' Over time, I stopped apologizing. 'She's autistic,' and a shrug. It's the social pressure that made me apologize before, but if Alex is in mental or physical pain because of a noise or a situation that's out of her control, that's not her fault.

Disabled people have to continually modify responses to sights, sounds, smells, and textures for the benefit of the 'neuro-typical' world. Alarms and announcements are created for those who can hear and not be bothered by the noise. Blaring noises don't help Alex or anyone else with audio sensitivities. They also don't help anyone who is Deaf or hard of hearing.

Most of our fellow passengers on the subway seem convinced that we cannot accommodate everyone, but in reality we live alongside many people of different abilities and disabilities. Everything that has been adapted in the classroom for Alex has worked positively – not just for her, but also for her classmates. Imagine if educators and governments focused on abled and disabled people as equal citizens.

Adaptations would benefit so many and in turn create more opportunities for everyone. The progress in adapting things has been fast during Covid, but it often benefits disabled people only by chance.

You can see it in how everyone transitioned to online learning during the pandemic. The option of learning online benefited students with learning disorders and anxieties, but it was a by-product of emergency ingenuity and not designed to help disabled learners. This example shows it's possible to create public services and shared experiences that support all abilities and sensitivities, even audio ones.

Alex's day program is located on the border of the city, just before Toronto turns into something else. It's an area filled with factories and industrial complexes. The last bus is packed with a variety of blue-collar workers. We get in and find a spot to stand at the back of the bus. Alex has taken off her headphones and turns to look out the windows. We pass many neon signs, and Alex responds with song. Her voice ranges from the lowest registers to the highest throughout our trip. As we arrive at our stop, she asks for her noise-cancelling headphones. We get off the bus, and outside of the day program we go over her social story of the day – a picture-based document that parses everyday situations into steps. Today it's all about headphones and choosing whether or not to wear them. Alex enjoys her music but needs to be able to control what she hears. As the audiologist explained to us, it's all about consent. It's important to give Alex the choice in her daily experiences. As I leave, Alex puts on her noise-cancelling headphones.

On my way back home from the day program, I look at my phone. Alex's application for accessible transportation, Wheel-Trans, has come through. Soon we'll be using it for our morning commutes.

As I wait for the bus, a fire truck with its sirens on full blast whizzes by. I, along with a few others waiting with me, put our hands to our ears.

## Plain Language Summary

• Jacqui and Alex write about their mother-daughter relationship and their experience commuting.

• Alex is Jacqui's adult autistic daughter. Together they travel by bus and subway to Alex's day program at the edge of Toronto.

• Alex has exceptional hearing and enjoys making music using GarageBand. She also finds some noises extremely irritating.

• Alex uses headphones on her commute and even at home to manage noise. She's working with an audiologist to expose herself to more sounds and become comfortable with different volumes.

• Alex's commute is full of noises that can be overwhelming. By consenting to wear or take off her headphones, Alex can have more control over her environment.

# Remembering Winter

## Emily Macrae

I was never the kid competing to slide the farthest or the fastest as winter snow melted into an ice sheet covering the entire schoolyard. At recess, other kids would race outside to play on the bumpy blue-grey surface that reflected the early spring sun. If I stepped onto the ice, my knees locked in fear and my arms strained for something to hold on to.

With one leg shorter than the other, I found that the repeated humiliations of gym class were never far from my mind at a school that treated Track and Field Day like a national holiday. I couldn't avoid letting down my teammates during relay races, but I could steer clear of embarrassment during recess. I knew that if I sprawled across the uneven ice, my pink marshmallow jacket and the snow pants that swished with each step would not be enough to pad my pride.

My aversion to icy surfaces started young. During a February fire drill in kindergarten, I slipped on snow, and my teacher (thank you, Mrs. Waters!) gathered me from the ground and walked with me until we reached the level linoleum of the school hallways. Like all my classmates, I had left the building in my indoor shoes. We didn't have time to put on winter boots that would have offered some traction before we filed outside to wait for the fire trucks.

Perhaps because of that initial humiliation, I took snow boots seriously as I grew up. I knew better than to try to slip through the season on sneakers, and I've never been tempted to boost my height with heels. Fluffy, flat-footed ankle boots were all the rage when I was in high school, but when I moved to Halifax for university, I switched to footwear more suited to the city that coined the term #StormChips. Even though many Maritimers hunker down with salty snacks when blizzards hit, each home is stocked with snow boots and metal-tipped snow scrapers to help residents navigate before and after a blast.

Winter is my favourite time of year, and I refuse to stay inside. No matter how cold it is, I head out in search of bird tracks in fresh snow or blue shadows across blanched fields. Over the course of four winters in Halifax, I tried everything from upscale Columbia pull-ons to Canadian Tire rubber boots supplemented with wool socks. No matter how much or how little I spent on boots, I always wore through them: my limp means that by the end of a season of long walks, I've rubbed holes into the toe of my right boot and the heel of my left.

I was lucky to grow up with parents who could carry that cost as my feet grew to adult sizes. Later, as an urban planning student and then an intern in the civil service, I extended my budget by trying to stretch boots into a second winter. I experimented with duct tape, plastic cement, and shoe sealant. But sturdy boots can do only so much if the sidewalks aren't shovelled. Walking to my first office job, I stepped with care, afraid of slipping and scraping my stockings or ripping my dress pants. It was on these trips through downtown Toronto's narrow side streets that I recognized the inequality of the city's approach to clearing snow.

A few blocks from home, I could walk along a main street where the sidewalks had been cleared by a city plow. But morning traffic was loud and trucks sprayed slush as they passed, so I usually wound through smaller streets where each neighbour was responsible for clearing the snow in front of their home. The result was a patchwork of sidewalks scraped clean by athletic early birds and pavement that became indistinguishable from surrounding snowbanks if no one shovelled. One day, after a fresh snowfall, I thanked fourteen different property owners clearing snow on my way to work. At other times, I took my frustration to social media, tweeting about the sorry state of sidewalks when it snowed. Even if I thought I could outwit winter sidewalks with snow boots and social media, my twin brother didn't have the same options.

In December 2017, we met up for dinner at a Thai restaurant where the staff were always quick to remove a chair and make space for my brother's wheelchair. The spring rolls were crisp and the mango salad was sunny. The meal felt like a tropical retreat from the slush that filled the roads and formed a crust around each curb. Turning down a side street with our bellies full, we moved slowly so the wheelchair could find traction on unshovelled sidewalks. Some strips of pavement were scraped and salted down to the concrete, but others were covered with churned snow the texture of coarse sand or slabs of ice more than an inch thick. Each property line presented a new challenge. Black ice where runoff from a driveway had frozen over an otherwise shovelled sidewalk. The sudden incline of climbing onto a patch of solidified slush. The indeterminate depth of a snowy puddle. Midway down a block full of these winter wild cards, my brother's huge power wheelchair got stuck.

The front castors spun but the main wheels sank in the snow.

My brother is an excellent driver. He can manoeuvre his wheelchair along crowded subway platforms without threatening the toes of his fellow commuters. He can navigate the narrow aisles of his favourite bookstore without disturbing the stacks of books sprawling in front of the shelves. He can back out of an ice cream shop without ever letting go of a cinnamon-spiced milkshake.

So, as his drive wheels spun in the snow, my brother adjusted his joystick to approach the ice from a different angle. No luck. I tried to give him a boost from behind, but the chair had settled into the grimy snow. Again he adjusted his angle and again his front wheels spun.

Our breath clouded under the street lights, and I tried to judge the distance in either direction. Forward to the end of the block, where we could wade into the roadway instead of risking more uncleared sidewalk. Backward to the previous curb cut, where we could turn into the road and try to avoid another block of the patchy property lines. But we were stranded in the middle of the block, and the distance in either direction was daunting. Neither pushing forward nor backtracking was an option because we still couldn't budge.

In search of ramen and rare books, I've helped my brother up steep ramps and down from uneven curbs more times than I can count. I know when to give a push so he can concentrate on steering at a moment when gravity might upend his chair. I know never to insult his independence by trying to drive for him and I know that lifting the chair is impossible for a single person to attempt.

But in that moment we needed leverage to raise the wheels from the pit of snow. I flexed my wrists and asked my brother for permission to invade his personal space. Using the handles at the back of the chair like parallel bars, I lifted myself off the sidewalk. My body rose as I shifted all my weight over the back of the chair. My boots dangled above the back wheels and my elbows cracked. Still not a millimetre of movement. The chair weighed hundreds of pounds, cost thousands of dollars, and required endless appointments to customize and repair, but couldn't barge through a Toronto winter. My entire body weight was not enough to nudge the chair out of the ice.

I don't remember how we got unstuck from the middle of that block. I do remember returning home exhausted and angry. No neighbours turned up to rescue us with shovels and salt. A ten-minute trip from the restaurant had taken twenty-five minutes. Our dinner was a distant memory, of a world where no one would ever get stranded in the midst of million-dollar homes because neighbours had not bothered to shovel after successive snowfalls. The problem of winter sidewalks is not unique to Toronto: when I shared the fear and frustration of that night on Twitter, I received stories from other neighbourhoods across the city and words of support from as far afield as Ottawa, Chicago, and Washington, DC.

East of the Rockies, winter is a reality for Canadian communities. Approaches from other cities show what works and what doesn't when it comes to keeping sidewalks clear and supporting mobility for disabled residents. The same year my brother and I got stuck in the snow, municipal staff cleared snow from 5,800 of Toronto's 7,029 kilometres of sidewalks. Residents were responsible for shovelling the remaining 20 per cent of sidewalks that were too narrow for city plows. At the time, the City of Toronto also offered assistance to elderly or disabled people who couldn't clear their own sidewalks. Although this service helped households avoid fines for lack of winter maintenance, it did nothing to support the mobility of people outside the home in the coldest months of the year.

More than half a million disabled Canadians consider themselves 'housebound,' and winter conditions are one contributing factor. In Toronto, the inconsistent maintenance of sidewalks on residential streets creates a perverse incentive against walking or riding around the city's densest neighbourhoods. Each winter, instead of visiting friends or attending events, thousands of Torontonians are stuck at home out of fear that the sidewalks we rely upon are not safe connections to our destinations.

In 2021, 8,157 households signed up – due to age or disability – for snow-shovelling services provided by the city. That means at least that many residents of Toronto face mobility challenges in winter. The real number is likely much higher. The 8,157 households did not include people who are not aware of the support program; people who have a non-disabled adult in their household; people who live in multi-unit housing and are not responsible for shovelling snow in front of their building; and people who live in other neighbourhoods where sidewalks were already plowed by the city. The number also excludes the thousands of Torontonians experiencing homelessness, many of whom are disabled. Statistics Canada indicates that 10.6 per cent of Canadians live with a disability that impacts their mobility. By this logic, one in ten Torontonians face barriers due to slippery sidewalks each winter.

Other Canadian cities have been quicker to implement a more equitable approach. Both Ottawa and Montreal clear the sidewalks of all residential streets. Montreal goes a step further by providing grants to community organizations to clear pathways and porches on private property for elderly and disabled residents who may not otherwise be able to reach the city-plowed sidewalks. Similarly, Ottawa matches people who are unable to shovel with contractors who provide winter maintenance and subsidizes the cost of snow-shovelling services for low-income residents.

In contrast, Edmonton sets standards for snow clearance but provides limited support for community members who are not able to shovel sidewalks. Only in 2021 did the city post opportunities on its website to 'grant funding to interested community leagues who wish to develop snow removal programming that supports seniors and persons with disabilities.' Although sidewalks are public infrastructure built by the city and serving all residents, Edmonton's snow-removal standards perpetuate the myths of personal responsibility and benevolent philanthropy by relying on property owners to shovel sidewalks and community leagues to develop programs to assist those unable to do so.

How might neighbours help one another while waiting for snow plows to arrive? How might open data track snow-clearing routes and convince skeptical taxpayers of the value of their investment? How might mutual aid or municipal services extend winter maintenance from public sidewalks to private front doors – a sometimes insurmountable distance in the snow?

Instead of encouraging collective action to maintain shared sidewalks, the pressure on individual property owners punishes residents who are unable to meet standards by imposing fines. Studies from cities across North America show that local fines are more likely to impact residents already living below the poverty line, working precariously, and facing systemic racism. Data from the City of Edmonton confirms that this approach to clearing sidewalks isn't working.

The fines aren't effective either. A November 2019 survey of more than 4,500 Edmonton residents shows that fewer than half of respondents were aware of the hundred-dollar fine for not shovelling. Only 3 per cent of respondents reported that receiving a ticket encouraged compliance with snow-removal standards. Yet residents weren't satisfied with the status quo. The survey shows that 65 per cent of respondents were not satisfied with their neighbours' shovelling, while almost half of respondents have fallen on a residential sidewalk that wasn't properly cleared.

As I know from my experiences in Toronto, it's not enough to rely on individual responsibility to shovel. Instead, all neighbourhoods need public investment to keep sidewalks safe, reduce injuries, and support winter mobility for residents.

The absence of consistent, equitable, and citywide supports to shovel sidewalks is especially surprising in Edmonton, since it was the first city in Canada to adopt a winter city strategy. Introduced in 2017, the strategy takes inspiration from Scandinavian communities and outlines ten goals to transform Edmonton 'into a World-Leading Winter City.' The document proposes actions to improve snow removal in business districts and pilot municipal snow-clearing services in residential areas. However, these practical measures are lost among ableist language that focuses on 'walkways' and travelling 'by foot' without once discussing the experiences of disabled residents. Instead of examining how to make sidewalks across the city more accessible for all residents, the strategy focuses on how measures like heated pavement and all-season patios could help local businesses.

Emphasis on commercial supports rather than community spaces shaped the outcomes of Edmonton's winter city strategy. After two years of the city distributing hot chocolate and providing blankets on patios, an evaluation of the strategy confirmed what any disabled person could have told you: negative perceptions of winter are most often linked to age, physical disability, and inadequate shovelling of sidewalks. Edmonton residents identified the greatest barrier to improved quality of life in winter as 'amenities for pedestrians/snow clearing of sidewalks, trails.' Instead of focusing on core services to improve the quality of life for all residents, the winter city strategy prioritized spectacle and marketing campaigns.

Four winters after my brother and I got stuck in the snow on a side street, Toronto City Council finally followed the examples of Montreal and Ottawa. In the final months of 2021, the city started taking responsibility for clearing snow from all sidewalks, including residential neighbourhoods where smaller plows or manual shovelling are needed. The celebratory tone of the city's 2021 news release unwittingly exposed how much work needs to be done in other communities: 'The proposed investment would make Toronto only the third major winter city in North America, along with Montreal and Ottawa, to employ a city-wide sidewalk snow clearing program.'

The absence of similar programs in Edmonton or Halifax – to say nothing of smaller cities and towns in between – reveals a lack of awareness of what winter weather means for disabled people. A lifetime after slipping in the schoolyard, I still fear embarrassing myself on the ice, ruining my work wardrobe, or busting an elbow. I still wear through my boots at a rate that defeats my budget but allows me to indulge in long walks in search of hot chocolate.

My brother and I have given up on going out for dinner when there's snow on the ground. I know we are not the only ones. Slippery conditions compound the isolation that disabled people face due to inaccessible buildings, inadequate educational or employment supports, and antiquated attitudes. Instead, as the buds appear each spring, my brother suggests we meet for dumplings or poutine or waffles in anticipation of a season of sidewalks unencumbered by neighbourly neglect or political priorities. Living on land shaped by snow and ice, if we seek to understand what accessible communities look and feel like, we must all prod at our plans and ask: What happens in winter?

## Plain Language Summary

- Emily writes about her earliest memories of slipping and falling on ice. It was embarrassing, so growing up she tried to wear good boots in winter to avoid falling.
- Emily limps, but her twin brother uses a wheelchair. He has a harder time getting around in the snow. On a walk with Emily, his wheelchair got stuck because someone had not shovelled the sidewalk.
- Emily writes about how different Canadian cities define responsibilities for snow shovelling. In Ottawa and Montreal, people can access supports for shovelling. In Edmonton, everyone must clear their own sidewalk.
- If sidewalks are not clear, people with disabilities have a hard time going outside in the winter. This makes isolation worse.

# Shifting Systems

# Fighting for Food: How We Won Hundreds of Millions for Poor Disabled People with Paperwork and Protests

## A. J. Withers

In the mid-2000s, I was part of a massive effort, called the Special Diet Campaign, that ultimately shifted hundreds of millions of dollars from government coffers to poor people's kitchen tables. This community struggle for income came to centre disabled people and disability demands, and we kept mobilizing in the face of unrelenting attempts to shut us down. Eventually, the government was able to quash the campaign, but its impacts are still evident today – twenty years after it began.

Poverty is a disability justice issue. Disabled people are much more likely (38 per cent) to live on less than $20,000 a year than non-disabled people (27 per cent). Indigenous people and women have higher rates of disability than the rest of the population, according to Statistics Canada; other studies show this is also true of Black people and trans people. Ableism is produced and experienced 'in and through' white supremacy, colonialism, capitalism, and cishetero-patriarchy. While not specifically addressing disability, Himani Bannerji, in *Thinking Through,* discusses how oppressions are co-consti-tuting and emerge in and through each other and capitalist relations historically and in the present.

Today, over half a million people collect social assistance in Ontario: just over 400,000 people receive Ontario Disability Support Program (ODSP) – or disability social assistance – and about 216,000 people receive Ontario Works (OW), often called 'welfare.' There are about 37,000 new ODSP applicants a year – almost all of these people will be on OW while they wait for their applications to go through. It can take people months, even years, to get their applications together. A large percentage of applicants are denied the benefit and have to appeal before they are accepted. It took me months to put the application together, and two and a half years in total from when I submitted it until I won my appeal.

There are also a lot of disabled folks on OW who don't apply for or qualify for ODSP. It took me years to convince my doctor to fill out my forms. Many folks don't have a supportive health care provider – or a health care provider at all. To apply for the benefit, one has to know about it. People who don't identify as disabled may not want to apply or may not think the benefits are applicable to them. Many simply can't handle the bureaucracy. Some won't appeal denials even though they would win – that is by design. Other people's disabilities might not be 'severe' enough, so they are disabled but forever stuck on OW. Disabled people on OW are still disabled – even if they don't get ODSP.

In 2005, I was trying to get by on the $164 a month I had left on my OW cheque after rent. I would have only had $120, but I got an extra $44 for my dietary needs. Toronto rents were much cheaper then. Today, if I were paying the average rent for the same place and was on OW, I would start off each month $34 in debt. And if I was on ODSP, I would have $581 a month to live off of after rent. Then, like now, folks on social assistance often had to choose between paying the rent and eating. I was socially isolated because I didn't have money for transit, especially not taxis, but I wasn't well enough to walk places. I also couldn't go out with my friends like everyone else could. Getting on ODSP meant that I went from one pair of pants to three and could take transit when I needed (though cabs were still pushing it). I was even able to go for the occasional coffee or meal out with a friend.

A group I had worked with, the Ontario Coalition Against Poverty (OCAP), had been fighting to raise social assistance rates since OW was cut 21.6 per cent in 1995. They started a Special Diet Campaign as part of a larger campaign to raise the rates. The Special Diet Allowance was up to $250 a month, or $3,000 a year, per person, including kids. OCAP realized that everyone on social assistance was at risk of malnutrition, so they could qualify for organic food ($190), bottled water ($30), and vitamins ($40), bringing them up to the $250 cap. The bottled water might seem like a stretch, but ultimately this was a medical prescription for money to prevent malnutrition. The campaign had three components: spread the word about the Special Diet Allowance, connect people with health providers who would support the sign-up process for the Special Diet (because so many providers couldn't be bothered), and provide direct action support if people were denied. This money more than doubled the amount I had to live on in a month.

I wasn't active in OCAP at the start of the Special Diet Campaign. I had cancer at the time, and I was on a break from the group, on the periphery of the organization. When I came back in the summer of 2005, OCAP was non-stop. The phone rang so much that we stopped answering it (before that was a thing). We changed the voice mail to instructions telling people how to get the Special Diet in the hopes they would hang up and go away.

In February or March 2005, OCAP held its first Special Diet Clinic. The clinics were all basically the same, although they became more efficient with time. OCAP members ran the front of the clinic, and we started files on each social assistance recipient who came through the door. The people requesting the Special Diet from OW/ODSP had to have a letter from a health provider saying they needed the diet, so doctors and nurse practitioners needed to provide documentation. We used a standard Special Diet form created for the campaign for everyone in the clinics. We would fill out the top of the form with basic information and have people sit and wait their turn. We would call them up when a provider was free, and the provider would have a conversation with the applicant and fill in their form.

In the right space and with the right number of health providers, we could see a hundred people in a few hours. But that was just a drop in the bucket. We tried to give people the information they needed to see their own doctors rather than come to our clinics, in order to broaden the number of people who could access the benefit. However, many on assistance didn't have a doctor at all, and many doctors simply refused to fill out social assistance forms.

The City of Toronto started fighting back just a few months into the campaign. OW and ODSP are provincial benefits, but OW was shifted onto the municipalities with neo-liberal downsizing under the Mike Harris provincial government. It meant the City paid the lion's share of the costs of OW and administered it. The City viewed increased food security of its poorest residents as a liability. In June 2005, just a few months after the first clinic, City-run OW offices (and provincially run ODSP offices in Toronto, for that matter) started unilaterally denying people's Special Diet applications.

OCAP started going to those offices with the denied recipients and doing direct action case actions. We did case actions throughout the campaign; because so many people were being hassled, we started doing group actions and dealing with everyone we knew who had issues at a particular office on a specific day. Group case actions were good because they increased the number of people and helped build solidarity between social assistance recipients.

We wouldn't disrupt folks who were simply waiting to talk to their workers – we didn't want to make the day harder for anyone on OW. Our aim was to use disruption to make business as usual impossible. We encouraged those folks with kids to bring them. Kids are great at causing chaos. Usually, we got a meeting with a manager or a supervisor fairly quickly, and usually the issue was resolved. We would almost always leave the office with a cheque in hand for the person's Special Diet (or a plan to get it). City staff didn't want us disrupting their offices, not only because we were annoying but also because we showed people on OW that they could fight back. If a case wasn't resolved, we let them know we would be back bigger and badder (and we were until we won).

The next month, in July 2005, the City introduced its own form for the Special Diet and said that everyone would be cut off and had to reapply using this new form – they could no longer be approved for the Special Diet Allowance without it. These were both bureaucratic attempts to restrict the benefit coming from the top. Through freedom of information request documents, it was confirmed that 'progressive' mayor David Miller's office was involved in trying to keep people off the benefit. We were able to defeat the first measure because it was blatantly illegal. However, the new-form rule stuck.

I returned to OCAP between these two moves by the City of Toronto. I had been on break from OCAP largely because of systemic disablism. Now, with the Special Diet Campaign, OCAP engaged with dozens, if not hundreds, of disabled people every week. Many in the leadership understood the need to incorporate accessibility, to centre disability demands and disabled people. New disabled members had also become involved. As with all anti-oppression learning, OCAP and its members made lots of mistakes, which I found frustrating and, at times, infuriating and hurtful. The simplest things, like using the word *lame* on a poster or nobody remembering to bring chairs for people to sit on at the rally, would happen.

One problem was that, back then, OCAP didn't have good examples to follow – radical groups weren't doing disability work unless they were disability groups themselves. We made an accessibility checklist for events and actions because things kept being missed. Today, there are lots of examples online of these checklists – that wasn't the case at the time. When OCAP tried to be innovative around disability inclusion, it would sometimes fail – protest marches tend to leave certain disabled people behind. I have been that person and it really sucks. So we decided to ask disabled folks to lead the march – that way disabled people would set the pace, and we wouldn't be forced to walk faster than we were comfortable with or capable of. It completely backfired, though, because a contingent of about six powerchair users took the lead and set a pace that no one could keep up with. OCAP members (including me) slowly learned how to make things more accessible and inclusive. But those of us who were disabled in the group had to suffer through others' learning, feel the brunt of their ableism, and, too often, we had to intervene along the way. However, with time, OCAP came to be exemplary of how groups can transform to centre disability.

One of the things people in OCAP had to learn – and that I also struggled with as someone on OW – was the divisions between disabled people. So much of our struggle for the Special Diet was focused municipally because people on OW were under attack. OW paid so much less than ODSP, and the City of Toronto was making policies to keep people on OW from getting money for food. Getting the maximum Special Diet Allowance meant a 47 per cent increase in income for a single person on OW but just a 26 per cent increase for someone on ODSP. People on ODSP wanted to focus on the province because the city didn't affect their benefits. Meanwhile, people on OW looked at people on ODSP, who were making almost twice as much as they were, and thought they were relatively well off. Why should they support people who were doing fine, they would ask.

Many in both groups would say that they were born in Canada and Canada should support 'its own' first. This was not only racist, it was an anti-Muslim dog whistle because so many Special Diet recipients and key campaign organizers were Somali moms (many of whom were also disabled). I developed a relatively standard reply to this. I would tell folks that the rich want to divide us, but if we are united, we can win. In practice, however, actually trying to build bridges between these groups was hard – especially given language differences. We worked across cultures and languages with lots of groups, but the Somali community was self-organized and consistently active and integral throughout the campaign.

I learned a lot about not taking for granted things that are deeply engrained as 'basic' in dominant culture. Muslim women, who often had large families, had busy routines that didn't fit with the standard activist meeting schedule, and they tended to live in communities ill-served by public transit. A meeting would involve riding three hours on transit, round trip, and three hours or more of discussion. Working across languages, we knew we weren't getting direct translations because sometimes the whole room would burst into laughter. But none of the non-Somali people were let in on the joke.

Even though there were ongoing divisions, we continued to fight for the benefit. By August 2005, OCAP said it had signed up four thousand people to the Special Diet. But the City initiated another attack on its social assistance recipients and on the benefit. Among the changes, the City included a review of every single Special Diet benefit to decide if they deemed it legitimate, and they required people to sign a medical release granting the City access to people's medical records. People on social assistance lose a lot of their privacy: social workers can even come inspect their homes. But now the City was demanding the right to conduct medical surveillance.

Families with 'multiple entitlements' – multiple members getting the Special Diet – were specifically targeted for review and denial. We understood this to be a racist dog whistle – depicting Somali families as fraudulent because large Somali families made up many, if not the majority, of the families with kids getting the Special Diet. Also, photocopies of forms would not be accepted – people had to get originals from their welfare workers, and the workers had to handwrite people's names at the top of the form. Why? There was no good reason for this other than to make getting the benefit harder and slower. We fought back by taking the clinics out of community centres and libraries and bringing them to the lawn of the provincial legislature. In September 2005, we announced we would hold a Mass Special Diet Clinic on October 3, 2005.

The logistics for this day were unbelievably complex, and we spent weeks planning it. People were bussed in from multiple communities that didn't have decent health providers. We organized people by area into four smaller clinics (Etobicoke, Scarborough, Downtown, Out

*A.J. Withers speaks at a Special Diet rally at Toronto city hall in 2009.*
*(Photo credit and copyright: John Bonnar.)*

of Town – each with a corresponding colour), and each person was given a handmade cardboard ticket. There were dozens of health care providers there that day. By this time, the providers had formed a group called Health Providers Against Poverty (HPAP), and they started organizing medical professionals. Near-life-size posters of the premier were printed: 'I owe you $250,' they said. We built a small stage on the lawn, with a generator and a large sound system. We had a meal. Various speakers pumped people up while we ate. Lines snaked across the lawn of the legislature. For people who couldn't stand in line, we had chairs, as well as access marshals helping with other access needs. Forty health providers were filling out forms. On that day, 1,100 people signed up for the Special Diet. As a result of one clinic, people on social assistance got $3.3 million over the following year.

The next month, the provincial government fundamentally altered the program. It wasn't diet-based anymore, but tied to specific medical conditions. We responded to this program change with a large march through the streets of Toronto, including a brief occupation of the lobby of the building where the minister in charge of the benefit lived.

By this time, OCAP had held twenty-five Special Diet Clinics. The clinics and the allowance were life-changing, and some people didn't need to stand in line for near-expired food at the food bank anymore. A mom relayed how relieved she was to give her kids vegetables regularly. One OW recipient told us about helping a family member who needed medical support that wasn't covered; with enough money for food, people on social assistance could better care for one another.

We continued to keep public pressure on both levels of government through that year. OCAP resumed the clinics in 2006, conducting five by the end of November, after working with HPAP to conclude that the new system made it harder to get the Special Diet, but it was still very possible. At some point, we also began referring people to one doctor downtown who saw many social assistance recipients for their Special Diet applications. In a sample of one thousand Special Diet applications, the Auditor General found that one health provider – no doubt this downtown provider – completed 20 per cent of them. Two complaints were lodged against him at the College of Physicians and Surgeons, filed by the provincial ministry in charge of social assistance and city councillor Rob Ford. They alleged that the doctor was 'disgraceful, dishonourable or unprofessional' for helping poor people get food. We kept fighting to make sure people got their entitlements.

In 2010, like most years, I watched the provincial budget being delivered on TV. Would this be the year I finally got a decent raise in the rates? I was on ODSP by now, so things were not quite so desperate – but they were still pretty desperate. It was a gut punch when I heard that the Special Diet would be eliminated and replaced with a nutritional supplement program from the Ministry of Health. That night, I accompanied a number of other OCAPers to the filming of TVO's budget discussion on The Agenda. When the host was interviewing the finance minister, we crashed it. We yelled at him on live television. I and others on social assistance told him what it meant to us to lose that money.

We got to work again, and our organizing was able to stop the Special Diet from being eliminated, but it went from being based on what kind of food people needed to a small number of medical conditions. This was done to be able to cut the Special Diet rolls and was effective in removing the benefit from many recipients.

The slashing of the Special Diet was a defeat, but the Special Diet Campaign changed people's lives. I knew people who were housed for the first time in years because they had that money and could finally afford both food and rent. One mom told us how beautiful it was to see her kids' faces the first time they ever ate fresh strawberries. Hundreds of millions of dollars continued to flow, even after OCAP stopped organizing the campaign. By 2013, an additional $200 million a year was flowing from the provincial coffers into the pockets of the poor. This money paid for rent, it paid for fresh fruit and favourite foods, it paid for new shoes, it paid for choices and dignity too often denied to social assistance recipients.

Sometimes people tell me that we 'went too far.' These are never the people who put food on their tables with the Special Diet. It is true there was a backlash because of the campaign – had we never taken action, the Special Diet might still be based on dietary need rather than medical diagnosis, and people might still be able to use photocopied forms. But we never would have won hundreds of millions of dollars for hundreds of thousands of people. The debate about whether or how hard disabled people should fight because of fears of a possible backlash is one for the privileged. If we fight back, there is a chance things might get worse; if we don't fight back, we know things can never get better.

## Plain Language Summary

- A. J. writes about fighting the government of Ontario and the City of Toronto so that disabled people could receive more money each month.
- A. J. has been organizing against poverty for more than twenty years. They describe organizing voice mail messages, sit-ins, and protests.

- To push for more money, organizers had to find ways to connect people who had different experiences. Organizers also had to learn to plan accessible events.
- In the early 2000s, disabled people receiving government assistance did not get enough money to live on. At that time, it was possible to apply for extra money for food. Now disabled people still don't get enough money to live on, but it is much harder to get additional money for food.
- The fight for more food money made a big difference in many people's lives. It also showed disabled people that it's possible to fight back.

# Breaking Barriers: My Journey as a Hard-of-Hearing Candidate in Toronto's Municipal Election

## Igor Samardzic

In the heart of downtown Toronto, where voices clamour for change and representation, I embarked on a journey that was both profoundly personal and emblematically political. Running for city council in 2022, I carried not just my hopes for a better community but also the invisible yet palpable weight of my disability. As a person who is hard of hearing and relies on hearing aids to navigate everyday life, my foray into the political arena was about public service, inclusivity, resilience, and the indomitable spirit of people living with disabilities.

I am an urban planner with a deep interest in all things city-related. I immigrated to Canada as a refugee in the early nineties, fleeing the war that led to the dissolution of Yugoslavia. This experience exposed me to the devastating consequences of war, including the destruction of our material world and the profound physiological and physical impacts of that destruction.

My decision to run for city council was fuelled by a desire to see a city that fully embraces diversity in all its forms, including disability. For too long, the voices of people with disabilities have been marginalized in political discourse, creating a glaring gap in representation. I wanted to bridge this gap, demonstrating that our perspectives are invaluable in shaping truly inclusive policies. The initial steps were fraught with hesitation, knowing the barriers that lay ahead, from navigating my own disability in such a public arena to the skepticism of voters unaccustomed to seeing candidates like me.

Living with a disability that affects hearing introduces a relentless stream of considerations, adaptations, and confrontations. My experience with hearing loss began at the age of twelve, transitioning from a world filled with clear sounds to one where those sounds gradually faded into silence. This progression toward severe hearing loss marked the beginning of a daily ritual where not a single day passes without acknowledging my disability. My hearing loss has been an unwavering companion for nearly two decades, shaping every aspect of my interaction with society.

For someone who has experienced life with and without a disability, the contrast is stark. My hearing loss dictates how I plan my day, from the moment I wake up to my interactions with the world around me. This condition influences my decisions on whether to engage in social settings, advocate for my needs, or choose silence over participation on particularly challenging days.

The mental calculus involved in living with hearing loss is exhausting. It encompasses scenarios where my disability might affect my ability to hear and participate in life's activities. Navigating the complexities of wearing hearing aids – contending with battery life, dealing with feedback from winter hats, and managing the hearing aids during physical activities – requires relentless adaptations. Adjusting to the nuances of communication in a world where masks and physical barriers have become commonplace adds another layer of complexity.

My experiences on the campaign trail revealed the fortitude required to navigate politics as a person with a disability. Every door knock, public forum, and interaction was an exercise in breaking down preconceived notions about equity and disability while fostering the resilience needed to persist against constant barriers. Communication barriers were the most immediate challenge, as political campaigns thrive on effective interaction. Being hard of hearing introduced complexities in engaging with constituents and media alike.

Running a campaign required innovative strategies not only to ensure my own inclusion but also to raise awareness about the broader issue of accessibility. My team – a mix of urban planners, designers, community advocates, and city builders – implemented multifaceted strategies shaped by the ongoing pandemic. The pandemic introduced complexities around masks, social distancing, and new norms of working from home. Despite using hearing aids, which assist but do not guarantee perfect hearing, I had to maintain an acute level of awareness. I rely heavily on facial cues, lip movements, and behavioural signals during conversations. Masks presented a significant challenge, making it incredibly difficult to hear someone when their voice was muffled and their lips were covered.

On the campaign trail, my usual intensity in focus was heightened. Representing voters added another level of responsibility, requiring me to be more aware and attentive, and to critically listen beyond my usual efforts. To manage the fatigue from this heightened attention, I periodically turned off my hearing aids, sitting or standing in silence to reset my mind for the next interaction.

In addition to these personal adjustments, my campaign also took coordinated action to enhance accessibility. My team ensured our materials and messaging were centred on accessibility, making our website one of the few accessible election-campaign sites. We also carefully chose contrasting colours for our branding to further support accessibility.

Interacting with the public involved educating many about the realities of living with hearing loss. I recall intense discussions with my team and family regarding the choice to use the word *disability* in the first sentence of the 'About Me' section on my campaign website. I believe in embracing my identity, thereby staying true to myself and representing people with disabilities who cannot conceal their condition. Despite concerns and warnings about limiting myself to a single identity and issue in such a visible manner, I prevailed, over-coming significant resistance and apprehension. Ultimately, this approach helped demystify my disability for voters, transforming it from a perceived weakness into a testament of strength and empathy.

I recognized my own experiences in the people I met who, like me, had a disability, but who were further discriminated against and oppressed by ableist policies, structures, and systems. My campaign took a holistic approach, informed by my lived experience and the experiences of disabled community members. It was important to campaign for exceeding accessibility standards in transit, public spaces, streets, and public buildings in Toronto. I advocated for the development and construction industries to address issues such as construction hoarding and staging. These temporary protections from building activities often spill onto sidewalks, bike lanes, or roadways, affecting typical paths of travel and creating inaccessible zones. The detours caused by construction hoarding and staging might be too narrow for some people to navigate or may dip into the roadway without ramps or cut curbs. My campaign advocated for improved standards, guidelines, and wayfinding that prioritize accessibility and offer better alternatives to closures of sidewalks, cycle tracks, and traffic lanes.

I also promoted the City of Toronto's Commercial Façade Improvement Grant Program, which provides funding to commercial property owners and tenants to enhance building facades, including improvements that increase accessibility, such as wheelchair ramps, accessible railings, and door openers that meet Accessibility for Ontarians with Disabilities Act standards. This initiative aims to create more inclusive, pleasant, and visually appealing streetscapes by supporting renovations that benefit both businesses and the community. However, there needs to be an expansion and more uptake for these grant programs, as the onus on opting in requires building owners – not the tenants operating businesses – to facilitate this process. As currently designed, the program lacks a convincing benefit to commercial landlords. Additionally, my campaign supported the expansion and full funding of the city's Community Crisis Response Program as a new approach to wellness and safety checks, informed by conversations with neighbours in encampments.

Too often, politicians and policy-makers focus only on disabled residents who can travel around town relatively easily, are housed, and contribute economically to our capitalistic society. These individuals are somewhat accepted by society and acknowledged for their presence. However, during my campaign, I had conversations with a range of community members and, for the first time, visited and interacted with unhoused individuals at an encampment in Clarence Square, located just north of Spadina Avenue and Front Street in downtown Toronto. This is one of many encampments of various sizes in Toronto. Several tents were present when I visited with a handful of residents living there.

When discussing disability and accessibility, even well-meaning advocates often fail to see, reference, or consider unhoused individuals. Listening to stories at the encampment revealed a darker side of how disability is framed in public discourse. For me, the 'othering' of unhoused individuals, many of whom have disabilities, highlighted a stark divide between those usually talked about when promoting accessibility and those left out of the conversation.

Although conversations with encampment residents were challenging, they shifted my understanding of disability. I realized that the communities I had been part of, which I believed included everyone, actually perpetuated a hierarchical view of who is accepted by society as having a disability. I had unintentionally excluded Torontonians who were unhoused due to my own lack of awareness and naïveté.

My journey through the municipal election was not just about advocating for change – it became a profound expedition into the heart of the city, unearthing stories of resilience, neglect, and the often-overlooked realities of living with a disability or disabilities. As I was welcomed into voters' homes and met with people with disabilities, the campaign illuminated the stark disparities between those fortunate enough to have options and others whose social mobility is stalled by systems of oppression and ableist policies. These intimate experiences in other people's homes brought to the forefront the profound invisibility of certain individuals and the systemic inadequacies that exacerbate their struggles.

The stark dichotomy between people with disabilities who had housing and others who were unhoused became glaringly apparent, revealing a complex narrative about perceptions of and categories for disability. To be considered disabled often means to be visible within the system – on disability support programs or securely housed (even if that means warehoused in an institution), thereby fitting into a neatly defined box. Yet, on the fringes, away from the safety nets or strictures of social programs and subsidized housing, there are countless individuals whose lives with disability are defined by invisibility.

I met residents who, despite disabilities that necessitated the use of wheelchairs, found themselves without a voice within the system or allies to amplify their calls to action. Their stories highlighted my own glaring oversights: the assumption that all people with disabilities are equally supported or recognized by neighbours, public programs, or decision makers. The reality, however, is a jarring mosaic of neglect and systemic failure.

These encounters underscored a lack of political will to deeply understand and consider the consequences of elected officials' actions – or inactions – on marginalized communities. The lack of accessible public washrooms, housing, the inaccessibility of transit, the dire shortage of and undignified pay for personal support workers, and the pervasive poverty that forces people with disabilities to panhandle despite receiving support like the Ontario Disability Support Program are all symptoms of a broader failure to consider the needs of all residents.

As I envision a more accessible city, I recognize the importance of listening to and amplifying stories of struggle and resilience from the disabled community. My perspective is shaped by the understanding that disability cannot be monolithically defined or addressed.

It is crucial that our policies, city planning, and societal attitudes evolve to acknowledge the complex realities faced by individuals with disabilities.

We, as disabled people, know that inclusivity hinges on recognizing these diverse experiences and ensuring that no one is left behind.

While the election's outcome is a matter of public record, the true measure of success lies beyond the ballot box. I hope my participation challenged stereotypes and pushed forward a conversation about the role of people with disabilities in public life. It demonstrated that accessibility is not just a matter of compliance but a cornerstone of a truly democratic society.

My experiences on the campaign trail show that the status quo is unacceptable, and the time for change is now. By confronting and addressing systemic barriers, residents and neighbours can begin to support the disabled community, transitioning from oppression to opportunity and from marginalization to full participation in society. This is crucial because not everyone can vote, but anyone living here can have a significant impact by getting involved and showing care. Building toward a more inclusive society is complex and challenging, but it is also necessary and achievable with the collective will and commitment to make it happen.

This entails not only re-evaluating and revising existing policies and practices but also actively involving people with disabilities in the decision-making process, ensuring our voices are heard, valued, and acted upon. It also means investing in infrastructure, programs, and services that genuinely meet our needs and foster independence and participation in society.

The journey does not end when the votes are counted. The lessons learned and the conversations sparked are stepping stones toward a more inclusive political landscape. As members of a community, each of us must continue to advocate for systemic changes that accommodate all forms of disability, ensuring that the political arena is accessible to everyone.

## Plain Language Summary

- Igor writes about running for city council in Toronto in 2022.
- He shares that it was a significant decision to include the word *disability* in the first sentence of the 'About Me' section on his campaign website.
- Living with hearing loss impacts many aspects of Igor's life, requiring him to adapt what he wears and pay extra attention to social interactions.
- His use of hearing aids also influenced how he communicated with residents of Toronto during his campaign.
- Listening to others with disabilities deepened Igor's understanding of ableism and motivated him to advocate for more equitable policies and programs.
- Convinced that maintaining the status quo is unacceptable, Igor is dedicated to involving people with disabilities in decision-making processes.

# Transportation Is Essential to Survival: An Advocacy Journey in Toronto

## Mazin Aribi

The Toronto Transit Commission is a public transport agency that has served Toronto since 1921. As one of the largest public transit systems in North America, the TTC is responsible for providing transportation options for millions of riders every year. In 2021, the TTC celebrated one hundred years of operations, but it was only twenty-five years ago that the first accessible subway station was built. It had taken many, many years to begin making the system accessible and inclusive. TTC riders with disabilities have faced – and continue to face – numerous challenges over the years.

In 1982, the TTC launched Wheel-Trans, a specialized door-to-door transportation service for riders with physical disabilities who were unable to use conventional TTC services. I first experienced the TTC's Wheel-Trans in 1989, after immigrating to Canada from a different land and culture. It was eye-opening for me to see how people with disabilities lived in Canada. Where I came from, there was nothing like Wheel-Trans. When I arrived in Toronto, Wheel-Trans made a big difference to me as a wheelchair user. From the start, I often thought about what could be done to maintain the service, improve it, and expand on it.

I also became curious about using the conventional transit system of buses, subways, and streetcars. At the time, in 1996, only five subway stations were accessible. Nonetheless, I planned a route from point A to point B. During my early trips on the TTC, I learned many things that would inform my advocacy in later years.

The first time I boarded a subway car, it was the old-style H4 train, with orange seats and no air conditioning. During my trip, I held on to the pole in the middle of the car. I was afraid that upon arrival at the next station, the train would slam on the brakes and send me flying. I took a risk; nobody had told me that the train usually arrives into the station gradually. But after that first trip I thought, 'Oh, that wasn't too bad.'

Another issue I encountered early on as a subway rider was the gap between the train and the platform. As I approached the subway to board, the front wheels of my wheelchair got caught in that gap. I was terrified. 'Wow, this is it,' I thought. 'I can't get in, I can't get out, and the train will move.'

I had heard a story about a guy whose backpack got stuck in the train doors and he was killed when the subway left the station. Later I learned that the TTC had improved its safety features, and the train will not move unless all the doors are completely shut. Nobody had told me that!

## A History of Accessibility on the TTC

The TTC began its journey toward accessibility in the early 1970s; in 1992 the Advisory Committee on Accessible Transit (ACAT) was formed. This committee was to provide the TTC with advice on how to improve accessibility for riders with disabilities and for seniors.

Despite these initiatives, accessibility remained a significant issue for the TTC throughout the 1980s and 1990s. Many TTC stations were not wheelchair accessible, and the design of buses and street-cars made it difficult for riders with disabilities to board and disembark safely.

In 1998, after seeing and experiencing first-hand the challenges and obstacles that exist on the conventional system, I decided to join ACAT. During my nearly twenty years of serving on the committee, I collaborated with ACAT members who were very passionate about their work. We took our role to heart and used our lived experience and heavy use of the conventional system and Wheel-Trans to constantly identify issues that could be brought to the table to be resolved or improved.

At the time, ACAT was structured to cover a wide range of issues, with five subcommittees: Design Review, Service Planning, Communications, Wheel-Trans Operations, and Administration. ACAT membership comprised fifteen individuals – at least eight with disabilities, as defined under the Ontario Human Rights Code. Several kinds of disabilities were represented, including physical or mobility, visual, hearing, communication, learning, mental health, and intellectual/developmental disabilities. There was also a minimum of two seniors and a maximum of three others who advocated for people with disabilities or who had a demonstrated knowledge of and interest in accessible transit issues.

## Challenges and Barriers Faced by Riders with Disabilities

One of the biggest challenges faced by TTC riders with disabilities has been physical barriers to access. Many TTC stations were built before accessibility standards were put in place, making it challenging and costly to retrofit them to be fully accessible. Additionally, some TTC vehicles were not designed with accessibility in mind (until a later date), making it difficult for riders with disabilities to board and disembark safely.

A lack of information about TTC services has also been a significant barrier for riders with disabilities. For example, the TTC's website and mobile app did not always provide accurate or up-to-date information about accessibility features at specific stations or on specific vehicles, making it difficult for riders with disabilities to plan their trips and navigate the TTC system.

Over the years, ACAT addressed many issues, including physical barriers to access and information available to TTC riders with disabilities. Just as I had gotten stuck between the train and the platform on my early trips using the subway, this was a common problem for other people using mobility devices. ACAT worked diligently to fix the gap between the train and the platform. There are different solutions, depending on whether the gap is horizontal or vertical or both. They have been implemented at quite a few stations. At Eglinton Station, a raised platform area meets the train and reduces the vertical gap, and solid rubber filler on the side of the platform reduces the horizontal gap. Before the fix, people were at risk of breaking their mobility devices, which happened in a few instances.

Another accomplishment of ACAT is the travel training now offered by Wheel-Trans. Any person, group, or organization interested in learning to navigate the conventional system can now book a one-on-one session with Wheel-Trans staff. When I started riding the subway and taking buses, there was so much I didn't know. I consider myself a guinea pig – all of us on ACAT were! We used the conventional system and reported back on what worked and what didn't work.

## Building Trust, Shifting Culture

At ACAT, we earned the TTC's respect and created culture change. For years the problem wasn't just infrastructure and information, it was also attitudes and lack of understanding. Some TTC leaders could not see that accessibility isn't just about inclusion: transportation is essential to survival.

One strategy we at ACAT used to change attitudes and build buy-in was to get TTC executives to experience transit as wheelchair users. We provided a power wheelchair and offered to lend it to Andy Byford, the CEO of the TTC at the time, to use on the transit system. Later, we invited Rick Leary, Byford's successor, to do the same. We asked both of them, 'Would you like to spend half a day travelling the TTC? We'd like you to see how it is to take transit using a wheelchair.'

They both liked the idea, so I planned an itinerary. We took a Wheel-Trans trip to the subway, changed subway lines, and transferred to a bus.

I warned Byford, 'You will notice that some people will not be very helpful.'

Andy said, 'What do you mean? Torontonians are very nice!'

I just replied, 'You will see.'

Sure enough, as he was exiting the train using a wheelchair, someone on foot cut him off.

There's an idea that riders in Toronto are polite. But over the years I've seen the way some fellow TTC passengers rush past disabled riders who need help or simply get in our way as we're trying to board or disembark. Despite what TTC leadership used to think, it's not enough to rely on the goodwill of other riders. At ACAT we implemented many policies to improve the TTC service. For example, the 'first on, last off' policy creates predictability for all passengers by establishing that the person with a mobility device should get on a TTC vehicle first and exit last.

Passengers with disabilities need consistent support and sustained funding to improve accessibility services. That's why ACAT's advocacy has been so important.

## Recent Developments

In recent years, the TTC has made significant strides in improving accessibility. As of 2023, fifty-five out of seventy-five TTC subway stations are wheelchair accessible, and the commission is working to retrofit the remaining stations that are not yet fully accessible. In 2014, the TTC also introduced for the first time new low-floor streetcars that are easier for riders with disabilities to board and disembark. Although work continues to make subway stations accessible, it is worth noting that all surface vehicles are now accessible.

The TTC has also made efforts to improve information and communication about accessibility features. The commission has launched a new website that provides detailed information about accessibility features at specific stations and on specific vehicles. Additionally, the TTC has introduced new descriptive accessibility pages and maps that inform and show riders the location of entrances, elevators, ramps, and other accessibility features.

I've travelled to other cities to see how they approach accessible transit. Whether I'm in Montreal or San Diego, as soon as I hop on a bus, I put on my advocacy hat and think about ways that Toronto's system could be improved. For example, San Diego has created a financial incentive for disabled riders to take conventional transit. When I visited, it cost disabled riders four dollars to use the door-to-door service but just one dollar to take a ride on the conventional system.

## Closing Thoughts

The TTC's journey toward accessibility has provided several important lessons for other public transportation agencies looking to improve accessibility. First and foremost, it is essential to involve riders with disabilities in the planning and decision-making process at the early stages. ACAT has been key to the TTC's accessibility efforts, and other agencies should consider establishing similar advisory committees to ensure that the voices of riders with disabilities are heard. ACAT advocated for blue priority seats. These seats are available on all TTC vehicles near the door and provide customers who are disabled, elderly, or pregnant with a designated spot to sit.

Second, it is important to recognize that improving accessibility is a long-term process that requires a sustained commitment in funding, policies, and government support. The TTC's efforts to retrofit its stations and vehicles have been ongoing for decades, and it has been costly and challenging at times.

I remember meeting with a high-ranking politician during my time as chair of ACAT. I was addressing the importance of maintaining consistency in budgeting to build an accessible and equitable transit system. Searching for a comparison, I said, 'A perfect accessible and equitable transit system is similar to a perfectly rounded pizza.' If you take out a slice of pizza (funding for accessibility), you won't have a perfect circle, and you won't have an equitable and accessible transit system either.

Unfortunately, the politician's response at that moment was 'Mmmm, I love pizza,' and my concerns were brushed away. As I was trying to explain, it is important to see the big picture to accommodate a growing population and the increasing need for accessibility. Therefore, moving beyond the minimum standards is essential.

Third, the TTC's efforts to improve accessibility have shown that technology can play a critical role in improving public transportation. The use of real-time information systems and automated vehicles can help make public transportation more convenient and accessible for all riders, including those with disabilities. Automatic stop announcements are another example of how technology can make transit more accessible for all riders.

Finally, the TTC's journey toward accessibility has highlighted the importance of collaboration and partnerships. The commission has worked closely with advocacy groups, government agencies, and private companies to improve accessibility, and these partnerships have been essential to the TTC's success.

## Plain Language Summary

• Mazin writes about his experiences as a wheelchair user and the past chair of the Advisory Committee on Accessible Transit (ACAT). This group works diligently to improve public transit in Toronto.

- When he first immigrated to Toronto, Mazin was very impressed by Wheel-Trans. It's a door-to-door bus service for people with disabilities. Later, he also learned to navigate the subway. At the time, only five subway stations were accessible.
- ACAT helped implement travel training for TTC riders with disabilities. Although Mazin taught himself how to use the subway, now people can get individual support in learning to use public transit. ACAT also worked to reduce the gap between the subway and the platform at many stations.
- Mazin describes the shifting attitudes of some TTC leaders. At meetings, he advocated for consistent funding for accessibility initiatives. He also showed two executives what it's like to ride the subway while using a wheelchair.
- Overall, Mazin recognizes that improving accessibility is a long-term process. He explains why it's essential to involve riders with disabilities in decisions from the start.

# 'It's a Good Tired'

## Jack and Zachary, Good Foot Couriers

*Good Foot is a registered charity that employs members of the neurodivergent community. Couriers trained, employed, and supported by Good Foot use public transit to make deliveries across the Greater Toronto Area.*

**Emily:** If somebody had never heard of Good Foot, how would you explain it to them?

**Zachary:** Have you seen the movie *Kiki's Delivery Service?* The premise of that movie is that there's this girl who's a witch. A thirteen-year-old girl who is a witch who goes to a new town for her training. She becomes friends with a baker and she decides to open a delivery service inside the bakery. So she delivers parcels on her broom to different parts of the city. It's not as easy to work as she thought, and her self-confidence keeps bumbling up her deliveries. So she gets into trouble and she gets caught in a gust of wind and she loses one of her parcels and she has to find it from some crows… So it's a really interesting movie, but I often find delivery to be like that.

I've been a courier with Good Foot for about eight years now. When things go smoothly it's wonderful. I have great customers, I get tipped sometimes. I get to familiarize myself with different parts of the city. I might actually talk to customers and get to know them. Sometimes I stop in to shops to buy things when I have a break. But when things don't go the way I want them to, it's a nightmare. I was delivering a bag of tea once and the bag ripped open and all the tea bags fell on the ground, so I had to shove them all into my bag. Then

I got to the shop, and it took me half an hour to unload everything and I felt so bad because I was holding up traffic in the store.

E: Anything you'd add, Jack?

Jack: It's fun. There's lots of walking. We mainly use the subway to get from point A to point B, and I like the environment – the staff is really friendly and supportive and accommodating. I feel comfortable, and to me that's something that's important. It's a good company and it provides employment, which is good. By the end of the day, I'm kind of exhausted, but it's a good tired. I feel like I did something that was worth it.

E: You mentioned that the team is really supportive and accommodating. On the flipside, what makes you a good courier? What do you bring to Good Foot?

J: I guess I'm a quick walker. I'm efficient and also I try not to complain that much. You can't really do much about the weather, sometimes it can be a bit difficult. I'm patient. Flexible. Some deliveries, they can really throw you a curve ball.

But I know my way around the city, which is good. So if there's an event going on, we can avoid it. Like let's just say, if we're doing deliveries around the Toronto International Film Festival – that's King Street – we can kind of work our way around that because it blocks off a lot of the street.

E: What about you, Zachary?

Z: I think the most obvious one is that I'm very schmoozy, which means I like to talk to people a lot. So that's very helpful because there's a lot of customer service stuff going on. I'm not great at adapting on the fly and I'm not the most flexible person. But I am good at listening to feedback, as long as it's not obnoxious feedback. Considering that I've made a lot of egregious mistakes in my eight years as a courier, some of which would probably have gotten me fired in other jobs, the fact that there's room for me to grow is good because I do have the potential to learn.

**E:** So what does your typical day look like as a courier?

**Z:** Well, my shift starts at 10:00 a.m. I'm a very slow riser but I hop on the bus and I might have something to eat at home or I might have a snack at the office. I usually have time to talk to some of the couriers who start their shift at the same time I do. Just, you know, chat. So my shift is from ten to two, because I'm only allowed to work for a certain number of hours a week and I have another job, and then on top of that, because of my Sabbath I can't work past a certain time, especially in the winter. I usually go all over the city, so I'm busing, I'm taking the streetcar, I'm taking the subway, and I keep in contact with dispatch via WhatsApp.

**E:** Have you gotten to know the other couriers?

**Z:** For the first four or five years, I actually wasn't very close with anyone at work. I didn't really pay attention to the social programs, and then when the pandemic hit and we were all furloughed, we had virtual tea time three times a week. I got to know more of my co-workers. Now at the office we socialize before our shift starts, so I get to talk to them here too.

**J:** Yeah, the social groups are really fun. Back in the summer we had a small group gathering at Pauper's Pub. We've done stuff like that before where we've had a picnic in Christie Pits with a group of the Good Foot staff and we'd get snacks and food, which was nice.

**E:** In general, what kinds of things do you deliver?

**J:** Sometimes we deliver boxes, envelopes, cookies.

**Z:** I was once given an express order. I had to deliver from a hospital someone's glasses and book. She had broken both of her arms and she was at home, but she had forgotten her book and glasses at the hospital. So I had to go to her house. She couldn't see me very well, but she was sooooo thankful! That was the most interesting delivery I've made.

**J:** I like the fact that we get to go to different places and see different parts of the city. Sometimes we're, like, picking up in Liberty Village and dropping off at Lawrence and Yonge. It's fun, you get to see a lot of things. When I make deliveries for the Night Baker [inhales], the whole store just smells like fresh cookies!

**E:** How does your work change at different times of the year? Today it's gross and rainy; it can get pretty hot in the summer.

**Z:** In my first year I actually delivered a package all the way out west. It took me the entire day because it was a snowstorm. I was waddling because the snow was yea high on my legs and I had boots and I was wearing protective gear and just treading my way through the snow. Also it could have an impact if it's really, really hot out. It's really just adjusting for the unexpected. We had one day where it was raining really heavily in the morning and then it turned into ice and snow in the afternoon, and you just gotta be prepared.

**E:** Before I started recording, you were both talking a bit about your neighbourhoods and what you're looking for – not just in terms of your work but where you live.

**J:** I'm close to Bloor West, like Runnymede. I like it because there's a bus stop, so I can easily take it down to the subway station. I'm also close to Dundas West subway station. So it's good to have both a bus and a subway nearby. Same with work – Good Foot is on Bathurst and a five-minute walk from Bathurst Station.

There's also a Tim Hortons near me, which is one of my go-tos. But I've been making my own lunches just to save money. Because nowadays when I go to Tim Hortons it's around nine dollars, and that's expensive. Just for a sandwich and a doughnut! You're not even getting coffee.

**E:** Zachary, before we started to record, you had mentioned some things about affordability too.

**Z:** I live near Bathurst and Glencairn, which is a very posh neighbourhood. I like it on the one hand because it's straight down to Bathurst Station on the number 7 bus. But at the same time, if it weren't for the fact that I'm living with my parents, I wouldn't be able to live in that neighbourhood.

Many Jewish people in Toronto live between Bathurst and St. Clair and Bathurst and Rutherford, but those are expensive areas. I'm observant and if I want to live near my synagogue and certain stores, it would be very difficult. I've walked an hour and forty-five minutes to get to the Prosserman Jewish Community Centre, but sometimes at the end of my Good Foot shift, if I'm really far away, I might Uber home.

**E:** You both mentioned that you have other jobs. Like, Jack, you're working at a coffee shop, and Zachary, did you say you're working at a grocery store?

**Z:** I work at No Frills, twice a week. So again, it's great because I can walk there. It's a forty-five-minute walk from my house. At my No

Frills job, I feel like the accommodations are more about fulfilling obligations. Being unionized does provide some job security, which helps.

Good Foot has been a lot more forgiving and accommodating of me than most employment. I think at the beginning I abused the sick days – I didn't really know what sick days were. These are all things that would have gotten me fired at other jobs. Good Foot has been just patient and accommodating and wants me to learn. They've been good for me with check-ins. I remember this one time where I made a huge mistake, and one of the support people just had a meeting with me to figure out what went wrong. So I really appreciate that.

**J:** I've been with Lil E since July. They also support people who are neurodiverse. I'm just learning a lot, and when you're starting something new, it can be a bit tiring, but in a good way; it's just a lot of information coming at you because you have to learn everything. It's fun making drinks for people, and customer service. I'm using different parts of my brain. It's good skills.

## Plain Language Summary

• This chapter is an interview with two couriers from Good Foot Delivery. Good Foot provides employment for people who are neurodivergent.

• The couriers talk about making deliveries using public transit and visiting new and interesting parts of the city to help clients.

• Zachary talks about adapting his deliveries when something goes wrong. He explains that Good Foot staff have been very supportive even when he makes mistakes.

• Jack adds that he has learned a lot working with Good Foot. He also likes the opportunity to hang out with and get to know other couriers.

• Both Zachary and Jack talk about affordability concerns living in Toronto. They each work a second job, besides making deliveries.

# Disability at the Desk and Beyond

## Anika Abdullah

### What Is Disability Employment?

For a disabled person, being employed is always framed as an achievement. But it is actually a necessity for survival in a capitalist society. There is no way to have a livable income in our system without participating in the workforce. The so-called income support provided by the Ontario Disability Support Program is 40 per cent below the legislative threshold for poverty,[1] effectively forcing many people with disabilities into cyclical poverty. Similar rates are consistent across Canada. For some people, employment also provides not only the income required to lead a dignified life but also self-fulfillment, in the same way that it does for non-disabled people. Capitalism frames employment as the foundation of self-growth and actualization. Many disabled people, including myself, a mobility scooter user with muscular dystrophy, seek jobs as a form of economic stability and personal satisfaction but end up facing partial accessibility and ableist practices that limit gainful employment. Often, our presence in workplaces is the first and only time that corporations engage with their painstakingly developed diversity, equity, and inclusion policies.

Businesses, non-profits, and government agencies may all assume that they are equal-opportunity employers because they adhere to the 'duty to accommodate' as it is broadly defined. The duty to accommodate means that employers must provide accommodations to the point of undue hardship (for instance, compromising the safety of others or requiring an expense that the organization can't carry). A lot of people will be familiar with the idea of providing adaptive technologies like computer equipment or software, or physical accessibility through renovations to create universal washrooms, accessible buildings, and barrier-free entrances, but these don't meet everyone's needs.

With a growing understanding of non-mobility disabilities, disabled people also have fought for many more accommodations needed to make workplaces inclusive for people with all types of disabilities. Flexible work hours and the option to work remotely support people with chronic illness and fatigue. Virtual meetings that can use captioning software include people who are D/deaf/deafened, hard-of-hearing, and others. Proactive policies mandating scent-free environments help people with multiple chemical sensitivities before they have to ask for an accommodation. Decompression spaces are private rooms where people can manage panic attacks or sensory overload safely and with dignity. These are only a few of the non-traditional accessibility accommodations that I or some of my colleagues, disabled and non-disabled alike, have used in recent years.

Since employment is a social area under the Ontario Human Rights Code and disability is a protected ground against discrimination, accommodations are a significant means of providing equity in the workplace. In Ontario, the Accessibility for Ontarians with Disabilities Act (AODA) of 2005 establishes requirements for employers to help prevent discrimination against people with disabilities, such as informing potential and current employees about available accommodations and/or developing an individual accommodation plan if requested. Despite these legal protections, there are foundational barriers to employment that are not addressed by existing legislative or regulatory frameworks like the AODA and its standards. For example, ableist job postings, an inaccessible built environment, and inadequate transportation options all block the participation and contributions of disabled talent. These barriers are remnants of a time when the workforce revolved around cis-gender white men.

## Accessibility Legislation and Employment Lands

Every organization, including municipalities and the provincial government, has obligations under the AODA. This act sets a minimum level of accessibility through the five standards of the Integrated Accessibility Standards Regulation: information and communication, employment, transportation, design of public spaces, and customer service. Each of these standards is limited in scope and leaves huge gaps when it comes to disability employment. For instance, the employment standard doesn't set a minimum for workplace design accessibility. The transportation standard covers things like the design of vehicles, fares, and operator training but doesn't cover crowding or the expanse of the network. These gaps are felt most by individuals with disabilities and places the onus on them to identify the gaps, request accommodation, or, in the worst-case scenario, abandon an employment opportunity due to insurmountable obstacles. Due to the narrow scope of accessibility legislation, some obstacles do not fall under the jurisdiction of the AODA.

In Ontario, employment lands are areas designated for business, created to protect jobs, attract investments, and retain existing industries. Although these areas are significant sources of work across several sectors, they are shaped by planning and land-use regulations rather than accessibility legislation. The Planning Act sets out how land use may be controlled and who the decision makers are for land-use planning. The Provincial Policy Statement (PPS) supports the Planning Act by establishing Ontario's goals and interests for land-use planning, such as providing for adequate housing and employment opportunities. Municipalities then deliver on these priorities through official plans, zoning bylaws, and other types of tools. There is no mention of coordination with or acknowledgement of the AODA or any accessibility-relevant standard/requirement within either the Planning Act or the PPS. However, municipalities must both produce their own official plans under the PPS and maintain a multi-year accessibility plan. Ontario's land-use planning system operates as a distinct and isolated entity that separates the PPS from the AODA rather than aligning with it under the Ontario Human Rights Code commitment to produce equitable outcomes for people with disabilities.

Lack of proximity to a range of spaces, including workplaces, is a key barrier facing disabled people, yet there is limited consideration given to supporting accessibility from within existing urban and regional planning processes. PPS provides the framework for 'provincially significant employment zones,' which are identified by municipalities and reviewed by the province. The goal of these zones is to maintain areas where economically important industries can operate in the long term. For instance, employment lands are a key site of manufacturing and warehousing businesses. These zones are primarily near major roadways and have a high concentration of employment. Yet the location of the zones – cut off from residential neighbourhoods and poorly served by public transportation – can pose significant barriers to disabled people seeking work.

There are currently thirty-one provincially significant employment zones registered by the Ontario government according to the standards set out in the PPS of 2020. With the draft of the latest PPS, released in spring 2023, weaker protections for employment lands open them up to the possibility of housing development. As a whole, these provincial policy changes mirror a shift in the planning profession. Although land-use professionals are moving toward recognizing the limitations of segregating employment lands from housing or community spaces, these changes have yet to be reflected in the daily lives of people with disabilities.

## How Does Disability Justice Apply to the Workplace?

Some employers have consciously engaged in equity, diversity, and inclusion analysis and initiated strategies to actively dismantle these barriers. But this process often requires people of marginalized backgrounds to rise, against the odds, into positions of power where they can ask the appropriate questions that instigate this level of not only reflection but implementation. If a disabled person is unable to access meeting rooms due to a lack of tactile surface indicators coordinated with accessible signage or is left out of communication due to the lack of an interpreter or captioning, how will they ever reach the decision-making table to ask the necessary questions regarding efforts toward equity in the workplace? The right to accommodation does not secure gainful employment and is not an effective enough tool on its own to bring people with disabilities to the forefront in the workplace. Disabled voices are not silenced so much as they are forgotten.

Remembering disabled voices requires learning about disabled histories. In 2015, Sins Invalid, a disability justice–based performance project, worked to create a framework that 'recognizes that we will be liberated as whole beings – as disabled, as queer, as brown, as black, as gender non-conforming, as trans, as women, as men, as non-binary gendered.' This framework became the 10 Principles of Disability Justice, which empower people with disabilities to live in their wholeness of self outside of the perceptions and stigma otherwise enforced upon us by capitalist and Eurocentric rhetoric. Just as workplaces and employers must move beyond norms designed for a narrow segment of the white male population, disability justice invites us all to commit to concepts of self-worth and community care that reject profit and productivity. The principles of disability justice are as follows:

1. Intersectionality
2. Leadership of those most impacted
3. Anti-capitalist politics
4. Cross-movement solidarity
5. Recognizing wholeness
6. Sustainability
7. Commitment to cross-disability solidarity

8. Interdependence
9. Collective access
10. Collective liberation

It is within this framework that I think about the foundational barriers to employment outlined above. In contrast to the pressure to work facing disabled people under capitalism, disability justice recognizes that a person's value cannot be measured by either their salary or their productivity in paid employment.

## Putting It All Together

Employment opportunities are often difficult to navigate for all job seekers due to a lack of plain language, transparency of salary or responsibilities, and intensive online forms that aren't compatible with a screen reader.[2] Furthermore, many job postings implicitly or explicitly state ableist work policies. Recognizing my own physical limitations as a person with muscular dystrophy, I have always applied only to jobs in roles like administration, data entry, or report-writing, with no listed requirements for physical labour. A quick search on a job board will show that physical requirements are listed on all types of job postings without any clear explanation of the regular tasks requiring physical strength and mobility. This requirement is prohibitive not only for people with disabilities but also for people who are aging, who may have chronic back or knee pain, pregnant people, and people of smaller stature. It is in conflict with the fourth and fifth principles of disability justice – cross-movement solidarity and recognizing wholeness. The emphasis on physical ability makes disabled job seekers, and others of minority backgrounds, feel as though they are less than, due to factors outside their control that may well be arbitrarily included in job postings.

In the face of these systemic barriers, disabled people may narrow their job search to roles and fields where they know their disability will not be an obstacle or can be easily accommodated. We can and do focus on applying to roles in places that are easy to reach via transit or personal vehicle. Yet, consistent with the logic of capitalism, which focuses on personal achievement and initiative, these are individual solutions to collective problems. Similarly, the geographic isolation of – and lack of accessible routes to – employment lands cannot be solved by disabled workers' personal determination or individual ingenuity. The lack of access to these locations compounds the barriers to employment faced by disabled people because employment lands host jobs of all types in all sectors and therefore represent significant economic opportunity. But only for workers who are able to show up and work on-site.

A broad solution to the complex barriers created by an inaccessible built environment and inadequate public transit is to reinvest in mixed-use development and innovate in job opportunities beyond employment lands. Employment lands are typically located in isolated areas with limited transit access and hundreds, if not thousands, of parking spots for the workers driving in. Concentrating jobs in peripheral areas is far from sustainable and inclusive: the transportation required to access these zones is not available to many people with disabilities.

The further disabled people live from work, the more likely we are to be reliant on transit. The lack of affordable accessible housing stock available in Canada exacerbates the distance between workers and workplaces. The gap between home and work is a greater barrier for disabled people compared to others because transit is not comfortable, safe, or reliable due to operating schedules that frequently change or do not sufficiently meet demand, causing significant delays. Employment opportunities available in employment lands can range from labour-intensive manufacturing to office administration, marketing, and bookkeeping – which can be done remotely with the correct technology. Without a strong remote work policy, there's a risk that people with disabilities will not pursue opportunities in employment lands because of the significant barriers experienced daily in getting to work. Just as I have self-selected out of jobs that list requirements for physical labour, other disabled workers may decide not to apply for jobs in designated employment lands because of the deficiency of transit and the outdated, inaccessible buildings affecting our collective access to the same opportunities as non-disabled counterparts.

Mixed-use developments can overcome these barriers by encouraging buildings that offer community spaces and housing alongside workspaces. In this way, combining sites of employment with residential areas can allow people to create their own walkable or rollable communities. Disability justice in this type of development is not only supported by collective access but is also inherently sustainable and intersectional, as these developments reduce vehicle reliance and attract people of all ages, races, and cultural backgrounds.

There are significant barriers to employment for people with disabilities at all levels, from corporate policies to the inaccessibility of the built environment. To achieve equitable and inclusive disability employment, employers in all fields must engage in reflective and introspective analysis of the foundational barriers they unwittingly perpetuate. A foundational barrier that neither individual employers nor disabled employees can dismantle on our own is the significant gap between the Accessibility for Ontarians with Disabilities Act, the Planning Act, and the land-use framework of the Provincial Policy Statement. This disconnect between policy, legislation, regulation, and enforcement compounds the effects of all barriers experienced by people with disabilities. In the process of dismantling these foundational barriers, we have an opportunity to achieve non-traditional accessibility accommodations and build toward a future where disability justice is greater than injustice.

## Plain Language Summary

- Anika writes about disability and employment. She explains that because government income support is so low, many disabled people must work to survive.
- But workplaces and employers are not always ready for disabled workers.
- Anika analyzes provincial rules in Ontario. She shows that one set of rules deals with accessibility but another set of rules deals with where workplaces should be located.
- The gap between these rules makes it harder for disabled people to find good jobs.
- Anika uses the framework of disability justice to show why disabled people may need to advocate for better hiring practices and working conditions. The challenge is that this is extra work, on top of a disabled person's workplace responsibilities.
- She suggests that blurring the lines between where people work and where people live could create stronger communities. These changes would especially help disabled people.

## Endnotes

1. DeClercq, Katherine and Abby O'Brien, 'Ontario has no immediate plans to increase social assistance funds despite "steadily growing" caseload: documents,' CP24, July 28, 2023, https://www.cp24.com/ news/ontario-has-no-immediate-plans-to-increase-social-assistance-funds-despite-steadily-growing-caseload-documents-1.6498456.

2. Reuschel, William, Michele McDonnall, and Darren Burton. 'The Accessibility and Usability of Online Job Applications for Screen Reader Users.' *Journal of Visual Impairment & Blindness*, 117, no. 6 (2023), 479–490. https://doi.org/10.1177/0145482X231216757

# Trauma Is a Patient Artist

## Paul Vienneau

**Emily Macrae:** I first became aware of your accessibility work when you took snow and ice along Halifax's Spring Garden Road into your own hands and started clearing intersections. Had you been tackling accessibility before then?

**Paul Vienneau:** So, I acquired my injury in August of 1991, when I was twenty-two years old. My music career started about three years before that, so after a two-year hospital stay, I still wanted to play music. I started booking short tours. I was living in Toronto at the time. I believe my first tour was a three-night stay at Bras d'Or Lake out in Cape Breton with a band called the Hopping Penguins.

It made me have to think about how am I going to fly? How am I going to get from the airport to my parents', where I was staying? From there to the gig and then at the hotel, what was the reality of that going to be? Like door widths, ramps, and all that. How am I going to get lifted up and down steps and onstage? It was a very fluid, in-the-moment exercise in creativity. In the art world we call it lateral thinking. It's an aesthetic strategy to not just accept what you're told. There's a way around a lot of stuff.

Over the years, as I travelled farther and farther with the band, I learned how to drive with hand controls. I would often travel separately from the band because they would get one of those big club vans, which was way too high for me to get into. I learned how to book my own hotel rooms, all those things. So I did very proactive advocacy for myself. Since then – I mean, that's been about thirty-two years, coming up on thirty-three now – I was glad to go some places and get ramps put up to stages and things like that. Nothing official – I was not calling myself an advocate or an activist. I was just a musician who was trying to make a living playing music.

I moved back to Halifax from Toronto in 2001. I spent some time in P.E.I. but returned to Halifax permanently in 2009. In my neighbourhood, there were things that could be easily fixed. The metal security bars outside Pete's Frootique – they had them for shopping carts so people wouldn't steal

*Winter 2015. Paul Vienneau poses with a big smile as he hugs his two shovels after a few hours of clearing out curb cuts and corners and liberating a few drains.*

them. But I found out that the shopping carts had that security feature where a magnet will trip as you walk away. The security bars were difficult to get around for me with a manual chair; somebody with a power chair or a scooter couldn't get through at all. They would have to find somebody to let them in through the parking garage.

So we got those bars cut out. It was such an easy sell. Every time you go in there, to this day, you can see where the bars used to be. It makes me feel good to know that people can take for granted that this entrance is completely liberated now. It shows the power of how, when you go to people, you can get them to be willing collaborators in change.

**EM:** Could you take us back to that winter in 2015? What pushed you into action?

**PV:** The winter of 2015 is spoken of in hushed tones in Nova Scotia as the worst winter that's ever happened to us. In November, we had our first snow. That season the City never plowed full widths down to the pavement on the curb cuts and corners on Spring Garden Road [which cuts through downtown Halifax]. The guy on the Bobcat, who was a contractor, would drive basically a straight line from Robie down to Barrington Street, which is like six or seven blocks. So he would plow half of the curb cuts effectively; they're each at an angle to that straight line.

After a thaw-freeze-thaw-freeze, it basically became ice. So I started talking to the Bobcat drivers when I would see them in McDonald's getting a coffee or something. I would personally ask them, 'I'm trying to get to Pete's Frootique to buy groceries, but the corner's only half-done. Would you mind just turning the wheel so that you go down into the road where the curb cut is lowest?' Their managers didn't get it. The municipal complaints line – 3-1-1 – didn't do anything.

It led to me deciding, I have to do something to draw attention to this. I called 3-1-1 a week ahead, and I said, 'I want to cross Spring Garden Road to go to my bank to pay my phone bill in person. Could you please send somebody down? The weather's been nice since the last snowstorm – I just need you to clear this crosswalk.' A week later, Thursday morning, I go and look, and it's even worse. It's a big giant cake of ice with a hole in the middle where there are grimy dog turds and cigarette butts. Just impassible. Even for an abled person, it would be a severe danger.

So I called back and I said, 'I'm going to go find a shovel and I'm going to go start it. If you could please send a crew down to clear this thing out for me, I'll buy them a coffee and shake their hand and go home and shut my stupid mouth.'

I come back with a shovel and a metal curtain rod I borrowed from the maintenance guy in my building. I spent six and a half hours banging this metal bar on the ice. I started out with 'I want to go pay my phone bill in person because I'm a big man, an adult man who wants to pay his phone bill.' It was all about me. But right away, people start showing up and telling me their stories. One of the first was a woman my mom's age. She told me she slipped and fell. So I reached out, gave her my hand, and helped her get over the grimy ice.

A week earlier she had fallen and hit her head on Quinpool Road. I've got probably five, six concussions and a traumatic brain injury from the time I got hit by a truck. I went, *If this was my mom, how heartbreaking would that be for me, how much rage would I feel?* So it expanded it out to, *It's for elderly people too. Like my mom.*

The beat cop who worked my area has two adopted boys from China who have disabilities. He says, 'What you're doing is something my boys could look up to.' It's hard to describe how that made me feel. I've only been a bass player my entire life.

Other people would tell me about an ultramarathon runner who snapped an ankle and had to have a plate put in. He's not going to be able to run at that level for the rest of his life. So it was about citizens' rights. You fall because the City's trying to save money; it affects the quality of your life. It's not just disabled people. We're the canary in the access coal mine because we're most affected by these things. What makes our lives possible makes your life a lot easier.

People would go, 'Oh, here, I'll do that for you,' and offer to take the shovel. But every person that day listened to me. I said, 'If you do this, somebody on a bus or on the sidewalk is going to take a picture of me sitting there passively and you saving me.' You can't control what people say about things, but for whatever reason, I decided I wanted to control the tiny bits of it that I could. They were all awesome about it. About listening and respecting my wishes. There are more things you can control than you think.

So that first day was only me for a reason. Then, after that, I started borrowing shovels. If anyone came up and said, 'Hey, let me do that for you,' I'd say, 'Hey, let's do it together.' The media loves to have supercripples or poor crippled bastards. I hate the C word. I don't think I'm empowering myself by using the words my enemies use about me. But the media loves that. You're either a Superman or you're a poor bastard. But for me it was about being a citizen. I wanted to be a citizen trying to solve problems.

**EM:** You've also called for stricter fines for the misuse of accessible parking spots. How's that going?

**PV:** I'd like to backtrack a bit. Back in 2017, there's the Bill C-59 Coalition. I'm really, really grateful to have been involved with this group. When the province announced an accessible Nova Scotia by 2030, my reaction was *That's a slogan, it's marketing*.

With the coalition, we had as much representation from different Deaf and disabled realities as possible. We met every weekend for months. Then the province gave everyone who needed to speak on the bill three days to get to the legislature to address the committee. People who have to call two weeks ahead of time for Access-A-Bus were given three days. People from Cape Breton were given three days to get to the legislature.

My first sentence was 'This process, by its very definition, is anti-democratic.' To their great credit, they took everything we said straight to heart. We talked about the realities of things like this. Why this is

*Paul Vienneau, Spring Garden Road portrait.*

not a democratic process. How, by design, they're keeping people away. Preventing us from talking about our own human rights.

When we came back the next year for more sessions, it was like a breath of fresh air. They had the CART [captioning] system, they had sign language interpreters. People were given a proper amount of time, and a lot of people came out.

**EM:** I'm curious about other aspects of your contributions at city hall.

**PV:** After helping with these things informally, I think it was 2018, I went to Jacques Dubé, the chief administrative officer, the guy who writes all the cheques and oversees everything. I had a meeting and I said, 'I'd like to make what I do a little bit more official so I'm not always initiating things.' He brought me in a week later to propose a position – the accessibility advisor to the chief administrative officer. So we would meet every couple of months, and I would make suggestions and observations.

The City had been talking for decades about making Grand Parade more accessible. It's a big paved space for concerts and events. But there are huge inclines leading into the square. So I kind of refreshed that conversation. I did an audit with Dr. Linda Campbell, my friend who is Deaf, to look at how we could make that better. Democracy is not some amorphous ether, it's not some theoretical idea. Democracy has to be physically accessible, as well as accessible in all the other ways.

When Covid happened, it was about democracy being accessible as well. Should Deaf people have to wait for a transcript of council meetings? Or should they be able to interact with it in real time, which everyone else takes for granted? It's so obvious, and in principle we all agreed it should be captioned. But for three or four months, the City couldn't make it work. Dr. Linda Campbell sent me five solutions, which I sent on to city hall. The next virtual council was accessible to everyone.

I didn't come up with the solutions, but I knew where to go for them, which is, duh, a Deaf person. Provincial and municipal government, they think they hold all the answers. They lack the humility to go to the people with the real experience and the real information.

Here's another example. The City decided they wanted to discourage parking and driving on the peninsula, basically downtown Halifax. The issue is that the peninsula is full of elderly and disabled people. They require either a vehicle to be able to live and work, or the services that help them live at home instead of in an institution. The people who help make their lives happen need parking and driving. Meals on Wheels. Religious leaders visiting. Family, home care, VON [Victorian Order of Nurses]. A million other things like that.

City hall, in a lot of ways, is still not including us in our destiny. For this and other reasons, I gave my notice to city hall and the public. I cannot be thinking about this for twenty-four hours a day when they continue to make the same mistakes over and over. I need to live my life again for myself. I think I managed to contribute to a bunch of things, but this is the last part of my life now, and I have things I really want to do.

**EM:** You're a photographer?

**PV:** Yeah, I do portrait photography and some abstract work. I've been studying and practising mentalism, a type of magic that uses effects mimicking extrasensory perception, memory arts, math skills, psychokinesis, telekinesis, mind reading, etc. I'm in a club and have been performing when I can. I'm hoping to do a Fringe show this summer.

I've also been in therapy for PTSD finally, for the last three months. Last summer, instead of spending time on Spring Garden Road, I spent every day in the Public Gardens by the duck pond. Or by the big tree near the Boer War statue. Doing breathing exercises. Or going to street corners and waiting for an ambulance to go by.

For years, when I heard an ambulance go by, I'd turn around and plug my ears so I wouldn't hear it or see it. Because it triggered the bejesus out of me. So my therapist said, 'Just let it happen.' The first time I did it, it was really empowering. I do that with big trucks that go by on the street. Some things are still really triggering, but I feel like more of an active participant in the process.

Some people have a meditative practice. For me it's my kindness practice – and I'm not trying to save everyone, I don't do it every day. The first winter I did the shovelling, that spring I started handing out bottles of water on Spring Garden Road. It was just a simple 'Would you like a drink of water?' With a smile. People are usually pretty suspicious. Because I look like somebody who should be asking for things. I don't want to control your actions. I just want you to have a drink of water on a hot day. It gives me that little spark of connection.

Today I went down to the entrance of my building on Spring Garden Road, and it was warm enough that I sat out there. Did my breathing exercises, watched the people pass by, did my PTSD exercises. It was a good day. I don't have to actually be actively working for it to be a good day. These days are for me.


## Plain Language Summary

• In this interview, Paul talks about accessibility and advocacy in Nova Scotia and beyond.
• When he first got injured, he was a musician. He had to figure out how to tour and perform. As an artist, he used creative thinking to deal with barriers.
• Later, Paul focused on accessibility in Halifax. One winter, he started shovelling an intersection that was blocked by snow and ice.
• He learned about how the city designs, builds, and maintains public spaces. He also learned about how neighbours can help each other.
• Paul worked with city hall and volunteered with other disabled people to push for other improvements.

# Dreaming Together

# The Invitation of a Crip Horizon

## Sean Lee

Throughout most of my adolescent life, I navigated an able-bodied world without much issue. True, I was visibly disabled – my back curved and jutted out with a hump; I was missing two-thirds of my ribs, causing the left side of my chest to collapse into my hips; and I was very short. But these were largely aesthetic troubles I could try to ignore. While I could not physically participate in some of the typical aspects of day-to-day life, and there was a bit of bullying that I just assumed came with the territory, being visibly disabled also had some perks – no gym class, and I could usually arrive to school late without much consequence. Some skip-the-line passes at Disney World too.

But something happened when I became older and my queerness entered the picture. Suddenly, I understood myself to be different, and not in a good way. I hadn't really ever felt undesirable before, but now, disability made me feel grotesque, maybe even monstrous. It wasn't necessarily the torpedo of queerness into my personhood itself that forced me to confront my disability, but rather a sudden urge to conform to able-bodiedness. Puberty made it abundantly clear that I was *different* in ways that I could avoid up until then. High school made me understand that the various rites of passage that were afforded so easily to those around me would be completely out of reach, and it was then that I realized, despite living with my disability all my life, I didn't *know* disability.

## Discovering Disability

The default way of understanding disability is the medical model, a system that underscores how disability manifests as an individual issue. Most disabled people are automatically subscribed and indoctrinated into this model, and unfortunately many don't get the opportunity to experience anything besides that. As an artist, I found myself searching for meaning in identity through my art. In college, I learned about the queer arts movement, the feminist art movement, the Black arts movement – and yet, curiously, disability was never presented with the same resonance. The relationship between disability and art was always relegated toward a charitable model instead, where disabled artists made art for therapeutic benefits rather than as self-actualized artists.

I felt that, as an artist, I was trying to piece together the whys and hows of my own experience of disability alone. But this brought me into researching disability, which helped me understand it as beyond a medical phenomenon. While the medical model has always presented disability as something isolated from the experience of the individual, my search helped me discover things like the social model of disability, which I found in a TED Talk given by the late Stella Young. Moments like these completely changed my perspective on how I approached my own disability through art. Models like the social model of disability parsed out the way society disables an individual and helped me understand the important role of access in our social contracts. As I continue my journey into disability community, I've found the social model is not perfect but it was an excellent launching point for myself at the time. Examining social systems helped me understand how compulsory able-bodiedness renders disability undesirable. And the process of this research and self-discovery lit in me a fire to resist its permeation.

It became important to my artistic practice that I do more than just explore my body on my own – I wanted someone else with whom to think these things through. I wanted to reach out to somebody – anybody – to try to better understand how disability lives beyond just myself. I was extremely lucky: that search paid off. I came across Eliza Chandler, the artistic director of Tangled Art + Disability, at a feminist unconference hosted at the Art Gallery of Ontario by TAG Feminist Art Gallery, curated by Allyson Mitchell and Deirdre Logue. In meeting Eliza, encountering Tangled, and finding other crip artists, I was introduced to disability art, culture, access, and the idea of disability community.

## Encountering Tangled

My experiences reflect disability activist Catherine Frazee's observation that many people come into 'Disabled Country' through the acts of gleaning and claiming – wherein we observe, we discover, and then we finally take back the narrative of disability on our own terms. In Dispatches from Disabled Country, she explains that none of us are born into Disabled Country, but instead, through the acts of gleaning and claiming, we each must follow our own path to entry. Belonging is a choice we make for ourselves, not one others can make for us. The gleaning, through Tangled, showed me that different kinds of worlds were possible. It revived in me a sense of belonging, thanks to my disability and not in spite of it. Having now been at Tangled since the launch of the gallery in downtown Toronto in 2016, I realize more than ever that I continue to glean, to learn, and to unlearn what it means to dwell in disability culture. The lands of Disability Country are like a vast galaxy encompassing a constellation of experiences, perspectives, and histories unique to each of us, yet held together in the sky. The art that comes out of disability culture has the capacity to claim, be disruptive, be political. As Frazee says, it is the art that bites back. But it can also be tender, soft, and gentle to us when the non-disableds tell us we are not enough.

## Disability Culture

Disability culture is challenging to define because historically it has been stripped from disabled people by ableist and medicalized rhetoric. Society often tells us that our bodies hold disability alone and that our bodies determine our future. We are told we don't participate culturally in disability because it is a personal failing and are taught instead to distance ourselves from individual deficit and overcome it. Disability is portrayed solely as a biological law, rather than a societal construction. The antidote to this narrative is disability culture, which rejects medicalization and isolation, emphasizing instead that we are the experts of our own bodies and can craft community rooted in disability. A shared culture reclaims disability through rituals and practices of access, sharing these 'hacks' as a way to forge community.

But even the word *community* can be inadequate when it's tasked to represent every nuanced faction of togetherness. Community is inevitably something we actively seek and learn. I sought community at a time of artistic discovery, and it led to my coming into curation as a form of community-building, a form of artistic expression, and a way of world-building toward something more just and equitable. How, within the complexity of our lived experiences, can we nurture a community that rejects the cultural compulsion to strive toward competition, capitalism, and neo-liberal concepts of productivity? These are the forces we must contend with if we want to radically experience disability community as something that gestures toward an anti-assimilationist politic. We have to be critical of a culture that, at best, only tolerates disability because there are experiences on the horizon that transcend the boundaries of ableism, moving us closer to a disabled future: a Crip Horizon.

## Crip Horizon

I've been using the phrase *Crip Horizon* to agitate out of a stagnant, one-dimensional future. It's a conceptual site and space for imagining a future otherwise. It's rooted in disability culture and characterized by a commitment to a politics of futurity. Building upon and expanding on the ideas of José Esteban Muñoz (2009) and Alison Kafer (2013), the Crip Horizon represents a forward-looking perspective that emphasizes the intersection of access and disability. Muñoz's 'queer utopianism' and Kafer's 'politics of crip futurity' both serve as foundations for this concept, emphasizing the importance of reimagining the future in the face of compulsory able-bodiedness. In creating this phrase, I'm looking toward not one future but the possibility of many.

The Crip Horizon harnesses the political potential that arises at the crossroads of access and disability, propelling disability culture toward an *elsewhere* and *elsewhen*, where we can dwell with disability. It requires not only the hope to believe in a better future but also the will and resilience to actively work toward it. This concept underscores the shared hope in an ever-moving future. This is where disability art plays a role in world-building and world-dismantling to imagine these alternative futurities. It resides at the intersection of a thirst for change, a critique of the present, and the determination to create a different and more promising tomorrow for those who have been historically denied the promise of a future.

For me, the Crip Horizon is the road we travel in Frazee's (2023) *Disabled Country*, immersing ourselves in disability culture and tasting access intimacy that quenches our thirst for a world that doesn't actively try to erase us.

I grew up trying to distance myself from my disability, and *Tangled* was the vehicle for me to enter Disabled Country – it helped awaken in me a sense of pride and identity. When I first began making art that reconciled my own thoughts around disability, I worked very much in isolation. My arts experience was cultivated to suit tastes that reflected a mainstream arts culture that never centred disability as a difference that mattered. On reflection, it might come as no surprise that I came into Tangled believing that to create access, we needed best practices and checklists, codes, and regulations. I initially focused on compliance-based methods of creating community that felt more a chore than a joy. At Tangled, I was shown a different way of experiencing disability and came to understand disability art as a movement driven by disabled people, for disabled people. Our experiences can't be quantified by a clean checklist because our experiences are not so tidy.

## Crip Curatorial Practices

To be honest, when I started at Tangled, I was an advocate for the check-box system of access because I didn't recognize the structural ways ableism was ingrained in our society. As I became more ensconced in disability culture, I began recognizing the ways the check-box methodology was ultimately employed under a neo-liberal maxim.

The check-box approach treats accessibility as a set of logistical standards, assuming access is a scientifically measurable outcome, people can be standardized, and a finite solution can be achieved. A more critical perspective on access, as described by disability scholar Aimi Hamraie (2017), is referred to as 'critical access.' This approach understands access as a political endeavour. It acknowledges that accessibility is an ongoing process that varies for different individuals.

Hamraie emphasizes that universal design, a popular concept in the early twenty-first century, represents an easy solution to accessibility. While universal design is often lauded for benefiting everyone, it aligns with neo-liberal capitalism by offering a 'one size fits all' solution. Disability scholar J. Logan Smilges (2023) adds that the emphasis on individual access needs ultimately distracts from the systemic ways ableism operates in our world and can inadvertently reinforce the status quo.

## Culture-Building Through Art

Tangled is the site of political engagement where I began my journey into Disabled Country and its many offerings on the landscape of disability culture. For me, disability culture – and future – remain an act of gleaning. We are in a moment when disability art has energized the cultural zeitgeist with urgent political nuance around accessibility, disability aesthetics, and curatorial practices. Art allows us to engage with access as a vital cultural aesthetic, not only reserved for spaces specific to disability but to become entangled in all facets of artistic production.

In 2021, Tangled reopened after the pandemic lockdowns with *Undeliverable*, an exhibition curated by Carmen Papalia. This exhibition focused on reclaiming the museum, based on the demands and desires of the disabled bodymind. It challenged conventional access by prioritizing the needs of crip artists over those of the audience, leading to an inherent embrace of the concept of Crip Time. The gallery's commitment to accommodating disabled artists extended into contracts that included a 'care clause,' developed by Tangled executive director Cyn Rozeboom. The care clause aims to ensure that artists' needs take precedence over institutional demands for a 'complete' exhibition and foster mutual accountability. *Undeliverable* demonstrated the potential to shift the clock to prioritize disabled bodies and minds, challenging traditional expectations of a 'complete' exhibition.

Traditional access elements, such as ASL translation, image description, and graphic recording, remain essential. However, access aesthetics go beyond mere accommodation; they transform art spaces and create more dynamic and socially transformative experiences. They can also take the form of rituals of care, like co-creating access riders for artists to take with them to their next exhibition. Tangled, for instance, in response to Covid-19, implemented remote options for visiting the gallery that are still in play today, allowing people to explore exhibitions from home and extending access beyond geographical boundaries.

## Conclusion

As we continue to fight for more just and equitable participation in the arts sector, I bring up the acts of gleaning and claiming one last time. Fostering a disability community cannot be limited to us – disabled artists, cultural workers, and activists – alone. Instead, it is a shared joy and responsibility, and it is through gleaning that we find ourselves gathering meaning in disability. Disability communities are constantly extending an invitation into our rituals and practices to those who find themselves unmoored in an unforgiving ableist terrain, offering a buoy to anchor themselves on the shores of the Crip Horizon. In solidarity we can come together across disability community to claim cultural space and find the joy in that elsewhere and elsewhen that crip community can provide.

## Plain Language Summary

• Sean describes growing up and learning about their identities as an artist and a curator. They studied many different arts movements in college. There wasn't much information available about disability and art.

• They gathered role models from internet research and books. Eventually Sean found other disabled artists and curators going through similar experiences.

• These experiences helped form Sean's personal understanding of disability community. Now Sean uses this knowledge to organize exhibits at Tangled Art + Disability. Tangled Art + Disability is an art gallery in downtown Toronto. It shows the work of disabled artists and offers many accessibility features.

• Sean has learned that a checklist is not enough to create accessible experiences for disabled artists and community members.

• As well as creating new ways to make and enjoy art, Sean encourages us to look to the future. The idea of a Crip Horizon means imagining a better future and actively working toward it.

## Bibliography

Frazee, Catherine, Christine Kelly, and Michael Orsini. *Dispatches from Disabled Country*. Vanoucver: UBC Press, 2023.

Hamraie, Aimi. *Building Access: Universal Design and the Politics of Disability*. Minneapolis: University of Minnesota Press, 2017.

Kafer, Alison. *Feminist, Queer, Crip*. Bloomington: Indiana University Press, 2013.

Muñoz, José Esteban. *Cruising Utopia: The Then and There of Queer Futurity*. New York: NYU Press, 2019.

Mykitiuk, Roxanne, Eliza Chandler, Nadine Changfoot, Carla Rice, and Andrea LaMarre. 'Cultivating Disability Arts in Ontario.' *The Review of Education/Pedagogy/Cultural Studies*, 40(3), 249–64, (2018). https://doi.org/10.1080/10714413.2018.1472482

# 'I Decided to Make My Disability Visible'

## Christa Couture

**Emily Macrae:** I first saw you onstage at what was then the SkyDome during what was at the time called the Canadian Aboriginal Music Awards. But you're not only a performing artist – how would you like to introduce yourself?

**Christa Couture:** At a dinner party last year, I was among a group of guests trying an exercise to introduce ourselves. The host instructed us to say three things folks need to know about us. The word *need* struck me – is what I want people to know about me different or the same from what I need them to know? It turns out, yes. I want people to know that I am a writer, a musician, a broadcaster, and a filmmaker. I want people to know that I am an artist, that I am driven to express myself and my experiences through storytelling. But I need them to know that I am Indigenous, queer, disabled, and a mom. I need people to know how I move in the world, how I love, and what kind of barriers I face.

**Jenny Hiseler:** It was wonderful watching you over social media enjoying the beach and joyfully walking in the rain with your new prosthesis. How has being water-resistant changed your experience of nature, of being out and about? Do you think rain resistance would impact your enjoyment of Toronto vs. Vancouver?

**CC:** My new prosthetic knee is water-resistant – a first, for me, since getting a microprocessor knee nine years ago. These knees are expensive – the knee I had for the first nine years was $40,000, largely paid for through crowdfunding in my community. That knee came with a warranty, but I was told clearly: The warranty does *not* cover water damage. Don't get it wet! I was told to be mindful of not just walking in the rain but of kneeling in grass. I love walking in rain. With my new knee, this love became stressful – I'd panic and find cover. Eventually I figured out to always carry a plastic bag with me, a little makeshift knee raincoat to protect it when needed. But now that the latest model is water-resistant, I'm able to be in the rain, to walk along a lake, to play with my daughter at a splash pad, without panic. It's wonderful to have that level of worry removed from how I can be outside.

**EM:** Beyond rain and waterfronts, how do Toronto and Vancouver compare in terms of navigating with a prosthesis – sometimes crutches, more recently a stroller? Vancouver has hills, Toronto has snowbanks …

**CC:** The biggest difference between navigating Toronto vs. Vancouver with a prosthesis is snow. Snow is an instant barrier for me and makes it very difficult to walk. In Vancouver, that would happen once a year. In Toronto, it can be weeks at a time that I simply can't leave the house as often as I'd like or need to. While I thought I was at least leaving very steep hills behind me by moving to Toronto, this city is deceptively hilly! Depending on the neighbourhood, encountering slopes and angles is as present here as in Vancouver.

**JH:** In your memoir, *How to Lose Everything*, you write about the energy it takes to live somewhere new. Where do you go when you need to recharge?

**CC:** Moving to a new city does take a lot of energy – learning directions and local culture, finding your new favourite coffee shop …

Nothing is automatic at first; everything takes work to discover. When I need to recharge, I go to the water, whichever water I'm living near. Or if that isn't an option, it's not a *place* I'll go to, but familiar people. There are two people in my life who are my closest, dearest friends. Connecting with one of them is one of my best ways to recharge.

**EM:** The impossibility of snowy sidewalks is something a lot of disabled people living in Toronto – and beyond – will recognize. It's also something many others have never had to notice. Tiny snowplows have started appearing on our streets to scrape at sidewalks. What do you want to see more of to make winter more navigable?

**CC:** During my first winter in Toronto, I arrived at my new prosthetist's office after a difficult – though I now know typical – journey through snow, slush, and ice, and asked: How do amputees get around outside here? My prosthetist replied simply: They don't. And he wasn't exaggerating – most of his clients would go from sheltered car parks or garages to another sheltered drop-off location when they did leave the house. I was very used to being outside year-round and taking transit all over the city. But with frequent snowfall that stuck around, I was encountering a new set of barriers. Snow instantly makes it difficult or impossible for me to walk. Regular, prompt clearing of sidewalks would make winter much more navigable, but many homeowners in Toronto don't clear snow – or don't have capacity to – which creates huge restrictions for folks like me or with strollers or other mobility needs.

**JH:** Often people say that they didn't really think of accessibility until they started pushing a stroller, but you experienced barriers to getting around before parenthood. Do you think your familiarity with occasionally using a wheelchair, and other accessibility considerations, prepared you at all for the changed mobility of being a parent?

**CC:** I was not at all prepared for the impact on mobility of parenting. I wanted so badly to parent, I don't think I allowed myself to truly consider the physical challenges that come with it – for any body, much less my disabled body. Between carrying more things, the amount of bending over, getting up and down off the floor, pushing strollers, clipping babies into car seats … to be honest, parenting has taken a large physical toll on my disabled body and I've had increased pain since my daughter was born. It's worth it! And I deal with it. But in my naïveté or denial, I didn't anticipate what those demands would be, and my experience with assistive devices didn't help me realize how inaccessible spaces also impact caregivers with strollers. Child care is very physical work, and without assistance, adaptation, or increased accessibility, it's very challenging.

**EM:** You've described your first microprocessor knee as 'the knee that folk music bought.' Could you say a bit more about networks of care in Canada's folk music scene? How do you support other artists and how have you been supported by musicians, friends, and fans?

**CC:** My first microprocessor knee was life-changing for one simple reason: I don't fall as often. Not falling at least once a week, feeling more confident and stable when I walk and stand and move, has been a huge gift, and it truly was a gift: the knee, at a cost of $40,000 and not covered by health care, was largely paid for through a crowd-funding campaign. I didn't realize the scale of care I had access to – across friends, families, and particularly colleagues – until that crowd-funding took place. With each donation that came in, I felt not only grateful for the financial support, but increasingly moved by the number of people who wanted to support me. And this was not a campaign others would get much out of, unlike when I'd crowdfunded my albums. This was just for me to have a better leg! Many folks, it turns out, wanted that for me too.

I do think, generally, people want to help, and that asking for help is the best way to open that connection. But also, the time I was crowdfunding my knee – which I would later call 'the knee that folk music bought' because of how strongly my career community of the folk music world in Canada contributed – was just a few years after my second son died, and that was just a few years after my first son died. The amount of support I received for the leg was partly because of community care, but it tapped into the previous years, when folks wanted deeply to support me but couldn't see a clear way how. The ask of support for the knee gave people a direct and impactful way to improve my quality of life. It was connected to my experience with grief, but it was a large part of my daily living. As the recipient of that fundraising, I became very aware of the difference that rallying around a cause can make. I contribute to mutual aid more often than I do to 'larger' organizations or causes because of this awareness – because the relationship is closer and more deeply felt.

**JH:** Was your disabled identity always part of your music career? Has disability always shaped your approach to storytelling or is that something that's surfaced over time?

**CC:** My disability identity was not always part of my music career and actually only became known to many through the crowdfunding campaign for the microprocessor knee. In fundraising for that knee, many folks in my broader community told me they didn't know I had only one leg! It wasn't a secret exactly, but I didn't volunteer the information and I dressed in a way that hid my prosthetic leg so that it wasn't visible at a glance. With the incredible experience of getting the microprocessor knee, I decided to make my disability visible by creating a floral cover for my prosthetic, 'the flower leg,' which became something I would then be known for or strongly identified with. I don't mind. It took time for me to feel confident and comfortable in my body in a way that I can celebrate my limb difference, and the flower leg feels like a celebration.

I remember saying to a friend, 'I don't want to be known as the singer with one leg,' and he replied, 'But you are a singer with one leg.' So simple! But it helped me consider why I was reluctant to share that part of my experience. To be fair, it wasn't just internalized ableism that held me back, but the very real truth that I would experience discrimination, like a promoter not wanting to book me if they're reluctant to make accommodations, or audiences making assumptions about the kind of art I create. Ultimately, disability has always shaped my storytelling because I have been disabled since I was thirteen; I can't extract disability from how I see the world or how I express myself. But how evident or central that influence is in my work has shifted over time as my confidence and understanding have grown.

**EM:** Thanks again for this conversation. Anything else you'd like to add?

**CC:** That understanding and confidence have not been gained in a vacuum. For all its downfalls, social media has played a large part in my education and self-discovery as a disabled person. The aspect of community and networking online is what led me to Mama Cax – an amputee, who has since passed, with incredible fashion, and the first person I saw who cut off one pant leg to reveal her prosthesis as a style choice; the Alternative Limb Project – a U.K.-based prosthetist who creates limbs as functional pieces of art and who inspired my floral cosmesis; Alexis Hillyard, aka Stump Kitchen – a congenital arm amputee who celebrates her limb difference in a way that deeply challenged my internalized shame about my stump; and Kaleigh Trace – the author of *Hot, Wet, and Shaking: How I Learned to Talk about Sex*, which was my first encounter with disability pride and disability justice. These connections brought me into a community of support that I hadn't had before social media. When Mama Cax shared my maternity photos in 2018, that caused them to go viral (the photos beautifully highlight my disability), which further connected me with disability community – and specifically those with limb difference – around the world. These networks have been invaluable to improving my self-worth, informing my politics, reducing my experience of isolation, and overall adding and creating meaning in my life and work.

## Plain Language Summary

- This is an interview between Christa Couture and this book's editor, Emily Macrae, and developmental editor, Jenny Hiseler.
- Christa is a writer, musician, broadcaster, and filmmaker. She is also Indigenous, queer, disabled, and a mom.
- Christa uses a prosthetic leg with a microprocessor knee. Her first one cost $40,000 and was largely paid for by crowdfunding in her community.
- Christa compares living in Toronto to living in Vancouver. Snow makes it very difficult for her to walk, so sometimes she can't leave the house as often as she'd like to. Rain can also be a barrier. Christa's first prosthesis with a microprocessor was not waterproof.
- Although she has been disabled since she was thirteen, Christa's disability identity was not always a part of her music career. The strong support of her community for the crowdfunding campaign helped her decide to make her disability visible by creating a floral cover for the new prosthesis.

# Cultural Resilience: The Intersection of Inuit Qaujimajatuqangit and Disability Justice

## Nicole Diakite, in collaboration with Abdoul-Karim Diakite and Noah Papatsie

To fully appreciate the connection between Inuit Qaujimajatuqangit (IQ) and disability justice, it's important to explore the historical context of Inuit communities in what is now Nunavut, Canada. The historical experiences of Inuit continue to shape cultural values and the approach to addressing disability issues. For centuries, Inuit have inhabited the Arctic region, adapting to one of the harshest environments on Earth. Inuit survival and adaptation strategies have been forged through generations of facing extreme climate conditions, limited resources, and isolation. In this context, the importance of community, interdependence, adaptability, and respect for nature – all central components of IQ – emerged as guiding principles for daily life. However, this historical context also involves ongoing encounters with colonization, cultural disruption, and health challenges that significantly impact Inuit communities. The history of colonialism brought major changes, including the forced relocation of Inuit families, the disruption of traditional practices, and exposure to new diseases and health issues.

The introduction of Western education and health care systems also played an important role in shaping the experience of those with disabilities within Nunavut. In many cases, the services provided by colonial governments were not culturally sensitive or tailored to the unique needs of Inuit individuals and communities. Furthermore, discrimination and social inequalities have been persistent consequences of colonialism. These inequalities often intersect with disability, as disabled Inuit individuals face multiple forms of discrimination, including racism, ableism, and other systemic barriers that limit opportunities and access to resources.

In this historical context, the emergence of disability justice as a framework for addressing the challenges faced by disabled individuals is especially relevant. Disability justice recognizes the connection of these issues and the need for a comprehensive approach to justice that considers not only disability but also the broader societal factors contributing to marginalization. Inuit communities' historical experiences of resilience, adaptability, and community support, as well as traditional knowledge and practices, have laid the foundation for a contemporary response to lived experiences of disability, ableism, and other forms of discrimination. The integration of IQ principles with disability justice represents a path toward addressing the historical injustices and inequalities faced by disabled Inuit, fostering a more inclusive and equitable society.

## Defining Disability: An Inuit Perspective

One important piece of the intersection between IQ and disability justice is the nuanced understanding of disability within Inuit communities: there is no direct translation or word for *disability* in Inuktut, the local languages. This absence shows the unique perspective of Inuit communities. Unlike Western societies, where disability is often framed as an individual's deficiency or medical condition, Inuit have historically embraced a more holistic perspective, deeply rooted in cultural values. Inuit culture has always emphasized the interconnectedness of all community members, each contributing to the collective well-being. Within this framework, individuals with impairments are not defined by limitations but rather by unique contributions to the community. Abilities and strengths are celebrated, and any support a person may require is considered a natural extension of the community's commitment to collective well-being. The absence of a direct word for *disability* challenges the dominant approach to assimilating people with disabilities. In this model, disabled people are often expected to conform to a predetermined norm or 'normalcy,' and if that is not possible, they face segregation or institutionalization. In contrast, Inuit communities have historically valued individual differences and emphasized adapting to each person's unique abilities.

The absence of a direct translation for *disability* provides insight into the complex dynamics of cultural preservation, identity, and the ongoing quest for justice across Inuit communities. The integration of IQ and disability justice is not just about addressing contemporary issues but also about preserving the essence of Inuit culture and challenging assimilation in all its forms.

## Inuit Qaujimajatuqangit: An Overview

Inuit Qaujimajatuqangit serves as the fundamental belief system guiding the lives of Inuit in the Arctic region of Nunavut, Canada. It's a way of looking at the world that focuses on community, respect for nature, and the interconnectedness of all living things. For Inuit, this wisdom has been a source of strength and resilience, enabling life in the harsh conditions of the Arctic. Over recent years, IQ has gained recognition as a valuable framework for addressing complex social issues, including disability inclusion. IQ is a comprehensive approach to life that includes cultural values, traditional knowledge, and practices passed down through generations. These principles shape not only the way Inuit interact with one another but also how communities relate to the environment.

At the heart of IQ is the concept of community and interconnectedness. Inuit firmly believe that individuals are deeply connected to family, community, and the land. In this world view, the well-being of one person is linked to the well-being of all. It's a culture that nurtures collaboration, ensuring that solutions are found collectively. Stories and oral traditions are not merely forms of entertainment; they serve as essential educational tools, making certain that wisdom and cultural knowledge are passed on.

While IQ prioritizes community and interconnectedness, disability justice tackles discrimination and oppression faced by disabled individuals and communities, advocating for fairness and inclusion. Disability justice is a framework for social justice that aims to address issues related to disability, solidarity, and sustainability. It recognizes that the challenges faced by disabled people and communities are intertwined with other forms of discrimination, such as racism, sexism, and ableism. This framework challenges the traditional disability rights movements by emphasizing intersectionality as a key component of achieving fairness. Disability justice opposes ableism, a system of discrimination and oppression against disabled individuals. It aims to challenge attitudes and practices that limit the inclusion of disabled people. There are ten principles of disability justice. Among them are:

1. *Intersectionality:* Disability justice recognizes that people have multiple social identities, such as race, gender, sexuality, and disability, that can intersect and intensify discrimination and marginalization.

2. *Interdependence:* Disability justice promotes the idea that every person has unique needs and abilities. It encourages a community-based approach where people support each other in ways that respect independence and self-determination.

3. *Collective Access:* Disability justice advocates for universal access and accommodation, recognizing that obstacles to access disproportionately affect marginalized communities. It seeks to remove these barriers to enable full participation.

Noah Papatsie is a prominent advocate and community leader in Nunavut. His personal journey exemplifies the intersection of Inuit Qaujimajatuqangit and disability justice principles. In response to questions about how IQ values and disability justice intersect in the context of Inuit culture and community life, Noah sheds light on the practical application of these principles and Inuit culture's profound impact on inclusivity and social justice in Nunavut.

## Noah's Story

Born and raised in Nunavut, Noah embodies the values of his heritage and the lessons passed down by his parents. He is a father of ten and a grandfather of two, and his life has been marked by a deep sense of responsibility to his family and community. He has a remarkable background as a former broadcaster and a dedicated member of city council, where he tirelessly advocated for the rights of people with disabilities. In the 1990s, Noah experienced a workplace accident that left him with a visual impairment. This significant event marked a turning point in his life. Noah faced the daunting task of adapting to a new way of life, learning to navigate an entirely different world. In the face of adversity, Noah became an unwavering advocate, inspired by the belief that 'challenges are not barriers.'

Noah's commitment extends beyond the boundaries of his community, as he actively engages in international work and serves on numerous committees dedicated to educating people about the rights of persons with disabilities. His advocacy work, rooted in the teachings of his parents, emphasizes the importance of community involvement and leadership. Noah is an advocate who exemplifies the idea that challenges can be surmounted with resilience, determination, and a strong sense of community. In conversation to prepare for this chapter, Noah elaborates on the role of inclusivity and storytelling, the importance of cultural sensitivity and advocacy, and the integration of IQ values in advancing disability rights and moving toward disability justice, not just as an individual but as a community.

## Understanding IQ and Its Application to Disability Justice

To explain the essence of IQ values and their application in the context of disability justice, Noah emphasizes the significance of unity and co-operation within the community, specifically Iqaluit, the capital city of Nunavut. He stresses the core values of sustaining, teaching, and respecting one another and fostering a strong sense of togetherness. This extends to caring for individuals, particularly those facing physical and mental health challenges. Noah elaborates on how Inuit tradition has been effectively leveraged to provide support to individuals with disabilities. The traditional application of IQ values centres on mutual support during challenging times, ensuring the ability to lead healthy lives. Noah also recognizes the delicate balance between adapting to the changing demands of contemporary society and preserving traditional knowledge and approaches to supporting people with disabilities. This underscores the pressing need for accessibility and participation rights, as he says, '[w]orking together as Inuit to sustain, teach, and respect each other. We take care of each other as a society, especially those with physical disadvantages and mental health challenges.'

## Application of IQ Principles to Address Disabilities

Noah's personal experiences, shaped by his upbringing within a community that increasingly recognized the importance of accessibility, provide a tangible illustration of how IQ principles can be applied to support people with disabilities. In his community, there was a growing awareness of the need to make sure that everyone could actively participate and access resources such as food and housing. This commitment to inclusion was not limited only to physical accessibility; it also extended to supporting the mental well-being of community members, recognizing that mental health is an integral aspect of overall quality of life. Noah's involvement in this ongoing process exemplifies the core values of nurturing healthy lifestyles that are at the heart of IQ. By actively working to make the community more inclusive and accessible, he not only contributes to improving the lives of those with disabilities but also strengthens the overall fabric of the community.

## Intersection of IQ and Disability Justice

Asked about his perception of the relationship between IQ and the principles of disability justice, Noah stresses the alignment between IQ's focus on equality, which extends to everyday life, and the fundamental tenets of disability justice, which revolve around the pursuit of justice while respecting individual differences. Noah's perspective reflects a profound understanding of the pivotal role that unity and collaboration play in achieving true inclusion. Furthermore, he emphasizes the importance of prioritizing mental health as a foundational step toward creating a more inclusive society. In doing so, he echoes core principles of disability justice, which recognize and address the interconnected aspects of individuals' identities and experiences. Moreover, Noah's focus on mental health parallels the increasing use of the word *bodymind* within disability justice organizing. This term highlights the ways a person's physical being and mental state are inseparable. Noah's perspective underscores how IQ and disability justice can work in tandem to build a fairer and more inclusive world. Inuit live worldwide, from Canada and Denmark to Greenland and even Russia. Due to forced relocation, the nomadic lifestyle has significantly changed and communities are seeking new forms of connections and inclusion across age, ability, and even time zones.

## Inclusivity and Storytelling

Noah notes that storytelling is a medium to instill empathy and broaden awareness, regardless of one's abilities. He particularly focuses on the role of music in promoting inclusivity, drawing parallels with the Inuit value of balance, which mirrors the way equity underpins disability justice. According to Noah, 'Abled – disability or not – storytelling is great; it is how we listen to one another. For generations stories were passed on to family as survival has always been the top priority with our remoteness and distance. And music always plays a great role in inclusion. Balance is important, and understanding our surroundings.' Noah's perspective highlights the enduring significance of storytelling in bridging gaps, forging connections, and promoting empathy – all of which contribute to a more inclusive and harmonious community.

## IQ Values and Advocacy for Disability

Noah stresses the significance of IQ values when advocating for disability rights, emphasizing the importance of mutual respect and understanding. He notes the integral role of Elders in the decision-making process and the necessity of collective efforts to enhance inclusion and justice. Noah's insights illuminate the tangible ways in which IQ values naturally align with and support the principles of disability justice, ultimately contributing to the creation of a more inclusive and equitable society in Nunavut. Noah notes the important role of cultural sensitivity in harmonizing IQ and disability justice to establish more inclusive and equitable practices. Respect for local people and the environment is the core of his approach to advocacy.

'Advocacy is important, especially with access, education, justice, promotion, and more, especially inclusion, and respecting the locals and the surroundings,' Noah says. 'We need to work together. Sustaining life is our mission – especially our environment.'

## Plain Language Summary

- This chapter is a collaboration by three people living in Iqaluit, Nunavut.
- Nicole, Abdoul-Karim, and Noah explain that Inuit Qaujimajatuq-angit is a way of looking at the world. It focuses on community, respect for nature, and the ways all living things are connected.
- Noah was born and raised in Nunavut. He talks about how his community and his culture shape his approach to disability advocacy.
- The culture, history, and environment of Inuit communities create a different understanding of disability. For example, there is no word for 'disability' in local languages.
- Now, as Inuit communities adapt to colonialism, people in Nunavut and other Arctic regions are looking for new ways to make sure everybody is included.

# Un beau défi: My Journey Fighting Multiple Sclerosis and the Climate Crisis

## Sébastien Jodoin

I remember the exact moment and place when MS entered my life. It was late October in 2015, around 11:00 a.m. I was in a coffee shop, working on an article on human rights and climate justice, when I suddenly felt the right side of my body go slightly numb.

Two days later, I began to have difficulty using my right leg and my right arm. I tripped while walking up a flight of stairs. I also felt an intense throbbing pain spread through all my joints. I felt a slight pressure around my torso – what I would later learn is called an 'MS hug.' My wife and I headed to the emergency room. After we'd waited for several hours, a team of three doctors came back with the results of my MRI scan. I recall seeing the senior neurologist encourage the young resident to share the diagnosis with me. I could tell he was nervous. He approached me and announced: 'It's MS. You have multiple sclerosis.'

Overwhelmed with emotion, I cried for a good solid minute. I did not know much about multiple sclerosis, just that it was scary. I thought of wheelchairs and Richard Pryor – the only celebrity I could think of who had lived with MS. Without any real idea of what lay ahead of me, I turned to my wife and exclaimed, 'Ça va être un beau défi' (this will be a great challenge).

It ended up being a lot harder than I had expected. There were many ups and downs in my first two years with MS. It certainly introduced a lot of uncertainty in my life, including in my career. I had spent close to a decade specializing in the fields of human rights and climate justice and was now in the first semester of a tenure-track position as a law professor at McGill University. The smart thing to do was to stick to what I knew, especially as the amount of work I could now complete was suddenly limited. Yet, my encounters with other people with MS and a never-ending series of medical appointments convinced me that I should shift my research agenda to focus on disability rights in the context of health law.

## Extreme Heat, Ice Vests, and Climate Vulnerability

The new direction my work would take was not apparent until the following summer. I live in Montreal, where the summers are hot and humid. Like 65 per cent of people with MS, I discovered that I was very sensitive to heat. Heat sensitivity in MS is not just inconvenient – it can significantly limit your quality of life by making it impossible to live without air conditioning and by restricting the types of activities you can do when it is hot outside. In the summer of 2016, it dawned on me that I and other people with MS were uniquely affected by the problem I had been working on for my whole adult life: climate change.

Due to increased concentrations of greenhouse gases in the atmosphere, the earth's global average temperature has increased by almost 1.5 degrees Celsius since the pre-industrial-level era – a trend that appears to be accelerating. The year 2023 was the warmest ever recorded, and ten of the warmest years have all occurred in the last two decades. This global heating is leading to higher average temperatures in the summer and more frequent and intense heat waves. While extreme heat may be an inconvenience for some, it can be deadly for many disabled people. For instance, in the Pacific heat dome that killed over six hundred people in British Columbia in June 2021, 91 per cent of the victims had a disability.

My new-found interest in the relationship between disability and climate change led me in 2016 to look for research that analyzed or addressed the disproportionate impacts of climate change for people with disabilities. I found a handful of insightful papers written by scholars in the field of disability studies, but almost nothing in the huge literature on climate change. Basically, climate scholars, activists, and policymakers were systematically ignoring disabled people. I was part of the problem. The year that MS came into my life, I was working with leading climate scholars and lawyers on a book on human rights and climate governance. Although our book had chapters on Indigenous Peoples, women, and children, the word *disability* does not appear in the index. My field had a lot to learn and a lot of work to do. As a disabled expert working on climate change, I realized that I was uniquely placed and even obliged to address this gap in knowledge. This is what led me to eventually co-create, in 2020, the only research program focused on disability-inclusive climate action.

I had more immediate concerns though. I was committed to finding a way to being able to spend time with my wife and daughter outside, in spite of my intolerance to heat. Surely someone had found a solution to coping with heat. As a privileged Montreal kid who had been to Disney World way too many times during my childhood, I began to wonder how people who wore mascot costumes could cope with the heat of Orlando in the summer. I soon discovered the online niche world of cooling apparel. I also realized that there were lots of people with disabilities who had come up with ways of staying cool in the summer or when exercising. I bought a cooling headband favoured by people undergoing chemotherapy, and I purchased a type of cooling vest that was highly recommended by an online community of people with MS who were committed to exercising outside. This device carried twelve little packs filled with a special liquid that froze at 9 degrees Celsius. It could keep your whole body cool for three hours. By wearing this vest, I was able to resume my summer activities.

While ice vests were critical for me in my first years with MS, I don't use them anymore. I eventually achieved a full recovery from all my physical symptoms, and I no longer experience heat sensitivity in the summer. This may be due to luck – genetic testing shows that I don't have the genes associated with more aggressive forms of MS. It mostly comes down to privilege though. My socio-economic status, education, and gender have made it possible for me to access excellent health care, including the most effective medical treatments for MS as well as the costly complementary practices that have been key to my recovery, involving yoga, weightlifting, a personal trainer, and a psychologist.

My atypical experience of fully overcoming heat sensitivity reveals another important truth about the climate vulnerability of people with disabilities. Whether or not someone is disproportionately affected by heat has little to do with their impairments. It is shaped by the broader patterns of privilege and discrimination that mediate things like whether an individual lives in a home with air conditioning or passive cooling, resides in a neighbourhood with lots of green spaces, has the funds and know-how to find and purchase specialized items like ice vests, has access to health care, or has doctors who believe in them and are ready to work with them.

When scholars refer to lived experience in their research, they often do so to recognize the long-overlooked value of the knowledge developed by historically marginalized groups such as women or Black or Indigenous people. As I discuss below, I too am committed to reflecting and foregrounding the perspectives of these groups in my work. Yet my lived experience as a *privileged* person with a disability has also motivated and shaped my overall research agenda at the intersections of disability and climate justice. My journey with MS reinforces the key insight of the scholars and activists who developed the social model of disability in the 1970s. It is the social, institutional, physical, and economic barriers in society, not the underlying medical impairment, that can be most disabling. This realization guides my efforts to understand the role that intersecting forms of privilege and discrimination play in generating, worsening, or alleviating the climate vulnerability of disabled people with different identities.

## Learning from and with People with Disabilities

Ice vests were not the first – nor the last – thing I learned about from my peers with disabilities. After my diagnosis, I discovered a vibrant and welcoming community of disabled people on social media. These individuals, mostly younger women with chronic illnesses, shared their struggles, victories, lessons learned, and tips and tricks for living life to the fullest despite the limitations and challenges that disease or society imposed on them. Their wisdom and expertise played a key role in my adjustment to life with MS and gave me a new-found appreciation for the value of lived experience as a form of knowledge.

I now know that activists and scholars alike are critical of the 'inspiration porn' that portrays disabled people as sources of inspiration for able-bodied people. These narratives can be harmful if they reinforce individualist tropes that suggest that courage and grit are all that is needed to overcome illness or disability. More often than not, such 'inspirational' stories also neglect to acknowledge that expensive adaptations, specialist care, or paid medical leave are not equally accessible to all disabled people. Unlike most mainstream depictions of disability, the blogs, Facebook groups, and Twitter threads I have found most insightful form a culture that is created by and for people with chronic illnesses. Through social media, disabled people build communities and share insider knowledge aimed at making *our lives* more comfortable, fulfilling, and joyful. These are what disabled scholar Arseli Dokumaci calls 'activist affordances.' By improvising innovative and ingenious ways of completing daily tasks, such as wearing an ice vest in the summer, people with disabilities imagine and build more habitable worlds for themselves.

The recognition that disabled people could be knowers and makers – a key point raised in the 'Crip Technoscience Manifesto' written by Aimi Hamraie and Kelly Fritsch – makes our systematic exclusion from efforts to build low-carbon and climate-resilient societies even more glaring. My experience of learning from others with MS and other chronic illnesses, online and in person, underscored the need to ensure that we are part of the process for developing and implementing equitable and effective climate solutions. In fact, if governments implemented many of the long-term demands of disability communities, it would significantly reduce the mortality and harm associated with climate impacts such as heat waves. With decent incomes, accessible housing, inclusive communities, excellent health care and support services, and programs to fight discrimination and stigma, disabled people would simply not be exposed to extreme heat to the same degree and would have the capacity to minimize its adverse effects.

Disabled expertise extends not only to the best ways of protecting us from the worse impacts of climate change, it also encompasses in-depth knowledge of universal design and accessibility that can ensure that solutions to reduce carbon emissions help address rather than reinforce disabling barriers in society. For instance, blind activists from the National Federation of the Blind figured out a while ago that electric cars could be dangerous because they emit no sound at the speeds they are driven in cities. Blind and partially sighted leaders lobbied the U.S. Congress to make it a requirement that all electric vehicles must emit a sound. This law will not only end up saving the lives of blind or low-vision pedestrians, it will enhance the safety of streets for everyone. Of course, I don't pretend to claim that electric vehicles are an effective solution to the climate crisis. They are also not designed to be accessible to most disabled people, especially wheelchair users. But this example illustrates what disabled people can contribute to the effort to solve the climate crisis: we know how to make things work for as many as possible.

I have made collaboration with people with disabilities a key element of the disability-inclusive climate action research program I lead at McGill. We have worked closely with disabled activists and organizations from all over the world, including those at the frontlines of the climate crisis in the global south. I am especially proud of the podcast series we've produced on the lived experience of climate justice of people with disabilities. Although I was a relative newcomer to the field of disability research and advocacy, I was struck by the openness of so many committed people who were willing to work with me and support our efforts to build linkages between disability and climate justice.

## Cultivating Hope

Close to a decade since my diagnosis with MS, I have lived up to my naive expectation that I would use this opportunity to grow as a person and a scholar. After years of therapy and reading an endless series of books about disability, mindfulness, Buddhism, and resilience, I am a more serene and optimistic individual today than I was in my early thirties. Perhaps the most valuable lesson I have learned from other disabled people is how to strike a delicate balance between cultivating acceptance and hope in the face of change and adversity. I continue to do everything I can to keep my MS at bay, but I know better than to think of disability (or wheelchairs, for that matter) as frightening. Likewise, I am still as committed as ever to addressing the climate crisis through my scholarship and activism, but I don't operate from a position of anxiety or fear. Yes, the world can be terrible and unjust. And yes, life can be hard. But there is no point in giving up the struggle. Life goes on and we must too. And it's easier to move forward if we work together as part of a larger community founded on care, equity, and the desire to build a better world.

## Plain Language Summary

• Sébastien writes about being diagnosed with multiple sclerosis. As a professor of law, he adapts his research to include disability.

- Sébastien also has to adapt to hot Montreal summers. He realizes that many disabled people are at risk due to global heating.
- Sébastien discovers that disabled people can find solutions to problems caused by heat. They share these ideas, challenge stereotypes, and build communities with other disabled people.
- The ways that people with disabilities care for one another and solve problems are important to keeping everyone safe as the planet warms.
- Collaboration is a key part of Sébastien's research into disability and climate change. He builds relationships with disabled leaders around the world.

# Wilderness Photography, Disability, and Me

## Nicolas Steenhout

### My Happy Place

It's a cool November morning. At 7:30 a.m. the sun is just cresting over the mountain. There's about 20 per cent cloud cover and a light breeze. I arrived about forty-five minutes ago, after a 2-kilometre walk on a gentle, maintained gravel path. On my way here, a bald eagle dropped a salmon head from a tree a metre ahead of me. It made me chuckle. 'It's raining salmon, y'all,' I told myself. I've already had time to set up my gear and observe bird activity. It's been too dark to take photos worth keeping. Doesn't mean I didn't try!

*Bald eagle sitting in a large fir tree.*

I'm in my zone, in my happy place. I am at one of my favourite spots to watch bald eagles during migration time. Here, I can relax. I can focus on the here and now. I can forget about work. About access barriers. I can just … be.

I've already observed a couple dozen bald eagles, both juveniles and adults. And a great blue heron. And trumpeter swans, and a half-dozen different kinds of ducks. I've also seen dark-eyed juncos and Steller's jays. And gulls. Lots and lots of gulls! I've heard a couple hummingbirds, though I didn't see those little ones this morning.

## About Me

I've told you about my happy place, and now it's time to tell you about me! I'm Nicolas Steenhout. I'm a French-Canadian guy currently living in rural Canada, out west, with my wife and my service dog. I rarely take the dog with me when I go birding though. He's well-behaved – he wouldn't chase birds. But birds and other wildlife give him the side-eye anyway.

I'm an ambulatory wheelchair user – I have good days and bad days – more or less mobile days. I can never tell from one day to the next what mode of transport I'll be using – wheelchair or feet. I've relied on a manual wheelchair for nearly thirty years. For a living, I'm a digital accessibility consultant. I help companies and organizations ensure their websites and web-based applications are accessible and usable by disabled people.

I love birdwatching, or birding, in the lingo of birdwatchers. And I love photography. Combining both really works for me. It's awesome! And yet there's a dose of ableism that seeps in. Ableism, in a nutshell, is prejudice or ignorance pointed at disabled people. It mostly happens when I encounter other people. It doesn't happen that often. But it happens.

## How It Started

Let me back up a bit. Let's talk about how I started going out in nature to photograph birds.

I've long been interested in photography, all the way back to my teenage years. I was using 35 mm film cameras back then. I even had a darkroom to process my photos. I wasn't taking photos of wildlife then; I was playing around with studio portraits and street photography.

I was always interested in taking photos of birds, but I never thought I had the right gear. I'd get some photos whenever I could. I captured some nice great blue heron photos in a park in Quebec. I managed a few nice photos of white-faced herons in New Zealand. Just before the pandemic, I was given a good lens. Then the pandemic happened. We were living in a very rural area. I was going out in nature a lot, and there were no other humans around. That's when I really began taking photos of birds. That's when I started calling myself a bird photographer. Before that, I was just a photographer who liked taking photos of birds.

In the few years since, I've turned into a birder. Taking photos of them, of course. But also learning the names and habits of the birds around me. I had to learn these things so I could get better photos. You'll be ready to photograph a bird as he flies off the branch if you've observed him wiggling his bottom, because you'll know that's a typical pre-flight behaviour.

Where do I find birds?

Birds are everywhere. We have so many options.

It can be hard to get to some locations. Extreme hiking in the backcountry is not typically the adventure most accessible to me as a wheelchair user. It's also not accessible to me on days when I'm ambulatory – sure, I can walk, but a long, arduous hike over steep terrain is still not within my reach. The good news for me, and for my disabled comrades, is that extreme backcountry hiking isn't a requirement for doing bird photography.

When I am lucky enough to travel to a new area, I look online for information about accessible nature trails. But accessibility-related information is often hard to find. Few websites for parks and reserves include this information. I often just take a chance and go exploring on my own. The trails, however, are not always passable for me. Sometimes I don't have the chance to venture much beyond the parking lot. Other times I can do a full circuit. Yet other times, I travel a hundred metres or so and come across a bridge I can't get onto. Mud, deep soft sand, and logs across the path are

*Anna's hummingbird.*

other typical barriers. But those hundred metres can yield some great bird sightings. Most of the time, it's not about how far you go – it's about paying attention to what's around you.

I've found that my best opportunities to get interesting photos involve nature parks with maintained trails. Typically, these are compacted gravel. Not the most fun to traverse with a wheelchair, but also not a blocker. City parks with paved trails are also an option. Did I mention birds are everywhere? Okay, so you're unlikely to come across bald eagles fishing for salmon in a city park. Let's face it, while birds-of-prey raptors are impressive, small songbirds are also fabulous. And if you look long enough, you'll find a myriad of different bird species, even in an urban park.

I spotted three different kinds of sparrows in a park in Montreal. I discovered four bird species I'd never seen before at a riverside park in Brandon, Manitoba. I guarantee you, my excitement over adding bird species to my 'life list' is pretty much all the way up there! As far as raptors go, I've spotted hawks and owls in parks in Vancouver and Chicago.

## Backyard Birding

Northern pygmy owl.

I also do a lot of birdwatching and bird photography right in my backyard. Yes, the backyard is an easy-to-get-to, mostly accessible, very handy spot to spend a bit of time looking for and finding birds. I can sit in my backyard and look and listen for birds when I don't have the time or opportunity to escape to the 'real' outdoors. I counted twenty-one different species of birds in my backyard one day in January a couple of years ago. Twenty-one!

During the spring migration, there are a lot of different songbirds in our backyard. And they attract the attention of different birds of prey. We had a northern pygmy owl hang around and feed on 'our' songbirds for a couple weeks. It's never fun to consider that birds eat birds. But they do – that's nature for you. Even when I lived in the city, there were birds in my backyard. Quite apart from the ever-present gulls, you can often find sparrows, ravens, cardinals, and so many other birds. It's amazing how many birds you can learn to identify when you start paying attention.

## Other Disabled Birders

I haven't had a chance to speak to very many other disabled bird-watchers – at least, none with visible impairments. But there's another person I'm in touch with regularly who is a birdwatcher and relies on mobility devices to get around. We've never met in person. They live in Europe, and I'm in North America. We haven't met, and yet we have similar experiences. We experience similar frustrations. We experience similar highs when we find a new-to-us bird. We share some of our photos and talk about the birds we see.

We discuss the joy of birdwatching – we don't need to talk about ableism. We don't need to discuss people's odd comments. We don't often talk about the mechanics of going birdwatching and photographing while disabled. We do, sometimes. We exchange tips and tricks from time to time. Or we talk about how awesome it is to discover a wooden boardwalk traversing a park. We know ableism exists. That information is there for us. We just know that the other understands what it's like – that it's part of our lived experience everywhere, including when we go out birdwatching. And we don't need to talk about it, specifically. But if and when we do, we also know that we can. And we know we won't have to give the Ableism 101 talk before we can discuss the experience. There's a lot of comfort and joy in that.

There are also groups of disabled birders. They advocate for more accessible trails. They get together to watch birds and spend time in community. This seems like a fantastic thing. But it's not for me. I do advocacy around accessibility in my day-to-day. I'm glad these groups exist, but if I were to join one, I'd end up just extending my daily work. Suddenly, my relaxing hobby would become advocacy. The nature of my nature trips would significantly change.

## People's Reactions

I've been using a wheelchair for well over two decades. By now, I'm kind of used to people's reactions to me doing 'unusual' activities. There's always someone who makes a remark, whether it's while I'm doing my weekly grocery shop or when I'm going to the fabric store.

I generally tune out the 'How fantastic that you're grocery-shopping for yourself' or 'How nice to see someone who's wheelchair-bound go out and about.' I mean, sure, such comments get to me occasionally, but I make a point to ignore them.

Ignoring comments is a lot more difficult when you are one of two people in the middle of nature though. The positive is that over the last several years, people's comments have come more from curiosity than from an ill-placed sense of admiration. Here are some of the things people have said to me, and my typical responses …

*Stranger:* I've never seen a guy in a wheelchair in the middle of nowhere like this.

*Me:* You've never seen a guy in a wheelchair in the middle of nowhere like this because a lot of us live in cities and don't really venture out in nature. But I've never seen you here in the middle of nowhere either. And I'm here every week, sometimes twice or thrice a week. You not seeing wheelchair users doesn't mean very much, does it?

*Stranger:* Weren't you using a wheelchair the last time I saw you here? Are you faking it?

*Me:* You possibly saw me using a wheelchair, yes. I'm not faking it. There are a lot of wheelchair users who are also ambulatory, depending on the day. On my more mobile days, I enjoy the additional reach I get by walking. I can get off the trail and get closer to the pond, for example. Or I can get nearer the blackberry bush if I need to.

*Stranger:* That looks difficult!

*Me:* Yes, it can be. Packed gravel paths are not super-easy. But they are doable. It's cheaper than going to the gym!

*Stranger:* You need a better wheelchair than that!

*Me:* A better wheelchair – yes, sure, there are wheelchairs designed to go off-roading. They are generally heavy and expensive. There are even power wheelchairs with tracks like tanks or backhoes. But that's even more expensive and heavy. No, my wheelchair is just fine, thank you very much. It's the chair I use every day. It fits in my car without too much trouble. I can handle it without assistance. Sure, it means a lot of trails are out of reach for me. But there are also a lot of trails I can access.

The thing is, people are generally ignorant about disabilities. Seeing a wheelchair user at the supermarket is unusual to start with. It shouldn't be, but there we are. Seeing a wheelchair user in nature ... Let's face it, I stick out like a sore thumb! I don't know what it is about the people I come across when I'm out there, with my camera, looking for my happy place. The majority of folks who talk to me are a lot more interested in the birds I've seen, or telling me about the rare bird they've seen and where to find it, than in asking about my wheelchair.

And that, in and of itself, is truly refreshing.

*Trumpeter swans on a pond in the early morning.*

## Enough Advocacy Is Enough (For Me)

I go out in nature to get away from work. Because I'm a disabled individual, that 'work' is never far. We routinely have to advocate for access. Steps at the entrance of a restaurant. Hotels refusing access because of a service dog. Elevators requiring a key, which is only available once you've been to the floor that requires an elevator to get to. Mobility parking spaces occupied by people without placards or permits. City buses with broken ramps. Rental units that are okay with pets, until you ask if they are wheelchair-accessible, and suddenly they don't accept pets. This is all part of the advocacy work I do most weeks – and this is only the personal advocacy work.

On top of personal advocacy, there's job-related advocacy – I push for accessibility in digital environments. I educate. I champion. I evangelize. I think about my next accessibility-related blog post. My next video to train developers or designers on accessibility. And, of course, there's the job itself. I'm frequently in my head, thinking about accessibility both in the built environment and in the digital world. I consistently advocate about accessibility, and when I'm not advocating, I'm thinking about advocating. I have to do advocacy for work. And I have to do advocacy so I can access places in my everyday life. It's exhausting. If I have a choice, I don't want to spend my free time on more advocacy.

## Photography Gear

I used to experience envy when I saw people with large tripods and huge lenses. I had FOMO – fear of missing out – *fer sure*. I don't own a huge, heavy lens. First, I can't afford it. And I can't carry one, nor the tripod needed to use these lenses. And I wouldn't want to. These days, I have really good gear myself. I currently use a Canon R7 and a 100 mm to 500 mm zoom lens. For me, it's a good combination in terms of camera quality, weight, and compactness. In fact, you don't even need to carry around a DSLR, or even a mirrorless camera. The disabled birder I chat with all the time has an older Canon Powershot camera. Their camera doesn't give them the reach mine gives me. That's okay, it's not about the photos.

## It's Not About the Photos

At least for me, bird photography is no longer about taking brilliant photos of birds. The photos are just an 'aide de mémoire.' A reminder of an experience I've had. Bird photography is about being out and about in nature. It's about enjoying the quiet. It's about soaking up nature. It's about observing the world around me. It's getting myself out of my head, out of continually thinking about work. It's stepping away from computers. In many ways, going out birdwatching and bird photographing is an excuse to go out in nature. I won't pretend to be 'one with nature.' I'm a visitor. An interloper even. A respectful one, I hope. Photography allows me to relive these opportunities. The moments in time when I spotted a bird and captured a photo.

*Bald eagle in flight, catching a salmon in a small river.*

I set up a few hundred of my photos as screen savers on my computer and on my smart TV. Each and every photo that cycles through brings me back to a moment. There's that hummingbird feeding from a flower that reminds me of being at a bird reserve on a hot summer morning. There's the white-faced heron walking in mud that reminds me of the wooden boardwalk in Russell, New Zealand. There's the bald eagle, beak open in a call that reminds me of an overnight stop on one of our RV trips. There's the house finch staring at me with a cheeky look in his eye that reminds me of sitting in my backyard and enjoying a cool morning break.

Every photo takes me back to a moment when I was in a good place. When I wasn't thinking about everything I do for work, for advocacy. Times when I'm not fighting or ignoring or otherwise dealing with ableism, a lack of access, or respect. Birding is my escape – a chance for me to be me, without thinking about the barriers that society puts in my way every day. It's comfortable not to fight, not to talk, not to think.

## Plain Language Summary

• Nic writes about spending time outdoors, connecting to nature and taking photos of birds.
• Nic has learned about and spotted birds in his backyard, in the parking lot of parks, and on nature trails.
• Because Nic sometimes uses a wheelchair, strangers ask him weird questions.
• Nic needs to advocate for better accessibility at his job and in everyday life. It's important for Nic that wildlife photography does not become more advocacy.

# Onward

Thank you, contributors, for your expertise. For the intimacy of having your stories written down even as we are each still evolving. All of us with disabilities are aware of the intimacy of proximity with health care professionals, the intimacy that starts at the skin, the intimacy of questions, pokes, stares. We also know the rare thrill of disabled friendship, of not having to say, of not needing to explain.

Thanks for engaging with the vulnerability of being known, alongside the everyday vulnerability of having assumptions made about you. We're grateful for all the people who have taken the time to contribute, amidst everything else you're doing. Thanks for the work and the words that you drew on. For the patience and perspectives you've shared. For giving credit to the friends, mentors, and elders who came before you and made change alongside you.

Thank you to everyone who couldn't participate. Because we're tired. Because we're sick. Because we're getting married. Because we're moving across the country. Because we're living our lives. Thank you to the people who are doing work in parallel on similar topics. Thank you to the people who are coming next.

# Appendices

## 1: Status of Accessibility Legislation in Canada (as of May 2024)

In Canada, national accessibility legislation lags almost thirty years behind the United States. The Americans with Disabilities Act (ADA) was passed in 1990 while the Accessible Canada Act (ACA) only became law in 2019. Many accessibility standards that would support the national legislation are still under development.

In the United States, the ADA covers federal, state, and local government programs and services. It also prohibits discrimination against people with disabilities in privately owned facilities, including businesses and medical offices. In contrast, the scope of Canada's ACA is much more narrow. It applies to matters under federal jurisdiction, such as banking, telecommunications, airlines, and railways.

In Canada, national legislation is supported by a range of human rights frameworks:

- The Canadian Charter of Rights and Freedoms
- The Canadian Human Rights Act
- Canada's commitments under the United Nations Convention on the Rights of Persons with Disabilities

Provincial and territorial legislation offers a patchwork of other standards and requirements. For example, Alberta does not have overarching legislation to support equal access for people with disabilities. Instead, accessibility and/or disability are mentioned in at least thirty different pieces of Alberta legislation.

### Canada
- Name of legislation: Accessible Canada Act, 2019

- Status of implementation: Aims to identify, remove, and prevent barriers that do not allow people with disabilities to be included in all areas of society by 2040.
- Additional context: Applies to the federal public sector, Crown corporations, and federally regulated industries, such as:
  - Railways, airplanes, and inter-provincial buses
  - Banks and mining companies
  - Television and radio

## Alberta
- n/a

## British Columbia
- Name of legislation: Accessible British Columbia Act, 2021
- Status of implementation: Public sector organizations are required to establish an accessibility committee and an accessibility plan, and build a tool to receive feedback on their accessibility. This includes schools, post-secondary institutions, municipalities, and public libraries.
- Additional context: Allows the Government of British Columbia, with the guidance of the Provincial Accessibility Committee, to develop new accessibility standards that will address barriers in areas including employment, education and transportation, buildings, and infrastructure.

## Manitoba
- Name of legislation: The Accessibility for Manitobans Act, 2013
- Status of implementation: The information and communications standard applies to the Manitoba government as of May 1, 2023, other public sector organizations on May 1, 2024, and all Manitoba employers by May 1, 2025.
  - Under the accessible transportation standard, any new buses purchased after January 1, 2027, are required to meet accessible

design requirements. Conventional transit operators have until January 1, 2042, to upgrade existing buses.
- Additional context: The Act consists of five standards:
  - Accessible customer service (regulation enacted in 2015)
  - Accessible employment (regulation enacted in 2019)
  - Accessible information and communication (regulation enacted in 2022)
  - Accessible transportation (regulation enacted in 2023)
  - Accessible design of outdoor public spaces (in development)

## New Brunswick
- Name of legislation: Accessibility Act, 2024
- Status of implementation: Aims to achieve a more accessible New Brunswick by 2040 by identifying, preventing, and removing barriers to accessibility.
- Additional context: The creation of accessibility standards related to:
  - Government services
  - Transportation
  - Education
  - Employment
  - The built environment
  - Housing
  - Information and communications
  - Sports and recreation

## Newfoundland and Labrador
- Name of legislation: Accessibility Act, 2021
- Status of implementation: This enabling legislation allows the Government of Newfoundland and Labrador to outline the principles and goals for an accessible province.
- Additional context: Public bodies are required to develop and make public accessibility plans.

## Northwest Territories

- n/a

## Nova Scotia

- Name of legislation: Accessibility Act, 2017
- Status of implementation: The Accessibility Advisory Board has established four committees that help make recommendations for accessibility standards.
- Additional context: Applies to the development of accessibility standards in:
  - Built environment
  - Education
  - Employment
  - Goods and services
  - Information and communication
  - Transportation

## Nunavut

- n/a

## Ontario

- Name of legislation: Accessibility for Ontarians with Disabilities Act, 2005
- Status of implementation: The purpose of the legislation is to 'achieve accessibility for Ontarians with disabilities' by 2025. There are different timelines for public sector organizations, businesses, and non-profits to develop plans and file reports. However, with the deadline of 2025 looming, independent reviewers, advocates, and members of the disabled community have heavily criticized progress toward this goal.
- Additional context: Sets requirements related to:
  - Employment
  - Customer service

- Information and communications
- Transportation
- Built environment

## Prince Edward Island
- n/a

## Quebec
- Name of legislation: Loi assurant l'exercice des droits des personnes handicapées en vue de leur intégration scolaire, professionnelle et sociale, 1978
- Status of implementation: Legislation updated in 2004. Supported by the 2009 policy À part entière : pour un véritable exercice du droit à l'égalité.
- Additional context: Calls for provincial ministries, municipalities, and public and private organizations to support the social participation of people with disabilities, especially in education and employment.

## Saskatchewan
- Name of legislation: The Accessible Saskatchewan Act, 2023
- Status of implementation: The Government of Saskatchewan and other public sector bodies must develop accessibility plans to address accessibility barriers that people experience when using provincial facilities, programs, and services.
- Additional context: Applies to areas that the provincial government is responsible for, such as provincially owned properties, cities and towns, parks, health care, and schools.

## Yukon
n/a

## 2: About Building Codes in Canada

A building code is a set of rules for the design and construction of buildings and other structures. The National Building Code of Canada is a model code. This means it can be adopted in its entirety or adapted by provinces and territories. The National Building Code references the Accessible Design for the Built Environment standard, which is a Canada-wide standard. The Government of Canada also has an accessibility standard that applies specifically to federal properties and facilities.

Provincial and territorial building codes outline minimum requirements that public and private infrastructure must meet. Alberta, British Columbia, Ontario, and Quebec each publish their own building codes. All other provinces and territories either adopt or adapt the National Building Code and the accessibility standards it references.

Municipalities must comply with relevant provincial/territorial and federal legislation. However, some cities and towns have developed their own accessibility guidelines that go above and beyond minimum requirements.

## 3: Income Support for People with Disabilities by Province or Territory

This section summarizes the maximum amount that a single person with a disability could have received in the calendar year of 2022. It combines total income from all government transfers, including tax credits and additional social assistance payments, where applicable. In each case, the combined income is well below the poverty line for each province or territory.

This summary does not include additional payments that may be disability-specific, such as supplements for assistive devices, home care, or dietary needs. In each case, additional benefits must be applied for individually and may be denied or cut based on government processes or political priorities. Even these additional benefits do not fully cover or account for the higher cost of living for disabled people.

The focus of this section is on a single person who qualifies for disability supports because couples face additional restrictions on both social assistance and earned income. The result is that disabled people across Canada must make impossible decisions about living with their partners, accessing government benefits, paying rent, and buying essentials.

This summary also does not reflect the full range of barriers to accessing disability-specific supports, which include working with supportive health care professionals and providing detailed documentation of disability.

## Alberta
- $11,268–$21,319
  - Note: The range reflects the rates of the Barriers to Full Employment and the Assured Income for the Severely Handicapped programs.

## British Columbia
- $18,054

## Manitoba
- $14,125

## New Brunswick
- $10,884

## Newfoundland and Labrador
- $20,400

## Northwest Territories
- $31,744

## Nova Scotia
- $12,687

## Nunavut
- $12,755

## Ontario
- $15,871

## Prince Edward Island
- $18,715

## Quebec
- $16,355

## Saskatchewan
- $17,039

## Yukon
- $23,825

*Adapted from: Laidley, Jennefer, and Tabbara, Mohy. Welfare in Canada, 2022. Toronto: Maytree Foundation, 2023. https://maytree.com/wp-content/uploads/Welfare_in_Canada_2022.pdf.*

# About the Contributors

**Emily Macrae (editor)** is a disabled writer, organizer, and twin. She has lived and worked in Toronto, Halifax, Vancouver, and rural Quebec; her work combines policy analysis and lived experience to build accessible urban and digital environments. Her words have appeared in *Canadian Architect*, *Spacing*, and NOW magazines, as well as publications in Britain and the United States.

**Jenny Hiseler (developmental editor)** is an accessibility professional who started her career as a wheelchair technician. Since then, she has worked with architects and designers, arts groups, universities, and more to make policies, spaces, things, and events more accessible. She still keeps tape measures at her desk.

**Anika Abdullah** is an accessibility specialist for the built environment with a background in urban planning and universal design. Integral to her work is her lived experience as a South Asian, disabled, immigrant woman. She is completing her graduate studies regarding accessibility in architecture project management at Toronto Metropolitan University while supporting clients to achieve universal accessibility. In her free time, she explores Toronto neighbourhoods and enjoys local art and cafés with her mobility scooter named Alice.

**Valdine Alycia** is a two-spirit Michif living alone in the subarctic. For fun, they volunteer as much as their health allows.

As a serious and passionate advocate for accessible transit, **Mazin Aribi** has been involved with the Toronto Transit Commission (TTC) in various volunteer positions for nearly twenty years. Mazin has worked to further the transit options of individuals with varying abilities. He has strong knowledge of the TTC and the Wheel-Trans system, and has served as vice-chair and chair of the Advisory Committee on

Accessible Transit at the TTC, where he performed system audits for accessibility and helped to develop plans to improve existing services in both Wheel-Trans and conventional service. Mazin seeks to raise awareness on issues affecting marginalized populations with the goal of eliminating barriers to using specialized and public transit.

**Courage Bacchus** is a former three-time Deaf Olympian sprinter. She began working as an actress in 2019 and has since performed in *The Black Drum, The Two Natashas, 21 Black Futures,* and season four of *The Corner* on Netflix. Courage has participated as an art collaborator with numerous theatre and film productions in Canada. She's held multiple positions, including as an interdisciplinary visual artist, art accessibility consultant, and activist for IBPOC Deaf art community to expand IBPOC Deaf artists' representation.

Born and raised in Winnipeg, Manitoba, **Corey Bialek** currently resides in Toronto, Ontario. He holds a master of science in planning degree from the University of Toronto and a bachelor's degree in geography from the University of Manitoba. Currently working as a sustainability analyst, Corey has a keen interest in city-building projects that work through an adaptation and resilience lens to manage the inexorable impacts of climate change, particularly as it relates to vulnerable groups.

**Adam Cohoon** is an artist with a disability, and an accessibility advocate and tech tester. Adam uses technology in artwork to develop compelling ideas and to explore ways to create a more exciting disability community. Adam has recently moved to the mobile realm and is learning to use mobile technology to help bring more creativity and culture to the world. Adam also actively advocates for creativity, innovation, and technology to bring everyone wider accessibility to the arts. Adam believes that, when possible, there should be more opportunities to bring arts and culture into people's homes through technology. Adam lives in Toronto.

**Athena Cooper** is an acrylic painter and creativity coach based in Calgary. Born with the rare genetic disorder osteogenesis imperfecta (a.k.a. 'brittle bone disease'), and a wheelchair user since the age of six, she creates paintings that explore what it means to live an ordinary disabled life. She is the winner of the 2023 Won Lee Prize, administered by the National accessArts Centre, celebrating creative excellence among Canadian visual artists living with disabilities. Her 2024 solo exhibit, *The Extraordinary, Ordinary Nature of Interabled Love*, highlighted the everyday moments of her life with her husband through a large series of paintings.

**Christa Couture** is an award-winning filmmaker, performing and recording artist, writer, and broadcaster. She is also proudly Indigenous (mixed Cree and Scandinavian), queer, disabled, and a mom. Her debut memoir, *How to Lose Everything*, is available from Douglas & McIntyre, and the series of short animated films inspired by the book is available on CBC Gem. Couture lived for many years in Vancouver, B.C., but now calls Toronto, Ontario, home.

**Nicole Diakite** has been the dedicated and forward-thinking executive director of Nunavummi Disabilities Makinnasauqtiit Society (NDMS) in Nunavut since 2016. Armed with a master's degree from Toronto Metropolitan University and currently pursuing a PhD in social work at McMaster University, Nicole sees her academic pursuits as deeply intertwined with her passion for social justice. Her doctoral research is an inspiring endeavour that seeks to shed light on the intricate inter-sections of disability and Indigeneity.

**Shay Erlich** is a disability justice world builder, artist, and disability educator whose work imagines a disability-centred world where disabled people are empowered to love themselves and live free from stigma, shame, and ableism. They are the founder and program lead for Pushmakers, a national initiative focused on excellence in manual wheelchair dance. They are also the founder of Ready For Access, a disability experience firm that offers professional development, workshops, and co-design to create superbly accessible experiences for disabled people.

Good Foot Delivery provides meaningful employment for the neurodivergent community through a reliable, professional courier service delivered via public transit and on foot. Jack has been working with Good Foot since 2015 and likes to build Legos and play video games when he's not making deliveries. Zachary has been a courier since 2016, likes to write about pop culture on his blog, and hopes to be a published author one day.

Nicole Hanson is an educator, community builder, Registered Professional Planner (RPP), and Member of the Canadian Institute of Planners (MCIP). Hanson has a combined honours degree in political science and urban studies, and a masters in environmental studies in urban and regional planning from York University. Within the planning profession, Hanson's contributions, work, and agency are anchored in equitable land-use planning and transparent development outcomes. Hanson has reviewed, analyzed, and processed complex development applications for a variety of land uses across Ontario.

Sébastien Jodoin is an associate professor in the Faculty of Law of McGill University, where he holds the Canada Research Chair in Human Rights, Health, and the Environment. Drawing on his lived experience with multiple sclerosis, Dr. Jodoin co-founded and directs the Disability-Inclusive Climate Action Research Programme. In 2023, he was awarded McGill University's Changemaker Prize, conferred upon scholars whose dedication to sharing their expertise with the media and the public has significantly impacted society.

**Kimberley Johnson** is a Canadian of African Nova Scotia descent. She works as a professional sign language interpreter specializing in the Canadian dialect of American Sign Language (ASL) and English. She has over twenty-five years' experience in this field and has worked across four provinces and the United States. Translation is a recent addition to her skill set and integrates her writing and editing work. She is currently developing inclusive, accessible yoga classes for her passion project turned business, Dancipation Wellness.

**Rabia Khedr** is dedicated to equity and justice for persons with disabilities, women, and diverse communities. Rabia most recently served as a director on the Accessibility Standards Canada board and a commissioner on the Ontario Human Rights Commission. She sits on the Minister's Disability Advisory Group. She is the national director of Disability Without Poverty and CEO of DEEN Support Services. A founder of Race and Disability Canada, she is also a board member of the Muslim Council of Peel and the Federation of Muslim Women. A motivational speaker and documentary commentator, Rabia draws on her lived experience of being blind and advocating for siblings with intellectual disabilities. She has received numerous awards for her humanitarian services, including a Queen Elizabeth II Diamond Jubilee Medal and the Daniel G. Hill Human Rights Award. Rabia holds a bachelor of arts (University of Toronto) and a master of arts (York University).

**Sean Lee** is an artist and curator exploring the assertion of disability art as the last avant-garde. Their methodology explores crip cultural practices as a means to resist normative idealities. Orienting toward a 'crip horizon,' Sean's practice explores the transformative possibilities of access aesthetics as an embodied politic that can desire the ways disability disrupts. Sean holds a BA in Arts Management and Studio from the University of Toronto, Scarborough, and is director of programming at Tangled Art + Disability.

**John Loeppky** is a disabled freelance journalist currently living and working on Treaty 6 territory in Saskatoon, Saskatchewan. He is an RTDNA and National Magazine Award winner, and his work has been published by *Healthline, VeryWell Mind, Defector,* CBC, the *Globe and Mail,* FiveThirtyEight, and a host of other outlets. Athletically, he is a two-time medal winner at the Canada Games. His goal in life is to have an entertaining obituary to read, and you can find him online at www.jloeppky.com.

**Sarah Manteuffel** is a community planner based in Winnipeg. She is a person with a disability (dwarfism) and passionately advocates for universal accessibility. In her professional work, Sarah fights for inclusivity in the planning profession to ensure every voice is at the table. She has written articles for planning and landscape architecture publications and has spoken at conferences on universal accessibility, the planning profession, and dwarfism awareness. Sarah is an avid karaoke fan, a fibre-artist, and a lover of pets.

**Alexandria Sakara McDonough** is a Toronto-based visual/digital/sound artist and word mixer. She has exhibited at the Bayside Gallery in Toronto in 2021 and 2023, and the Royal Ontario Museum in 2022. Her themes include communication as a minimally verbal autistic through popular culture and art from the nineties to the present, particularly music, station bumpers, and children's public television programming.

**Sonali Menezes** is a Hamilton-based multidisciplinary artist and writer. She makes art as a way to find meaning under the weight of capitalism and the unending anxiety of the climate crisis. Her zines live in personal and public zine libraries worldwide. Sonali is currently working on the manuscript for her first book, an expanded version of her popular zine *Depression Cooking.*

**David Meyers** is a Black, cis, disabled man and a settler who has worked in Toronto's community sector for over twenty years. David collaborates with disabled people, disability rights networks, and non-profits to collectively disrupt ableist injustices that oppress disabled people, including legislated poverty and inaccessible housing. He pursues progress toward an accessible Canada through engaging in accessibility education, disability community organizing, and government relations. David currently works as a senior manager at the Centre for Independent Living in Toronto (CILT).

**Angelo Muredda** is a Toronto-based film critic, teacher, and programmer whose work has appeared in *Cinema Scope*, *Sharp Magazine*, *The Walrus*, and *Film Freak Central*. He holds a PhD in English on representations of disability in Canadian fiction and film from the University of Toronto. He teaches in the Department of English at Humber College.

**Dorothy Ellen Palmer** is an award-winning disabled, senior writer, accessibility advocate, retired English/drama teacher, and union activist. She has published over forty works of fiction and nonfiction in literary and disability journals; three novels, including *When Fenelon Falls* (Coach House, 2010); and a memoir, *Falling for Myself* (Wolsak & Wynn, 2019). Winner of the 2022 Susan Crean Award for Non-Fiction and the 2020 Helen Henderson Award for disability journalism, she lives in Burlington, Ontario, with her mobility scooter, Rosie.

**Igor Samardzic** is a community activist and city builder with extensive experience as a volunteer and planner in both the public and private sectors. His work supports accessible public transit, cycling infrastructure, affordable housing, community arts, and public space activations. Igor contributes to numerous non-profits and social enterprises, advocating for people with disabilities and championing a more equitable and livable city for all Torontonians.

**Nicolas Steenhout** is a disabled speaker, trainer, and consultant on the topics of digital accessibility and disability inclusion. He started as a web developer in the mid-nineties. Nicolas quickly realized that accessibility work in the digital space is as important as accessibility in the built environment. He has since worked with Fortune 500 companies, universities, and non-profit organizations in Canada, the United States, New Zealand, and Australia. Nicolas spends as much time as possible exploring nature and looking for birds with his camera.

**Claire Steep** studied English at St Andrews University, where she became an expert in all things literary and the correct way to brew tea (the microwave does not feature). It's also where she discovered the ID cane and why she is (as far as she knows) the go-to expert on the white cane on-screen. When not cataloguing televised white canes, she's a sort-of spy whose work is carefully supervised by some very silly dachsunds and a cat with an outstanding glower.

**Jacqueline Valencia** is a Toronto-based writer, essayist, and activist who earned her honours BA in English at the University of Toronto. Jacqueline was the organizer of the 2015 'Toronto Poetry Talks: Racism and Sexism in the Craft' and is the author of several prose works in anthologies and the writer of books of poetry, including *There Is No Escape Out of Time* from Insomniac Press.

**Paul Vienneau** is and has been many things: a son, a brother, a bass guitarist, an abstract and portrait photographer, an advocate and activist, a magician and mentalist, and a cat dad. His nickname is 'The Asshole with a Shovel,' a self-given and ironic title. The irony lies in his refusal to work angry, instead shining a light on issues affecting disabled citizens in Halifax.

A. J. Withers is a queer, trans, non-binary, disabled activist, artist, and academic. They wrote a book about the Ontario Coalition Against Poverty and municipal policy: *Fight to Win: Inside Poor People's Organizing* (Fernwood). They are also the author of *Disability Politics and Theory* (Fernwood) and *A Violent History of Benevolence: Interlocking Oppression in the Moral Economies of Social Working* (with Chris Chapman, University of Toronto Press).

Typeset in Albertina and Circular Std.

Printed at the Coach House on bpNichol Lane in Toronto, Ontario, on Rolland paper, which was manufactured in Saint-Jérôme, Quebec. This book was printed with vegetable-based ink on a 1973 Heidelberg KORD offset litho press. Its pages were folded on a Baumfolder, gathered by hand, bound on a Sulby Auto-Mina-binda, and trimmed on a Polar single-knife cutter.

Coach House is located in Toronto, which is on the traditional territory of many nations, including the Mississaugas of the Credit, the Anishnabeg, the Chippewa, the Haudenosaunee, and the Wendat peoples, and is now home to many diverse First Nations, Inuit, and Métis peoples. We acknowledge that Toronto is covered by Treaty 13 with the Mississaugas of the Credit. We are grateful to live and work on this land.

Edited by Emily Macrae
Designed by Crystal Sikma
Cover design by David Gee

Coach House Books
80 bpNichol Lane
Toronto ON M5S 3J4
Canada

mail@chbooks.com
www.chbooks.com